World education report 1995

World education report 1995

UNESCO Publishing
OXFORD

Published in 1995 by the United Nations
Educational, Scientific and Cultural Organization
7, Place de Fontenoy, 75352 Paris 07 SP
Printed by Mateu Cromo

Graphics by Visit-Graph, Boulogne-Billancourt

ISBN 92-3-103180-5

Foreword

In the year in which we commemorate the fiftieth anniversary of the adoption of UNESCO's Constitution, it is fitting to recall the belief of UNESCO's founders in the possibility of 'full and equal opportunities for education for all'. In those days it was a very distant goal. Barely half the world's adults could read and write; in Asia the proportion was approximately one adult in three, and in Africa it was only one adult in six. In every region, the majority of illiterate adults were women.

UNESCO was created 'for the purpose of advancing, through the educational and scientific and cultural relations of the peoples of the world, the objectives of international peace and of the common welfare of mankind for which the United Nations Organization was established and which its Charter proclaims'. Without the provision of 'full and equal opportunities for education for all', UNESCO's founders realized, this purpose could not be achieved.

If the provision of education is more widespread today than fifty years ago, the goal of 'education for all' is still far from being attained. It is not only between societies that imbalances in educational opportunity are apparent, but also within them: between rich and poor people, between urban and rural areas, between different ethnic groups, and between men and women. Yet at a time such as the present, when so many societies are under strain internally, it is more than ever vital that education plays its full role in helping to strengthen the bonds of solidarity and democracy which hold society together. The International Year of the Family (1994) has reminded the world of the most important of these bonds, and the International Year for Tolerance this year highlights the dangers of excluding, marginalizing and rejecting people who are simply different from ourselves.

This report, the third in UNESCO's series of *World Education Reports,* focuses on the largest single category of persons denied equality of educational opportunity in the world today: women and girls. So often maltreated and abused, as the Fourth World Conference on Women (Beijing, 1995) vigorously deplored, women represent two-thirds of the world's illiterate adults, while girls form a similar proportion the world's out-of-school young people. Such an asymmetry in the exercise of the right to education is not only a denial of equal opportunity but also limits the contribution of education to development and undermines its capacity to nurture respect for human rights generally. Addressing this flagrant injustice to women is indissociable from the task of creating a more equitable, sustainable and peaceful world. The report concludes – appropriately – by recalling the contribution that education everywhere can and must make to the promotion of peace, human rights and democracy.

Federico Mayor
Director-General of UNESCO

Contents

List of figures, boxes and tables

Figures, tables and the chart for which no source is indicated have been drawn from the database of UNESCO's Division of Statistics. In these figures and tables, where a regional breakdown is shown, there is an overlap between the two regions of sub-Saharan Africa and the Arab States (see Explanatory Notes to Appendix II on page 103).

Figures

Chart

Boxes

Tables

Text tables

Regional tables

World Education Indicators

Acknowledgements

THE information presented in this report is drawn selectively from the full range of information available to the UNESCO Secretariat from both official and unofficial sources.

In preparing the report, including Appendix III (World Education Indicators), the Secretariat received specific advice and suggestions from a number of people outside the Organization whose contributions are gratefully acknowledged: Ronnie Andersson, Michal Beller, Gabriel Cárceles Breis, Amrung Chantavanich, Michel Debeauvais, Isabelle Deblé, Mostafa El Hddigui, Ahmed Elsheikh (Arab League Educational, Cultural and Scientific Organization), Naomi Gafni, Heinz Gilomen, Caroline Gipps, Rafica Hammoud, Horst Itner, Robert Johnston (United Nations Statistical Division), Bettina Knauth (Statistical Office of the European Union), Helmut Köhler, Gilbert de Landsheere, Douglas J. Lynd, Barry McGaw, Katherine Namuddu, Neville Postlethwaite, George Psacharopoulos (World Bank), Rati Ram, Olga Remenets, Claude Sauvageot, Wendy Simpson (Organisation for Economic Co-operation and Development), Magda Soares, Max Van Herpen, Herbert J. Walberg and Robert Wood. None of these necessarily agrees with the views expressed in the report.

Appendix IV (Reports, publications and periodicals) was prepared by Benedict Faccini, with the assistance of Sandrine Antunes.

1
Introduction

INTERNATIONAL concern to ensure that women participate fully in humanity's quest for sustainable development and peace has been growing. This is evident in the attention which has been given to issues pertaining to women in the series of world conferences, convened by organizations of the United Nations system since the end of the cold war, to consider the major challenges facing humanity today: the World Conference on Education for All (1990), the World Summit for Children (1990), the United Nations Conference on Environment and Development (1992), the World Conference on Human Rights (1993), the International Conference on Population and Development (1994), the World Summit for Social Development (1995) and the Fourth World Conference on Women (1995). It is through the actions of women as much as men, these conferences have affirmed, that the hoped-for transformation of the human condition must be achieved.

The role of education in preparing both men and women for that task is increasingly recognized as crucial, appropriately so in this fiftieth anniversary year of UNESCO's Constitution. More than just skills and capabilities are needed: without shared values, it is realized, common action cannot be devised, either within societies or among them. Without the universally shared experience of 'full and equal opportunities for education for all', such values can not be easily formed, and a secure and lasting peace, rooted in 'the intellectual and moral solidarity of mankind' (Box 1.1), can hardly be attained.

Box 1.1

To construct the defences of peace

The Governments of the States Parties to this Constitution on behalf of their peoples declare:

That since wars begin in the minds of men, it is in the minds of men that the defences of peace must be constructed;

That ignorance of each other's ways and lives has been a common cause, throughout the history of mankind, of that suspicion and mistrust between the peoples of the world through which their differences have all too often broken into war;

That the great and terrible war which has now ended was a war made possible by the denial of the democratic principles of the dignity, equality and mutual respect of men, and by the propagation, in their place, through ignorance and prejudice, of the doctrine of the inequality of men and races;

That the wide diffusion of culture, and the education of humanity for justice and liberty and peace are indispensable to the dignity of man and constitute a sacred duty which all the nations must fulfil in a spirit of mutual assistance and concern;

That a peace based exclusively upon the political and economic arrangements of governments would not be a peace which could secure the unanimous, lasting and sincere support of the peoples of the world, and that the peace must therefore be founded, if it is not to fail, upon the intellectual and moral solidarity of mankind.

For these reasons, the States Parties to this Constitution, believing in full and equal opportunities for education for all, in the unrestricted pursuit of objective truth, and in the free exchange of ideas and knowledge, are agreed and determined to develop and to increase the means of communication between their peoples and to employ these means for the purposes of mutual understanding and a truer and more perfect knowledge of each other's lives;

In consequence whereof they do hereby create the United Nations Educational, Scientific and Cultural Organization for the purpose of advancing, through the educational and scientific and cultural relations of the peoples of the world, the objectives of international peace and of the common welfare of mankind for which the United Nations Organization was established and which its Charter proclaims.

Source: Preamble of UNESCO's Constitution, adopted in London on 16 November 1945.

Women and girls globally constitute the largest single category of persons denied 'full and equal opportunities for education for all'. Their education is the main theme of this report.

The report examines recent global trends and developments in the education of women and girls, and assesses the progress being made towards equality of opportunity. The context also is evoked: a time when profound changes are occurring, both within societies and in the global political, economic and cultural environment. There are signs of a shift in values (Box 1.2) and of a renewed demand for education to help inculcate those principles which are conducive to peace, human rights and democracy that finally must constitute the fabric of the 'intellectual and moral solidarity of mankind'.

Global standards

Since UNESCO's earliest days, most notably in the *Convention Against Discrimination in Education* (1960), the denial of equal educational opportunities to women and girls has been recognized internationally as a fundamental challenge to the dignity of the person, indeed, as a limitation of the scope of human rights that undermines the capability of education itself to nurture those values of solidarity and mutual obligation that ultimately hold society together and help to ensure social cohesion.

As in the case of other global standards in fields such as health, employment or the environment, the effort needed to implement equal educational opportunities for men and women is not the same for every country. Historically, few (if any) countries have provided equal educational opportunities for the two sexes in the early stages of the development of their education systems, and the call today for all countries to strive to attain this standard is clearly more difficult to implement in some regions of the world than in others. The world's education systems are at different stages

Box 1.2
'Values in Transition'

The impression grows that we are at the end of a long period of secularization. People are beginning to assert that it is impossible for them to realize their full humanity in a totally secularized world where no value is assigned to immeasurable qualities such as rectitude, sharing, mutual obligation, inner peace, harmony with nature, and so forth. The resurgence of fundamentalism is only one manifestation of this process, and it is not in all cases a reactionary impulse. The morality of social and political structures is now being challenged from many other quarters as well.

The progression toward ˙individualism also seems to be reaching a point of diminishing returns. The process of individualization, so successful in releasing enormous creative power, at some point begins to erode the bonds between people. It weakens the nation, the community, and even the family. It has also, at the national level, eroded the commitment to multilateral cooperation in dealing with pressing global issues. Instead we see increasing evidence of regional and global unilateralism.

It is often simply impossible to know which movements, trends, or practices may prove to be significant in the long term. Spontaneous currents arise unexpectedly to alter the course of history – the Gandhian movement in India is one example. Recent decades have been characterized by profound shifts in the values held by significant groups of people. These shifts, which are both a result and a source of social change, occur simultaneously in disparate and sometimes conflicting directions. Some look back to a revival of traditional values; others look to other cultural traditions or attempt to define an entirely new configuration of values.

Source: Soedjatmoko, 'Values in Transition', in Kathleen Newland and Kamala Chandrakirana Soedjatmoko (eds.), *Transforming Humanity: the Visionary Writings of Soedjatmoko*, pp. 148–9, Tokyo, United Nations University Press, 1994.

of development in terms of both their overall capacities to accommodate participants and the ranges of educational experiences that they can provide. Moreover, each has evolved within a specific economic, social and cultural context. Just to provide any child with education is a bigger challenge in some regions of the world than in others, if only because of rapid population growth and higher proportions of young people in the total population (Figure 1.1). Indeed, these constraints apply particularly in those regions where the challenge to provide equal educational opportunities for men and women is most pronounced.

In order to facilitate the discussion in the report, two aspects of the concept of 'equal educational opportunity' are distinguished: participation and process. The former is understood to refer to equal opportunity to participate in education as such, while the latter is understood to

Figure 1.2
Estimated world population[1] aged 6–11 and 12–17 enrolled in formal education and out of school, 1995

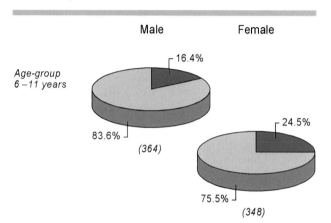

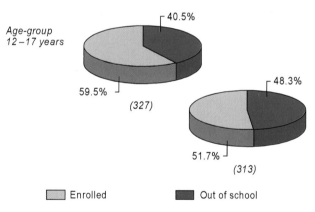

1. Figures in parentheses refer to total population of the corresponding age-groups, expressed in millions.

Figure 1.1
The changing age-structure of the world's population, by region, 1980–2000

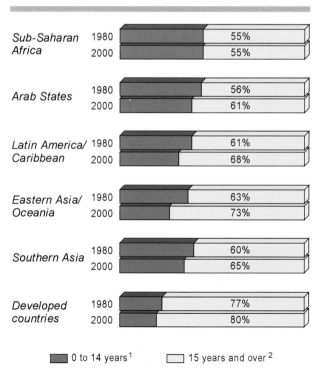

1. Percentage ratio of the population in the 0 to 14 years age-group to total population.
2. Percentage ratio of the population in the 15 years and over age-group to total population.

refer to equal opportunity and treatment during the educational process. Under the first heading, consideration will mainly be given to questions concerning women's and girls' access to education, and hence the focus will largely be on developing countries; these questions are considered in Chapter 2. Under the second heading, consideration will mainly be given to questions concerning the nature and content of the education which is provided to women and girls. The fundamental issues involved are basically common to developed and developing countries; they are considered in Chapter 3.

Access and participation

Over a billion young people – nearly one-fifth of the world's population – are enrolled in formal education today, compared to around 300 million or one-tenth of the world's population in 1953, the earliest year for which UNESCO has global estimates of enrolment.

Girls are less likely than boys to be enrolled in school. In the age-group 6–11, which corresponds broadly to that of primary or first-level education, nearly a quarter (24.5 per cent) of the world's girls are estimated to be out of school (85 million) compared to around one-sixth (16.4 per cent) of the world's boys (60 million) (Figure 1.2).

Largely as a consequence of this long-standing

Figure 1.3
Estimated number (millions)
of literate and illiterate males and females
aged 15 and over in developing countries,
by region, 1995

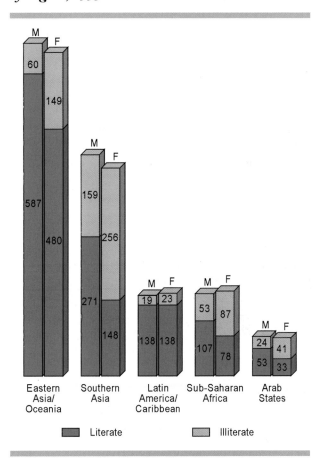

imbalance in participation in formal education, the literacy rate of the world's women (71.2 per cent) is significantly lower than that of men (83.6 per cent), although the gap is slowly closing (Table 1.1).

Nearly two-thirds of the world's illiterate adults are women (565 million) (see Appendix II, Table 2); most of them live in the developing regions of Africa, Asia and Latin America (Figure 1.3).

The changing global patterns and trends of these male-female imbalances in literacy, and access to and participation in education, are

Table 1.1
Estimated adult literacy rates,[1]
by region, 1980 and 1995

	1980			1995		
	MF	M	F	MF	M	F
WORLD	69.5	77.2	61.9	77.4	83.6	71.2
Developing countries of which:	58.0	68.9	46.8	70.4	78.9	61.7
Sub-Saharan Africa	40.2	51.8	29.2	56.8	66.6	47.3
Arab States	40.8	55.0	26.2	56.6	68.4	44.2
Latin America/Caribbean	79.7	82.1	77.5	86.6	87.7	85.5
Eastern Asia/Oceania	69.3	80.4	58.0	83.6	90.6	76.3
of which: China	66.0	78.6	52.7	81.5	89.9	72.7
Southern Asia	39.1	52.8	24.5	50.2	62.9	36.6
of which: India	40.8	55.3	25.3	52.0	65.5	37.7
Least developed countries	36.5	48.3	24.9	48.8	59.5	38.1
Developed countries	96.6	98.0	95.4	98.7	98.9	98.4

1. Percentage of literate adults in the population aged 15 years and over (see Appendix II, Table 3).

Box 1.3
'The vast majority of single-parent families are headed by women'

In France, according to the 1990 population census, one in every eight families is a single-parent household. This corresponds to the European average, far behind Sweden and Denmark but well ahead of Spain and Italy. Single-parent families represent nearly 1.2 million adults who live with two million children under the age of 25. They have been steadily on the rise over the past twenty years, but the most substantial change is linked to the composition of the family unit. Today, most cases are the consequence of divorce, whereas widowhood was once the main cause. Overall, in the past twenty years the number of single-parent families has increased by 63 per cent, while the number of families with divorced parents and single parents has quadrupled.

The vast majority of single-parent families are headed by women. Their circumstances vary widely with regard to age, number of children, profession, income and life-style.

[...]

Divorced men and women make up the largest group of parents who live without a spouse. The rise in divorce, which has reached the rate of 100,000 per year, explains the fact that single-parent families have gained ground so rapidly over the past twenty years or so.

[...]

Even though cases of single-parent families vary widely, they have some points in common. They are usually made up of women with children. They live in medium-sized or large cities, hence they tend to live in apartment buildings more than couples with children do. They are less often home owners. They work primarily in the service sector and more specifically in the public sector. Although some earn a good living, average income remains lower than that of a dual-income couple, not to mention the fact that women's salaries are on average inferior to men's. Special allowances are granted to the most impoverished. They experience severe child-care problems and generally have very little time to help children with their homework or meet their teachers.

Source: Institut National de la Statistique et des Études Économiques (INSEE), *Les familles monoparentales*, pp. 6–8, Paris, INSEE, 1994.

examined in Chapter 2, where the presentation, as in previous editions of the *World Education Report,* draws heavily on UNESCO's unique international education statistics database.

Contents and purposes

The provision of increased opportunities for access to education has been only one part of the global challenge of ensuring equal educational opportunities for women. The other part concerns the nature of the educational experience provided: what kind of education? Do girls have equal opportunities with boys to learn the same things, to study the same subjects and fields? Are tests and examinations fair to girls? Are teaching practices effective for both sexes?

These questions are critical for an understanding of what women can obtain from their education; they are considered in Chapter 3. The issues involved are complex, and touch on many fundamental matters relating to both the purposes of education and the respective roles of men and women in the wider economy and society. Traditionally, in most countries, the type of education provided for girls was strongly influenced by the assumption that much (if not most) of their time as adults would be devoted to household activities and raising a family. This assumption is still widely held, but it has not forestalled the shift over the past century of more than half the world's women from mainly household to mainly market-based activity, a development which has accelerated in recent decades in all regions of the world. Moreover, with majorities of both men and women now working outside the home, their family roles are less well-defined. In fact, the notion of 'family' itself has begun subtly to change meaning: single-parent families, usually women with young children, are on the rise in many countries (Box 1.3). In the industrial societies, the break-up of the traditional two-parent household has hit women especially hard; in a majority of

---

Box 1.4
A warning (1937)

When Maria Montessori gave her first public lecture on the theme of education for peace – in 1932, at Nice, at a Congress of the International Bureau of Education – she was almost dismayed by her realization of the novelty of this idea. Rather than make a frontal attack on the subject, she therefore chose an imaginative, persuasive approach.

She went back through history some twenty centuries and spoke at some length on the mysteriously recurring plague which took, over the years, a toll of millions and millions of lives. This had continued until men of learning, scrutinizing the invisible universe, discovered the microbe that was responsible for the scourge, and halted its reproductive process by drawing up certain vital rules of hygiene and inducing society to adopt them. As a result, modern man is physically healthier than his ancestors.

Having thus built up a proper basis for comparisons, Maria Montessori carried her argument further: 'War is like plague,' she said, 'and it leaves us bewil-

dered. But just as a new physical constitution was needed to defeat plague, so we need a new spiritual constitution to help us put an end to war. [...]'

Five years later she stressed this point again: 'Education in its present form encourages the child's sense of isolation and his pursuit of his own interests,' she said. 'Children are taught not to help one another, not to prompt those who do not know something, to think of nothing but their own advancement, to aim solely at winning prizes in competition with their companions. And these pathetic egotists, mentally wearied as experimental psychology reveals them to be, then go out into the world, where they live side by side like grains of sand in the desert – every one cut off from his neighbour, and all sterile. If a gale arises, this human dust, with no spiritual essence to give it life, will be swept away in a death-dealing whirlwind.'

Source: Maria Remmidi, 'Maria Montessori, A Vision of Mankind Transformed', *The UNESCO Courier*, Vol. XVII, No. 4, 1964, pp. 18, 20.

---

cases they are left with the responsibility of raising the children while at the same time becoming the sole source of earnings, the fathers often being unable (or even refusing) to provide support. It has been estimated that more than half of this generation of children in some industrial countries will spend part of their childhood living apart from one of their parents, usually the father. In these circumstances it is hardly surprising that women today are becoming more concerned about education. For what sort of life did their education prepare them? For family and household? For a competitive labour market? For both?

And the men: what did they get out of their education? Are their sons and daughters to be educated likewise?

Indeed, has education itself contributed in some way to the loosening of bonds in society? This question has been posed before: nearly sixty years ago, reflecting on the condition of education in Europe at that time, a distinguished educator and early proponent of education for peace who later became associated with UNESCO, warned of the consequences of neglecting education's nobler purposes (Box 1.4). These purposes are recalled in Chapter 4.

2
The education
of women and girls

I N a majority of countries still, the literacy rate of women is significantly lower than that of men. In sixty-six countries – a third of the membership of the United Nations – the gap between the male and female adult literacy rates is estimated to be larger than 10 percentage points, and in forty countries it is estimated to be larger than 20 percentage points (Chart 1). Few other indicators capture as decisively the imbalance in the status of men and of women in society as does this simple measure.

Yet the gap between the male and female literacy rates is not just a statement about men and women and the educational opportunities which have been provided for them. It is also a statement about the society's development, and its capacity and willingness to provide such opportunities. Literacy, educational opportunity and development are inseparable.

Largely because of the efforts of the United Nations over the past two decades to bring women's rights to the forefront of national policy-

Chart 1
World male-female literacy gaps, 1995

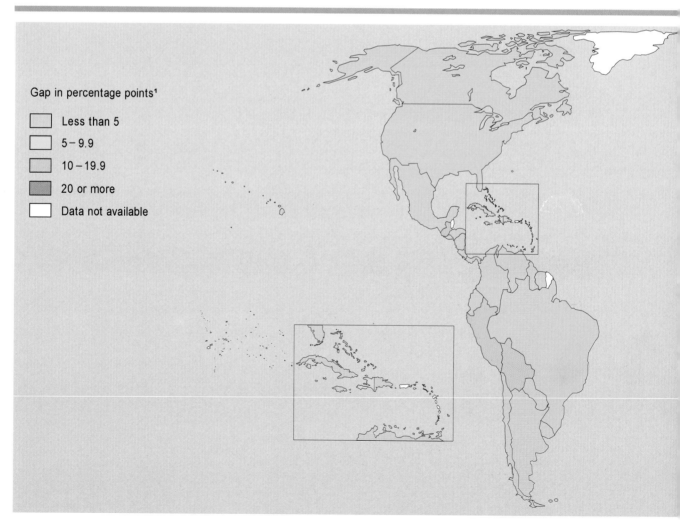

Gap in percentage points[1]

- Less than 5
- 5 – 9.9
- 10 – 19.9
- 20 or more
- Data not available

1. Estimated percentage of adult males aged 15 years and over who are literate minus the corresponding percentage of adult females.

makers' concerns and thinking about development, there is now a much greater international understanding and appreciation of the complex nature of the relationship between the education of men and women and the development process. The four World Conferences on Women held in Mexico City (1975), Copenhagen (1980), Nairobi (1985) and Beijing (1995), as well as the United Nations' Decade for Women: Equality, Development and Peace (1976–1985) and the three United Nations' conferences on population held in Bucharest (1974), Mexico City (1984) and Cairo (1994), have helped stimulate a body of international research and inquiry that has begun to expose the real costs for society of neglecting to ensure women's right to equal educational opportunity.

Key elements of this shift in thinking are recalled briefly in the section which follows, while the remainder of the chapter considers the changing patterns of male and female participation in education.

Development imperatives

Fundamental aspects of population growth, and of economic, social and cultural change, it is now realized, cannot be understood unless the closest attention is given to the position of women in society and to their education in particular.

The prospects of a continuing slowdown in the world's population growth and its implications for sustainable development and the future global 'quality of life' have emerged in recent years as a powerful instrumental consideration in favour of the education of women in those regions of the world (especially Africa and Asia) where population growth is still high. Much depends, it has been estimated, on the 'demographic transition' in these regions (cf. *World Economic and Social Survey 1994,* pp. 208–14, New York, United Nations, 1994): whether there is a change from population growth paths characterized by high fertility and high mortality rates to paths of low fertility and low mortality rates, as happened over the past century in the now-industrialized countries. Women's education has been recognized as a critical factor in the likelihood of this change, because of its influence on both fertility and mortality rates: better educated women having fewer and healthier children, and better health themselves, than women with little or no education.

Mortality rates are currently falling faster than fertility rates, hence much recent research has focused on fertility. Yet although the correlation of women's education with various aspects of their reproductive behaviour is now well-established (e.g., Figure 2.1), there still is argument among specialists over the way in which education actually exerts an influence, as noted in the *World Education Report 1993.* The majority of the explanations which have been put forward to date have recognized that several processes are involved, ranging from the direct effects of schooling on knowledge, skills, values and attitudes to the indirect effects of postponement of marriage and greater access to the kinds of employment and careers which often are incompatible with having large families. There is general agreement that the duration of formal education is critical: when all the various background factors (rural/urban location, income levels, etc.), as well as the husbands' education, are also taken into account, it is women who have received six or seven, or more, years of schooling whose fertility behaviour would appear to have been decisively affected. This has suggested of course that the completion of primary or basic education is a kind of watershed in the global topography of population and development, if not the determining factor in the 'demographic transition'.

Certainly, in every country the young woman who has received a complete basic education is potentially much better able to manage her life in a changing economic, social and cultural environment, than if she were without education. Married and with children, it is argued, the real significance of her education becomes apparent: her ability to communicate with and educate others, especially her own children, in a fundamentally different way than if she were illiterate. Philosophers of education who have hailed women's literacy as a 'liberation' from the traditional life cycle have therefore retained essentially the same insight into the development process that is suggested by the demographers' correlations.

Besides the 'demographic transition', the world of work has been the other major area where advances have been made in the past two decades in understanding the implications of women's education for development. Although economists are still handicapped by methodological difficulties in giving a complete empirical account of the value of women's work, since a substantial proportion of the world's women do not work for wages and women's household activity is not valued in the market (Box 2.1), they have concluded that the social 'rates of return' on investment in women's education are generally high, indeed that they are comparable if not higher than

Figure 2.1
Women's education and fertility behaviour in developing countries

A. Mean number of children,[1] by level of education

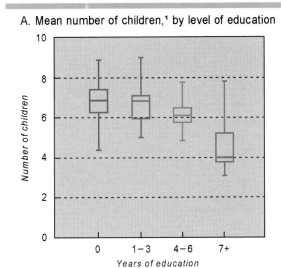

B. Total fertility rate,[2] by level of education

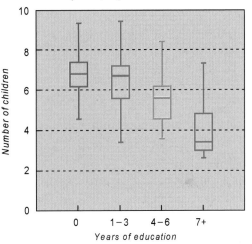

C. Mean desired family size,[3] by level of education

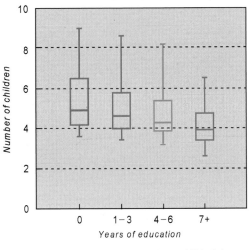

D. Mean age at marriage, by level of education

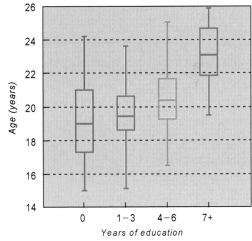

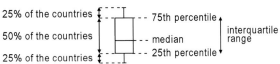

Note: The distance between the ends of the lines extending from each box shows the range of values observed across all countries with the relevant data available; the box itself spans the 25th to the 75th percentile values (the interquartile range), a measure of dispersion. The median or 50th percentile value is shown by a horizontal line through the box. For example, with reference to figure A above: in 50 per cent of the countries for which data are available, women with one to three years of education had given birth on average to between six and seven children. In 25 per cent of the countries they had given birth to between seven and nine children, and in another 25 per cent of the countries they had given birth to between five and six children. In contrast, for women with seven or more years of education, in 75 per cent of the countries such women had given birth on average to five or less children, and in 50 per cent of the countries to four or less children.

1. Mean number of children ever born for ever-married or all women aged 40–49 years.
2. Average number of children born per women aged 15–49 based on the five years preceding the survey.
3. Mean number of children desired by ever-married women aged 15–49, adjusted for age differences between educational groups within each country.

Source: Based on *Fertility Behaviour in the Context of Development. Evidence from the World Fertility Survey,* Tables 112, 115 and 119, pp. 224–33, New York, United Nations, 1987.

Box 2.1
The exclusion of women's household work from the national income (GDP)

Economic activity is perhaps the most difficult of the concepts used in population censuses. [...] In determining economic activity, the activity status of the person being reported on must first be established, since this defines the size of the economically active population, which is the foundation of the study of economic activity of the country. In examining the questions used in determining the activity status of individuals, it will be observed that almost all involve some measurement of 'work'. Hence, the concept of work which is applied will significantly influence the results obtained. In fact, a perceived expansion in female participation rate in many countries can result in part from improved techniques for data collection brought about by an increased awareness of women's work as economic activity. This is particularly applicable in economies with a relatively large informal sector and has a greater effect in relation to women than to men.

[...] The definition of participation in economic activity by the population has become broader in scope over the years. In 1954, for example, the [ILO] definition was: 'Persons who perform some work for pay or profit'. By 1966 it was enlarged to represent: 'All persons of either sex who furnish the supply of labour

for the production of economic goods and services'. The 1982 ILO revision enlarged the concept even further to include: 'All persons of either sex who furnish the supply of labour for the production of economic goods and services as defined by the United Nations System of National Accounts and Balances'.

[...] The 1982 definition [...] clarifies the concept of the 'production boundary'. The definition given by the ILO, with reference to the United Nations System of National Accounts and Balances covers:

'all market production and certain types of non-market production, including production and processing of primary products for own consumption, own-account construction and other production of fixed assets for own use. It excludes unpaid activities such as unpaid domestic activities and volunteer community services'. [...]

The exclusion of household work from the production boundary is currently the subject of much debate.

Source: United Nations, *Methods of Measuring Women's Economic Activity. Technical Report*, pp. 30–2, New York, United Nations, 1993. (ST/ESA/STAT/SER.F/59.)

---

the rates of return on many forms of investment in physical capital infrastructure.

Other lines of economic research also have opened up new perspectives on the whole development process. Possibly the most significant advances in understanding have been in respect to the role of women in agriculture (e.g., Box 2.2), a sector which still is central to the development prospects of most countries in the poorer and more populous regions of the world. Many observers and critics had previously charged that development programmes and projects had tended to underestimate women's needs for information and training, indeed, often to ignore them ('invisible farmers') altogether. Efforts to respond to such needs, it is also now realized, are unlikely to be successful if rural women have not first received a basic education.

One of the most critical factors to emerge from recent studies of women's economic status is the right to own property, notably land. In many countries, women's rights in this respect are still severely circumscribed, limiting their access to bank credit especially, even where they are responsible for working the land. As yet, few countries have developed successful programmes along the lines, for example, of Bangladesh's well-known Grameen Bank, which has managed to overcome such constraints while at the same time encouraging women borrowers to improve their education and business skills.

In general, research on the nature and extent of women's participation in economic activity outside the household in both the industrial and developing countries has confirmed fears that the more limited educational opportunities available

Box 2.2
'Gender-based distinctions in agriculture'

A number of questions can be raised about the linkages between gender-based distinctions in agriculture, on the one hand, and characteristics of the individual, the household, the farm, the community, and the national and international economic and political system, on the other.

[...]

Answers to these questions are critical to the planning process, both for agricultural and employment policy making and for project identification and design. [...] Consider the data on *sex specialisation by crop and task* among Tiv households at a project site in Nigeria. Because women do virtually all of the weeding, processing, and crop storage, training to reduce crop losses due to pests or spoilage would have to be designed specifically for women if such policies are to succeed. Improved yields would add to women's overall work load, perhaps creating labour bottlenecks at harvest and processing time that reduce time spent on food preparation and child-care. Because yams, cassava, and maize are 'women's crops' as measured by labour inputs whereas millet, sorghum, and water-melon draw more male labour, shifts in cropping patterns would affect male and female time use differently. In addition, projected changes in net returns to labour reveal that whereas both sexes share increased returns from some crops (e.g. yams), for others the returns from men's work accrue largely to women (e.g. cowpeas), or vice versa. The group that controls the distribution of the crop or its proceeds reaps most of the benefits of increased production, leaving the other with little incentive to work harder.

Examples of task specialisation from southern Asia suggest additional scenarios resulting from agricultural policies or project interventions. Because the hand processing of paddy in Bangladesh is largely women's work, the introduction of automated rice mills following rural electrification can undermine the livelihood of tens of thousands of rural women. Planners might concentrate instead on designing intermediate technology to retain women's control over earnings from rice processing while reducing the drudgery of the *dheki*.[1] If labour displacement is inevitable, alternative employment opportunities would need to be created for village women, in agriculture or in agro-based small industries or services. In the semi-arid villages of southern India, female farm labourers who do weeding would be displaced by the introduction of herbicides. With few alternative sources of employment, the more labour-intensive methods appear preferable. In contrast, the spread of cotton and of irrigated paddy production in neighbouring villages intensifies the demand for female wage labour and raises household incomes.

1. Place where women mill the rice in the traditional way. (Ed.'s note.)

Source: Ruth Dixon-Mueller, *Women's Work in Third World Agriculture; Concepts and Indicators*, pp. 119–21, Geneva, International Labour Office, 1985. (Women, Work and Development, 9.)

---

to women and girls tend to condemn them to subordinate and sometimes menial roles in most industries and occupations, while at the same time prejudicing the employment and career development prospects of those women whose educational attainments are equal or superior to those of males. In most labour markets there are large wage gaps, with women on average, according to World Bank estimates, earning only 60–70 per cent as much as men.

While such gaps often just represent pure discrimination – denial of equal pay for equal work – the fact remains that in much of the world today women are more likely to be illiterate and to have received less education than men, and hence are more vulnerable to economic discrimination. Eradication of illiteracy and provision of equal educational opportunities for women are therefore fundamental imperatives if a global economic culture that is fair to women is ever to emerge.

Growing numbers of illiterates

While literacy rates are rising in all major regions of the world, and male-female literacy gaps – as was noted in the previous chapter (Table 1.1,

Figure 2.2
**Trends in male and female adult literacy rates
in the Sahelian countries, 1980–1995[1]**

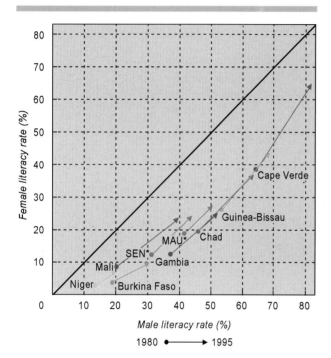

* MAU: Mauritania; SEN: Senegal.

1. See also Appendix I, pp. 95–7.

The difficulty which many countries have in reducing the absolute number of illiterate adults is illustrated by the case of Egypt (Figure 2.3), where although the overall adult literacy rate is estimated to have increased from 40 per cent to 51 per cent between 1980 and 1995, the absolute number of illiterate adults (both male and female) increased from nearly 16 million to nearly 19 million over the same period. Eventually, if Egypt's provision of primary or basic education to the younger generation continues to expand faster than

Figure 2.3
**Estimated literate and illiterate
population (millions) in Egypt, by age-group,
1980 and 1995**

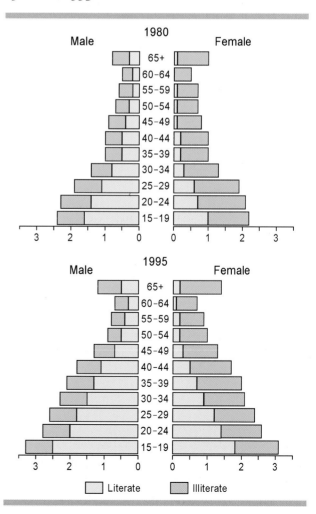

p. 19) – are slowly closing at the global and regional levels, there still are many individual countries – for example, those in the Sahel (Figure 2.2) – where the male-female literacy gap is not closing despite increases in both their male and female literacy rates.

Moreover, although the absolute number of illiterate adults appears to have levelled off globally (Appendix II, Table 2), it still is increasing in certain regions, notably sub-Saharan Africa, the Arab States and Southern Asia, with women again forming a substantial majority in each case. Indeed, the absolute number of illiterate adults is estimated to have increased in the period 1980–1995 in fifty out of the sixty-three countries in these regions for which UNESCO has data (Appendix III, Table 2).

Box 2.3
UNESCO's literacy prize-winners in 1995

Having examined twenty-five nominations, twenty-two of them submitted by governments and three by non-governmental organizations, in compliance with the stipulations and criteria of the General Rules governing the Award of Prizes for Meritorious Work in Literacy, the Jury has unanimously decided:

Firstly, to confer *The International Reading Association Literacy Award*
to *Literacy New Brunswick Inc. Canada* for its *Community Academic Services Program* (CASP), for:
(1) having created through the mobilization of the community an extensive network of learning facilities to provide instruction in literacy and other basic skills, available without payment of fees to all individuals regardless of age and background;
(2) the wide use made of non-formal approaches adapted to the needs and convenience of individual learners;
(3) the firm commitment to cultural pluralism shown by the use of both English and French as languages of instruction; and
(4) the excellent results achieved in dramatically reducing the drop-out rate in literacy courses and improving achievement levels.

Secondly, to award *The Noma Prize*
to the *PKK (Pembinaan Kesejahteraan-Keluarga) Family Welfare Movement*, in Indonesia, for:
(1) having created a national movement conducted by the wives of civil servants and dedicated to the education and social welfare of women which since its establishment in 1968 has been extended to all levels of government from the national to the local and presently counts over 50,000 learning groups;
(2) having emphasized the fundamental importance of educating women and girls as a means of contributing to long-term family welfare in a rapidly changing world; and
(3) having demonstrated the effectiveness of combining literacy and post-literacy activities with income generating activities as a means of encouraging learning, alleviating poverty and promoting family welfare.

Thirdly, to award *The King Sejong Literacy Prize*
to the *All-China Women's Federation* (ACWF), the largest non-governmental organization of Chinese women, for:
(1) its efforts to educate women in a nation in which over 70 per cent of illiterates are females;
(2) operating a large-scale campaign in co-operation with both governmental and non-governmental institutions in rural areas in order to teach literacy skills to peasant women within the framework of a highly motivating non-formal skills training programme known as 'Dual studies and Emulation'; and
(3) having created the first ever women's literacy prize to recognize outstanding contributions by individuals and organizations in China's vast and successful literacy campaign;
and to the *Pilot Literacy, Post-literacy and Training Project for the Improvement of the Quality of Life of Rural Women* (PROCALMUC) in Ecuador, for:
(1) having launched, with the support of UNESCO, UNICEF and WFP, an exemplary non-formal literacy and adult education pilot programme for rural women in order to raise education levels, improve health and nutrition, and promote the social and economic betterment of both the participants and their families;
(2) having adopted a comprehensive approach to the struggle for development in which both governmental and community organizations play an active role and share resources and expertise in order to maximize programme effectiveness; and
(3) having included out-of-school children of both sexes in its programmes while, at the same time, working with families and institutions to reduce the school drop-out rate in rural areas.

Source: International Reading Association Literacy Award, Noma Prize and King Sejong Literacy Prize, 1995, pp. 1–2, Paris, UNESCO, 1995. (Statement by the Jury of the Literacy Prizes.)

population, the absolute number of illiterate adults will start to fall. In the meantime, however, which could be decades, Egypt and many other countries face the prospect of having large and growing numbers of illiterate citizens despite progress in reducing the overall rate of illiteracy; the majority of these citizens are likely to be women unless special measures are taken. Some countries are already taking such measures (Box 2.3), but in many countries there still is a mistaken belief that the problem of adult illiteracy will soon go away because of progress in expanding the provision of primary or basic education for the younger generation.

Trends in school enrolment

The global imbalance in female-male participation in formal education that was noted in the preceding chapter is basically due to imbalances in the less developed regions of the world. However, the trends over the last thirty years or so (except possibly in sub-Saharan Africa, where enrolment ratios levelled off in the 1980s) indicate a narrowing of male-female gaps in participation at the different levels of education in most regions (Figure 2.4). In Eastern Asia/Oceania and Latin America/Caribbean the first-level gross enrolment ratios for both males and females exceed 100 per cent, indicating theoretically at least the full participation of both sexes at this level, although the enrolments in fact include large numbers of over-age children; the latter also account for significant proportions of the first-level enrolments in sub-Saharan Africa, the Arab States and Southern Asia.

In the Latin America and Caribbean region and in the developed countries the male-female disparity in enrolment ratios has effectively disappeared at all levels; indeed, in many countries at the second and third levels the disparity is in favour of females (Figures 2.5 and 2.6), a recent development which has mostly occurred over the last decade and which is not yet fully understood. It is indicated in Figure 2.5 by those countries where the overall female/male 'participation ratio' (i.e. female gross enrolment ratio divided by the male gross enrolment ratio) is higher than 100 per cent. In the southern African countries (Botswana, Lesotho, Namibia and South Africa) at the second and third levels, for example, the main reason is

thought to be early school-leaving and migration of boys in search of work in the mines or commercial agriculture. No such ready explanation is available to account for the situation in many Latin American and Caribbean countries, or in certain countries in other regions such as Sri Lanka and the Philippines, the Gulf countries such as Qatar and the United Arab Emirates, or the majority of the industrial countries, where the female/male participation ratio at the second and/or third level is in favour of females. Doubtless there are multiple explanations, each country being to some extent unique, but the possible emergence of a global trend towards the longer participation in education of females compared with males can not be altogether excluded; it is evoked again later in both the present and next chapter.

Turning to the majority of countries where the female/male participation ratios at all levels favour males, two general points need to be made. First, it should be noted that the female/male participation ratios are broadly correlated with the female enrolment ratios themselves (cf. Appendix I, pp. 99–100). In other words, in countries where females participate almost as much as males, females are more likely to be enrolled anyway, and vice versa. The opposite also applies: in countries where females participate much less than males, females are less likely to be enrolled at all. There are of course individual exceptions to this pattern, but the overall tendency remains: the disparity in participation between girls and boys tends to diminish as the participation of girls improves. It is the tendency to 'hold back' the enrolment of girls more than of boys which essentially causes the pattern of female-male participation disparities in the world, as if girls have to climb a hill which gets less steep or 'difficult' the further up they climb, i.e. as larger proportions of them get into school.

Second, the disparities in participation are only partly related to the different levels of overall development (GNP per capita) of the countries concerned, although the disparities certainly are more

Figure 2.4
Trends in estimated male and female gross enrolment ratios,[1]
by level of education and region, 1960–2000

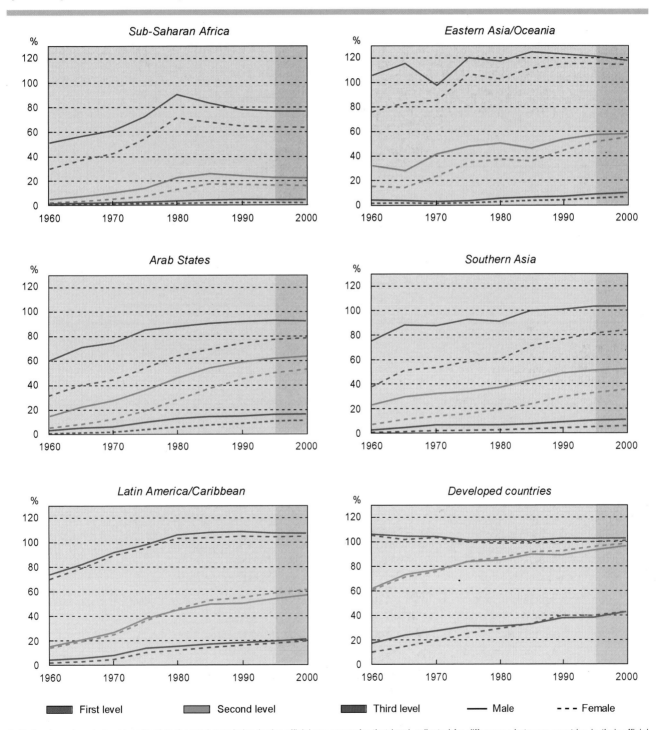

1. Ratio of enrolment at a given level to the total population in the official age-group for that level, adjusted for differences between countries in their official age-groups.

Figure 2.5
GNP per capita and female/male participation ratio[1] in the first and second levels of education, 1992

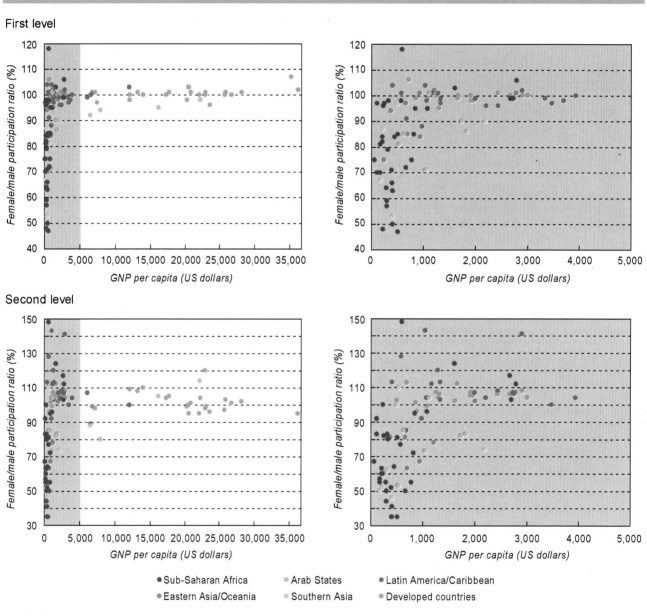

First level

Second level

- Sub-Saharan Africa
- Arab States
- Latin America/Caribbean
- Eastern Asia/Oceania
- Southern Asia
- Developed countries

1. Ratio of female gross enrolment ratio to male gross enrolment ratio.

common among the poorer countries. Among countries with a GNP per capita of less than US$500 in 1992, the female/male participation ratio in first-level education ranges from under 50 per cent (where the gross enrolment ratio for girls is less than half the corresponding ratio for boys) to nearly 100 per cent (where the gross enrolment ratio for girls is equal to that of boys), e.g., Guinea (47 per cent), Chad (48 per cent), Benin (50 per cent), Pakistan (53 per cent) and

Figure 2.6
GNP per capita and percentage of female students in third-level education, 1992

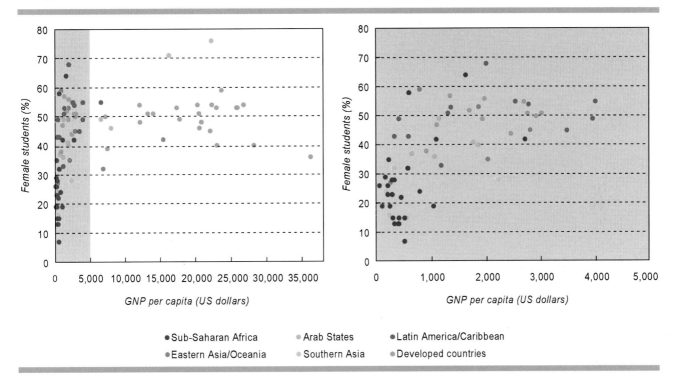

Niger (57 per cent), compared with Kenya (98 per cent), Rwanda (97 per cent), Tajikistan (97 per cent), United Republic of Tanzania (97 per cent) and Madagascar (96 per cent). Clearly, a complex mixture of socio-cultural and economic factors is involved in each case and global generalizations about the reasons for such differences cannot easily be formulated.

Although the majority of countries where the female/male participation ratio in first-level education is low are in sub-Saharan Africa, many of the sub-Saharan African countries are not large in terms of total population, so the impact of their low female/male participation ratios on the global female/male educational imbalance is less dramatic than if their populations were on the same scale as some of the Asian countries for example. This becomes apparent if attention is directed to the absolute numbers of boys and girls in the world who are out of school.

School access and drop-out

Out-of-school children either never entered school or entered and dropped out early. Although the entry into school of over-age children is still common in many parts of the world, in most countries it can reasonably be assumed that if a child has not entered the first grade of primary education by 11 years of age then he/she is unlikely ever to enter school. Estimates of the percentage of children in the 6–11 years age-group who are enrolled in school in a given country therefore broadly indicate the likelihood of entering school in that country.

In sub-Saharan Africa today less than half of 6–11 year-old girls are estimated to be in school (Table 2.1). More than half of the girls in that region therefore are unlikely ever to receive any formal education; in Southern Asia the figure is more than one-third, and in the Arab States region it is more than a quarter. However, because of its larger population, the Southern Asian region shares equally with sub-Saharan Africa the largest number of out-of-school girls in the 6–11 years age-group (Figure 2.7), and in both regions – but more so in Southern Asia – girls constitute a majority of the out-of-school youth in this age-group. In sub-Saharan Africa the numbers of both girls and boys out-of-school are estimated to be still growing.

For 12–17 year-olds, the net enrolment ratios in all regions are much lower, and hence the numbers of out-of-school girls are much larger than for the 6–11 year-olds. The weight of the large populated Asian regions compared with sub-Saharan Africa is also more apparent. In the Eastern Asia/Oceania region, the smaller number of girls than of boys out of school in the 12–17 years old age-group is basically due to the smaller number of girls than of boys in the estimated total population of that age-group.

It is not *a priori obvious* which of the two factors, access or drop out, is more important today in accounting for the global imbalance in the educational enrolment of boys and girls. The situation undoubtedly differs from country to country. There has not up to now been any systematic cross-national analysis of the weight of these two factors. Yet at both national and international levels the issue clearly is important for the design of appropriate policies and programmes aiming to

Figure 2.7
Estimated numbers of out-of-school youth in developing countries, 1990 and 2000 (millions)

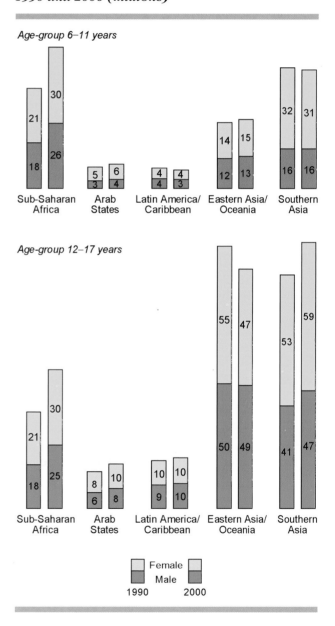

Table 2.1
Estimated net enrolment ratios for the age-groups 6–11, 12–17 and 18–23 years,[1] by region, 1995

| | 6–11 | | 12–17 | | 18–23 | |
	M	F	M	F	M	F
Sub-Saharan Africa	55.2	47.4	46.0	35.3	9.7	4.9
Arab States	83.9	71.6	59.2	47.1	24.5	16.3
Latin America/Caribbean	88.5	87.5	68.4	67.4	26.1	26.3
Eastern Asia/Oceania	88.6	85.5	54.7	51.4	19.5	13.6
Southern Asia	84.3	65.6	50.5	32.2	12.4	6.6
Developed countries	92.3	91.7	87.1	88.5	40.8	42.7

1. Percentage ratio of the number of enrolled pupils/students in each age-group to the total population in the age-group.

increase the educational participation of girls. Is school drop-out and early withdrawal from school the main problem? Or is it the unwillingness of parents to send girls to school at all?

There is evidence to suggest that drop-out and early withdrawal from school, while being an important factor in reducing the enrolments of both girls and boys, may be less important globally than has often been thought in accounting for the lower educational participation of girls *compared with boys*. Among countries where there is a major problem of survival through the first four grades of primary education – possibly the minimum participation for acquiring permanent literacy and numeracy – there are almost as many countries where girls survive longer than boys than the other way round (Figure 2.8). In both cases anyway, with a few exceptions (Afghanistan, Burkina Faso, Chad, Lesotho, Togo and Zaire), the girls' and boys' survival rates are very close.

In general, it would seem that in countries where there is a major problem of girls' survival in school through the first four grades of primary education, there also is likely to be an equally serious problem of boys' survival too. Poor survival by girls, therefore, can hardly be the only explanation of the global imbalance in girls' and boys' participation in primary education, at least in the first four grades. The likelihood of getting into school in the first place also needs to be taken into account.

'School life expectancies'

New statistical measures are needed in order to settle the question of the relative importance of school access and drop-out (or 'survival') in accounting for imbalances in girls' and boys' participation in formal education. One such measure is the 'school life expectancy', which was defined in the *World Education Report 1993* as the number of years of formal education that a person of a given age can expect to receive in the future,

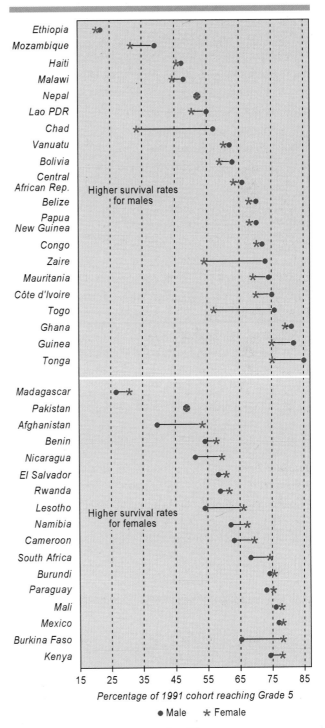

Figure 2.8
Male and female survival rates[1] to Grade 5 in selected countries,[2] 1992

Percentage of 1991 cohort reaching Grade 5
● Male   ✳ Female

1. See Appendix III, 'Explanatory notes', p. 115.
2. Countries where the female survival rate was less than 80%.

Table 2.2
Male and female school life expectancy and school survival expectancy
in selected developing and developed countries,[1] *1992*

					Developing countries					
	School life expectancy (years)		School survival expectancy (years)			School life expectancy (years)		School survival expectancy (years)	
	Male	Female	Male	Female		Male	Female	Male	Female
Sub-Saharan Africa					*Latin America/Caribbean*				
Botswana	10.4	10.9	10.5	10.9	Argentina	13.0	13.5	13.0	13.5
Burkina Faso	3.4	2.1	9.0	8.5	Bahamas	12.2	13.1	12.2	13.1
Burundi	5.1	4.0	9.3	8.5	Barbados	12.8	12.9	12.8	12.9
Gambia	6.1	4.0	9.2	8.2	Belize	10.4	10.3	10.4	10.3
Guinea	3.8	1.6	10.4	8.6	Bolivia	10.5	8.9	10.5	8.9
Lesotho	7.8	9.5	11.3	10.6	Chile	11.8	11.8	11.8	11.8
Malawi	6.3	5.0	8.8	8.4	Costa Rica	9.6	9.4	10.2	9.8
Mali	2.3	1.2	9.2	8.3	Cuba	11.8	12.9	11.8	12.9
Mozambique	4.0	2.9	7.6	7.4	Dominican Republic	10.1	10.4	11.1	10.4
Namibia	12.0	13.0	13.5	13.3	El Salvador	8.7	8.5	10.5	10.2
Niger	2.8	1.4	8.4	7.9	Jamaica	10.9	11.1	10.9	11.1
Rwanda	5.9	5.5	7.2	6.8	Nicaragua	8.4	8.7	10.1	10.1
Senegal	5.6	3.6	9.8	8.8	Panama	11.0	11.3	11.6	11.9
South Africa	11.7	12.2	12.8	12.7	Paraguay	8.6	8.3	8.9	8.7
Togo	10.6	5.9	11.3	9.5	Trinidad and Tobago	10.6	10.6	10.6	10.6
Zaire	6.7	4.4	11.5	9.2	Venezuela	10.4	10.7	11.3	11.4
Mean	*6.5*	*5.5*	*9.9*	*9.3*	*Mean*	*10.7*	*10.8*	*11.1*	*11.1*
Arab States					*Asia/Oceania*				
Algeria	11.0	9.2	11.0	9.6	Bangladesh	5.9	4.4	5.9	4.5
Bahrain	12.5	13.2	12.5	13.2	Brunei Darussalam	11.2	11.2	11.5	12.0
Egypt	10.8	8.8	11.1	10.5	Indonesia	10.1	9.1	10.1	9.1
Iraq	9.4	7.1	11.1	9.7	Iran, Islamic Republic of	9.9	7.6	10.3	8.8
Jordan	11.4	11.6	11.4	11.6	Lao People's				
Morocco	8.0	5.7	9.9	9.3	Democratic Republic	7.9	5.5	10.0	9.1
Oman	8.4	7.4	11.7	10.4	Philippines	10.7	10.9	10.7	10.9
Qatar	10.5	11.8	12.6	14.3	Republic of Korea	14.3	13.0	14.3	13.0
Saudi Arabia	8.6	7.7	13.0	12.4	Vanuatu	7.3	6.5	8.1	7.8
Syrian Arab Republic	10.2	8.7	10.2	9.1	*Mean*	*9.7*	*8.5*	*10.1*	*9.4*
Tunisia	10.9	9.7	10.9	9.7					
United Arab Emirates	10.7	11.7	10.7	11.7	*Mean for*				
Mean	*10.2*	*9.4*	*11.3*	*11.0*	*developing countries*	*9.1*	*8.5*	*10.6*	*10.2*

1. Countries for which the relevant data are available to UNESCO.

assuming that the probability of his or her being enrolled at any particular future age is equal to the current enrolment ratio for the population of that age. The school life expectancy therefore is a synthetic or summary measure of expected overall participation in the whole education system: for a 5-year-old it summarizes his or her expected par-

ticipation from entry into primary school up to the end of formal education.

In this report, for the first time, estimates of school life expectancies are shown separately for males and females (Table 2.2; see also Appendix III, Table 3). Another measure is also introduced: 'school survival expectancy', which is basi-

Developed countries	School life expectancy (years)		School survival expectancy (years)	
	Male	*Female*	*Male*	*Female*
Northern America				
Canada	17.2	17.9	17.2	17.9
United States	15.6	16.3	15.6	16.3
Europe				
Austria	14.9	14.2	14.9	14.2
Belgium	14.4	14.4	14.7	14.4
Bulgaria	11.4	11.9	12.2	12.6
Croatia	11.1	11.3	12.6	12.7
Denmark	14.9	15.4	14.9	15.4
Estonia	12.1	12.7	13.0	13.5
France	14.3	15.0	14.3	15.0
Germany	15.0	14.2	15.7	14.5
Greece	13.2	13.2	13.2	13.2
Hungary	12.0	12.0	12.0	12.0
Ireland	12.9	13.3	12.9	13.3
Malta	13.3	12.8	13.3	12.8
Netherlands	15.7	15.2	16.4	15.5
Norway	15.3	15.6	15.3	15.6
Poland	12.0	12.3	12.0	12.3
Romania	10.9	10.7	11.0	11.0
Spain	14.4	15.0	14.4	15.0
Sweden	13.6	14.0	13.6	14.0
Switzerland	14.6	13.6	15.2	13.8
United Kingdom	14.7	15.0	14.7	15.0
Asia/Oceania				
Australia	13.4	13.9	13.4	13.9
New Zealand	15.2	15.5	15.2	15.5
Mean for developed countries	*13.8*	*14.0*	*13.8*	*14.1*

cally a school life expectancy just *for those persons who get into school* (Appendix I, pp. 95–6). In countries where virtually all children get into school, the school life and school survival expectancies will normally be the same. In other countries where a certain proportion of children never get into school, the school life expectancy will be lower than the school survival expectancy, the difference being accounted for by the possibility of never entering school at all.

Comparisons between these two measures offer many new and important insights into the educational participation of boys and girls in both developed and developing countries; in particular, as will be seen below, they help to settle questions concerning the relative importance of school access and drop-out (or 'survival').

As regards the developed countries, it may be noted firstly that there are very few differences between the school life and school survival expectancies, which is to be expected since virtually all children enter formal education. In the handful of cases (Belgium, Bulgaria, Croatia, Estonia, Germany, Netherlands, Romania and Switzerland) where the estimated school life expectancies are lower than the corresponding school survival expectancies, this is probably due either to a small proportion of children not being recorded as entering formal education, or to an overestimate of the size of the population in the reference age-group.

Secondly, it may be noted that the school life expectancies of girls tend to be higher than those of boys; at least this is the case in fifteen out of the twenty-four developed countries for which the relevant data are available. The gap in favour of girls is especially pronounced (i.e., 0.5 years or more) in Australia, Bulgaria, Canada, Denmark, Estonia, France, Spain and United States. It seems that in the industrial countries there is a tendency for boys to leave the formal education system for the world of work earlier than girls. The reasons for this are not fully understood. Several explanations are possible, ranging from earlier and/or better employment opportunities available to boys, to better academic performances (and hence easier access to higher education) by girls. It could also be the case, in view of the difficulties that women generally have in getting fair treatment in the world of work outside the household, that girls in the industrial countries, having now

Figure 2.9
Trends in male and female school life expectancy in selected Arab countries,[1] 1980–1992

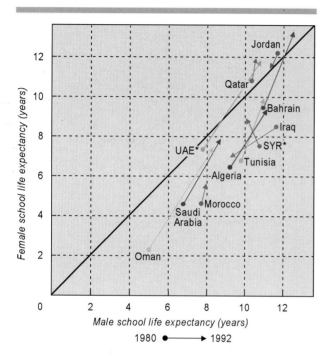

* SYR: Syrian Arab Republic; UAE: United Arab Emirates.

1. Countries for which data are available for both dates.

Secondly, it may be noted that the countries where the gap in school life expectancies is most in favour of boys are generally those where the school life expectancies of both boys and girls are low; these countries are mostly located in sub-Saharan Africa, but they also include some countries in the Arab States Region, e.g. Algeria, Egypt, Iraq, Morocco, Syrian Arab Republic and Tunisia, where the school life expectancies of both girls and boys generally are higher.

Thirdly, it may be noted that in those countries where the school life expectancy of girls is very low, there is less of a gap between girls and boys in their school survival expectancies than in their school life expectancies. In other words, there is less of a gap between boys and girls in their school life expectancies *once they get into school* than before they get into school. The education system, it seems, is less 'unfair' to girls than the economic, social and cultural conditions which limit their access to school in the first place. This suggests that the real challenge for national policy-makers in many of the poorest countries is less one of ensuring that girls are retained once they get into school, than of devising ways and

pretty well achieved parity of participation in education with boys, are striving harder than boys to get high levels of formal qualification in order to strengthen their chances in the labour market. Clearly, the whole phenomenon merits deeper investigation.

As regards the developing countries, it may be noted firstly that the school life expectancies of girls tend to be somewhat lower than those of boys, which is to be expected since in many developing countries higher proportions of girls than of boys never get into school at all. Even so, in seventeen out of the fifty-two developing countries for which the relevant data are available to UNESCO, the girls have slightly higher school life expectancies than boys; this is particularly marked in the Latin America/Caribbean region.

Table 2.3
Male and female school life expectancy (years) in selected Asian and Latin American/Caribbean countries,[1] 1980 and 1992

	1980		1992	
	Male	Female	Male	Female
Bangladesh	5.0	2.8	5.9	4.4
Barbados	12.1	12.3	12.8	12.9
Bolivia	9.2	7.5	10.5	8.9
Brunei Darussalam	10.6	10.6	11.2	11.2
Costa Rica	9.7	9.7	9.6	9.4
Jamaica	10.4	11.0	10.9	11.1
Nicaragua	8.4	8.7	8.4	8.7
Panama	10.9	11.3	11.0	11.3
Philippines	10.1	10.5	10.7	10.9
Republic of Korea	12.3	11.1	14.3	13.0
Trinidad and Tobago	10.9	10.9	10.6	10.6

1. Countries for which data are available for both dates.

Figure 2.10
Female and male school life expectancy (years),[1] in selected countries,[2] 1965–1992

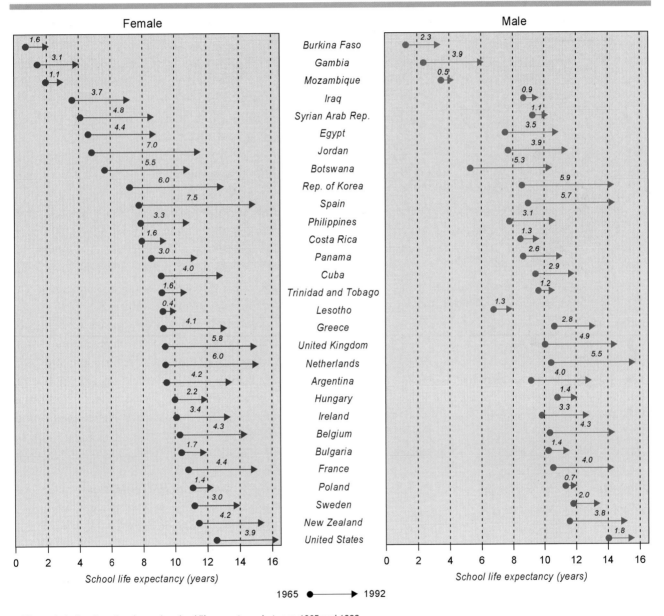

| | Female | | Male | |

Female / Male

School life expectancy (years)

1. Figures in italics show the change in school life expectancy between 1965 and 1992.
2. Countries for which data are available for both dates.

means of encouraging parents to send their girls to school at all.

Finally, it may be useful to note certain trends in the school life expectancies. In nine out of eleven countries in the Arab States Region for which the relevant data are available to UNESCO for both 1980 and 1992, the improvement between the two dates in the school life expectancy was greater for girls than it was for boys (Figure 2.9). Among the Asian and Latin

Figure 2.11
**Urban population and female/male
participation ratio[1] in the first and second
levels of education, 1992**

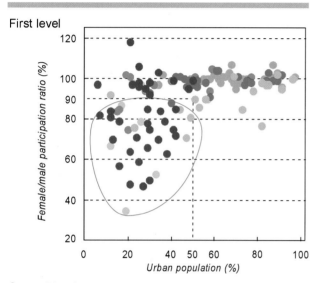

First level

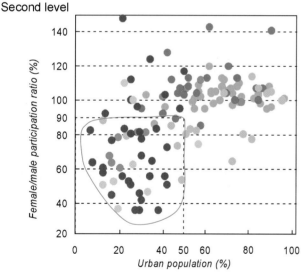

Second level

● Sub-Saharan Africa   ● Arab States   ● Latin America/Caribbean
● Eastern Asia/Oceania   ● Southern Asia   ● Developed countries

1. Ratio of female gross enrolment ratio to male gross enrolment ratio.

American/Caribbean countries for which such data are available (Table 2.3), the changes in the school life expectancies between the two dates for both girls and boys generally were small, except in the Republic of Korea, Bolivia and Bangladesh.

In Bangladesh there was a significant narrowing of the male-female gap.

Among the twenty-nine countries for which data are available to UNESCO for both 1992 and 1965 (the earliest date for which school life expectancies were previously estimated by UNESCO), twenty-five countries increased the opportunities for girls more than for boys, and in five countries (Iraq, Mozambique, Poland, Syrian Arab Republic and the United States) the improvement for girls was more than double that for boys (Figure 2.10, p. 41).

The general picture which emerges from the examination of the school life and school survival expectancies above confirms suggestions which emerged earlier from the examination of the enrolment ratios. In particular, it seems that in the developed countries and in many countries in the Latin American/Caribbean region, as well as in a small but probably growing number of countries in other regions, there is essentially no real difference in the opportunities available to boys and girls for participation as such in the formal education system, and there even are are signs of a tendency for girls to stay longer in the system than boys. Globally, however, these countries are a minority; developing countries especially in sub-Saharan Africa and Asia, are not fully represented in Table 2.2. In probably well over 100 countries the overall participation of girls in the formal education system is certainly still significantly lower than that of boys.

Priorities for action

In the majority of countries where the educational participation of girls relative to that of boys is low, the population is mainly rural, although in a global perspective this by itself is not necessarily a decisive factor (Figure 2.11). The actual socio-economic, cultural and educational conditions in the rural areas are relevant, and these vary from country to country, in some cases (Box 2.4, and

Box 2.4
Problem areas in Bolivia's education

Problem areas include persistent absolute and functional illiteracy, scarce provision of state education, exclusion and drop-out, irrational distribution and lack of training of teaching staff, shortage of financial resources and the gap between human resources training and demand. The most serious problems continue to be poor quality and lack of equality in Bolivian education.

Absolute and functional illiteracy
Persistent illiteracy of the population, especially among rural women (50 per cent) is a direct result of exclusion and dropping out of school. [...]

Of the total illiterate population, 70 per cent live in rural areas and 68 per cent are women.

Availability of state and private education
In Bolivia, the state is the main provider of educational services. [...] State education accounts for 88 per cent of enrolments (including state-funded schools administered by the Catholic Church and some non-governmental organizations).

In rural locations, education is provided almost entirely by the state.

Private education accounts for 12 per cent of total national enrolments, in approximately 500 establishments. The schools with the highest levels of achievement are generally very expensive and cater for élite social groups in the big cities.

Exclusion and drop-out
In primary education, the education system takes care of approximately 60 per cent of school-age children in rural locations and 87 per cent in urban locations. [...]

Exclusion rates increase in lower-secondary education and even more so in upper-secondary and higher education. Only 43 per cent of the urban primary-school intake progress beyond the fifth grade. Scarce provision creates such problems as the fact that 55 per cent of rural schools offer only Grades one to three at the primary level, and the incompatibility between the school calendar and the farming calendar in rural communities. [...]

From a national point of view, the greatest divergencies in drop-out rate are seen between the city and the countryside. They are even greater than between the sexes, although the female drop-out rate is slightly higher in both cases. The rural drop-out rate can be as high as 70 per cent. This phenomenon occurs primarily during the first year of schooling. Only 1.4 per cent of boys and a bare 0.7 per cent of girls finish secondary school.

Irrational distribution of teaching staff
There are 67,555 teachers in Bolivia, more than 60 per cent of whom work in the city. The teacher/student ratio is 1:18 as a national average, but this does not reflect the real situation, since there is an excess of teaching staff in urban locations – in some cases the ratio being 1:7, whereas there is a lack of teachers in rural locations and remote communities have to settle for a poorly trained teacher, or face losing their teacher altogether, with no replacement available for that location. [...]

Discrimination and inequality
As may be seen, we have been unable to fulfil all the objectives proposed in the 1955 reform, whose aim was to incorporate the indigenous population into the education system (at that time the vast majority lived in rural areas). Academic failure rates and the poor quality of education are problems that chiefly prevail in rural locations and in disadvantaged peri-urban zones, for the most part occupied by migrants. [...]

The current content of education reflects discriminatory practices and ideas that show little respect for ethnic, cultural and linguistic diversity or gender awareness.

Unfair distribution of financial resources
Some 98 per cent of the education budget goes towards teachers' salaries, whereas only 2 per cent is allocated for other purposes. Virtually none of the remaining funds are invested in the rural sector. There is usually a strong tendency to allot the resources to urban locations.

The outlook
The Government has announced that it is vital to implement drastic changes through steady, gradual and long-term reform. It has been estimated that it will take approximately twenty years to transform the system completely.

Source: Informe nacional sobre el desarrollo de la educación, pp. 42–5, La Paz, Ministerio de Desarrollo Humano, Secretaría General de Educación, Dirección General de Planeamiento Educativo, 1993. (National report presented at the 44th session of the International Conference on Education, Geneva, 1994.)

perhaps those countries circled in Figure 2.11) being more discouraging to the educational participation of girls compared with boys than in other cases.

Most analysts and commentators have stressed that out-of-school factors in the family and community are probably more important than in-school factors. There is general agreement that

---

Table 2.4
Percentages of female teachers in the first and second levels of education, by region, 1980 and 1992

	1980		1992	
	First level	Second level	First level	Second level
WORLD TOTAL	53	41	57	47
Developing countries of which:	44	32	50	39
Sub-Saharan Africa	34	33	42	33
Arab States	42	32	52	40
Latin America/Caribbean	76	47	77	48
Eastern Asia/Oceania	41	29	49	38
of which: China	37	25	45	34
Southern Asia	29	27	31	35
of which: India	27	27	28	34
Least developed countries	28	23	34	24
Developed countries of which:	77	52	80	58
Northern America	81	46	83	54
Asia/Oceania	67	48	72	53
Europe/Russian Federation	79	55	81	60

Box 2.5
Strategies to promote the education of girls in Zimbabwe

The Ministry [of Education and Culture] has over the past two years adopted and implemented several strategies to promote the education of girls, some of which are the following:

(a) It has relaxed conditions and criteria for girls' admission to certain levels of education (positive discrimination);

(b) It has continued to offer scholarships, bursaries and other concessions to girls, particularly the gifted and deprived girls;

(c) It has given deliberate attention and publicity to 'successful' females, with a view to focusing people's attention on them as models for other females to emulate;

(d) It has favoured females in promotion procedures, even when they are less deserving than their male competitors, if only to provide role models for the girl-child and give women hope;

(e) It has encouraged the offering of a unitary curriculum which has no gender biases (not 'woodwork for boys, needlework for girls');

(f) It has adopted sexual neutrality in the development, selection and use of teaching/learning materials, choice of language, role models, school structures, and other activities;

(g) A scholarship fund has been set aside for girls seeking entry into the Advanced Level of the General Certificate of Education (6th Form).

Source: The Development of Education, 1992–1994: National Report from Zimbabwe, p. 17, Harare, Ministry of Education and Culture, Ministry of Higher Education, 1994. (National report presented at the 44th session of the International Conference on Education, Geneva, 1994.)

---

family poverty, whether in rural or urban areas, is probably the most important reason for holding girls back from school or causing their early withdrawal, although this is often re-inforced by cultural norms and traditional conceptions of the division of labour in the household for tasks ranging from the care of younger siblings to fetching water and collecting firewood that are less favourable to girls' than to boys' participation in school.

It has been observed that women and girls in many of the poorer parts of the world are locked into a cycle of poverty and early marriages, with illiterate mothers bringing up illiterate daughters who are married off early into yet another cycle of poverty, illiteracy, high fertility and early mortality. Breaking up this cycle, it is recognized, requires more than just educational intervention; comprehensive development that transforms the basic conditions of rural (and urban) community life is needed. Education, both formal and non-formal (especially for adults), needs to be part of this transformation, but other community infra-structure (e.g., water wells, fuel/energy supplies, easily accessible health clinics, etc.) also is neces-sary, not to speak of improved employment and income-earning opportunities.

The education authorities by themselves nor-mally can do little to create such conditions. They have more scope for action in regard to in-school factors and conditions which are specific to edu-cation (e.g., Box 2.5).

Among the in-school factors which generally are considered to have an important influence on the attendance of girls, the presence of female teachers has often been highlighted, since parents in many countries sometimes are reluctant to allow their daughters to be taught by male teachers. In a global perspective, the educational participation of girls relative to that of boys certainly is corre-lated with the presence of female teachers (Fig-ure 2.12; see also Appendix I, pp. 99–100), more so than with the country's income level or per-centage of rural population, although all these factors are to some extent interrelated. Female teachers are in the minority in first-level education in both sub-Saharan Africa and Southern Asia, es-pecially the latter (Table 2.4). As noted earlier, it is in these two regions that the challenge to increase the school attendance of girls is most pronounced.

The strategic importance of the teaching pro-fession for the advancement of women has prob-ably been underestimated up to now by national policy-makers. Historically, in the industrial countries, teaching was one of the earliest and most successful career paths that women took in entering the world of work outside the house-hold. Quite aside from the encouragement which an increased presence of female teachers in the schools could give to parents who are reluctant to send their daughters to school, the teaching pro-fession itself in most developing countries today is one of the few 'modern' wage-paying occu-

Figure 2.12

Percentage of female teachers and female/male participation ratio[1] in the first and second levels of education, 1992

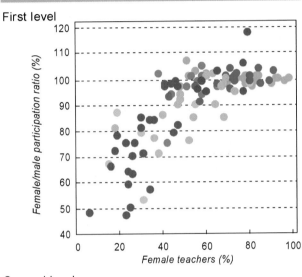

First level

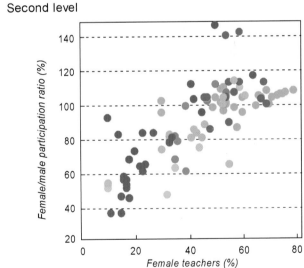

Second level

● Sub-Saharan Africa ● Arab States ● Latin America/Caribbean
● Eastern Asia/Oceania ● Southern Asia ● Developed countries

1. Ratio of female gross enrolment ratio to male gross enrolment ratio.

pations which the national authorities have the power to ensure is relatively free of discriminat-ory entry conditions for women while at the same time giving a certain measure of social protection (maternity leave, etc.). In that perspective, review

---

Box 2.6
Call for action on girls' education in Africa

This Conference calls upon
- Governments to undertake analytic assessment of the social and educational situation of girls and women with the active participation of women's organizations and other NGOs, political and traditional leaders and representative of various population groups with special emphasis on the co-operate bodies;
- Governments to give priority to quality and equity and administration targets for improving girls' education within the framework of national development plans;
- Governments of those countries in which the disparity between boys and girls in school is more than 10 per cent of the target population to eliminate such disparities by the year 2000;
- Governments to prepare and implement strategies to achieve such targets making the girl-child the focus of education planning and development;
- Governments and in particular the ministries of education to ensure that by 1995, all teachers have received training on gender issues and that such issues be incorporated in the conventional teacher training programme and the school curriculum;
- Governments introduce and reinforce regulations which will eliminate the employment of school-age girls as household help without opportunities for education;
- Governments to monitor the progress in their achievement and by 1995 to make the first progress report to the nation, the sub-region and to the region and also in the global context to report progress to the EFA Forum and United Nations World Conference on Women in 1995, and thereafter to present biennial reports;

- regional, bilateral and international agencies and NGOs, to make the education of girls the number one priority in their development programmes and also to give priority to the development of rural water, roads and electricity which will ease the workload of the mother and hence the girl-child;
- wives of heads of states, ministers and parliamentarians to form a pressure group for ensuring the education and welfare of the girl-child;
- educators to draw on the positive aspects of historical, cultural, and religious heritage as a means of improving education quality and equity;
- the Organization of African Unity to give priority to the education of the girl-child in the agenda of its upcoming OAU meeting in Cairo and further to take affirmative action in reducing the disparity between education of boys and girls as a follow-up to the Dakar consensus with special reference to the target to eliminate these disparities by the year 2000;
- the United Nations in its agenda for the upcoming World Conference on Women to put girls' education on the agenda and to include a round table on girls' education;
- Governments and the international community to recognize and make reference to this declaration, as of today, as the Ouagadougou Declaration.

Source: The Ouagadougou Declaration, adopted by the Pan-African Conference on the Education of Girls, organized under UNESCO's Priority Africa Programme and the UNESCO/UNICEF Joint Committee on Education in Co-operation with the Government of Burkina Faso, Ouagadougou, Burkina Faso, 28 March–1 April 1993.

---

of the current conditions for access to teacher education programmes could be a priority area for action in many countries.

In some countries it is difficult to post newly trained unmarried female teachers to rural schools, and they tend to congregate in the towns thus further aggravating urban-rural imbalances in the school attendance of girls. In these cases, married women teachers living in rural areas would appear to be a key resource, meriting special incentives. They are needed too for non-formal education programmes aiming to teach literacy and other basic 'life-skills' to women and adolescent girls who never entered or who dropped out early from the formal system. There potentially are benefits in terms of community attitudes towards girls' schooling: literate mothers, it has often been observed, are more likely to strive to ensure that their daughters receive a basic education than mothers who are illiterate.

Prospects

The international political commitment in favour of the education of women and girls has never been stronger than today. Most countries now accept that the education of women and girls must have priority in their education policies. This was agreed by the World Conference on Education for All (Jomtien, 1990), by the Pan-African Conference on the Education of Girls (Ouagadougou, 1993) (Box 2.6) and by the Education for All Summit of Nine High-Population Countries (Delhi, 1993).

Nevertheless, while these conferences have been extremely important in helping to create an educational policy environment favourable to the education of women and girls, they cannot substitute for active political leadership and pressure at the national level. In that connection, mention should be made of the influential role of the Forum for African Women Educationalists (FAWE), a partnership of thirty to forty African women cabinet ministers, women vice-chancellors of universities and other senior women policy-makers in education and related fields, which was created in 1992 with the goal of mutual assistance and collaboration in developing national capabilities to accelerate female participation in education at all levels.

In general, the prospects of achieving rapid advances in the educational participation of girls in countries where their participation is currently most limited are tied up with these countries' development prospects overall. As was noted earlier at several points in this chapter, the biggest male-female gaps in literacy and participation in formal education tend to be in countries where the levels of literacy and educational participation are low for both males and females. In at least forty countries today, the gross enrolment ratio of girls in first-level education still is less than 100 per cent, yet in thirty of them the gross enrolment ratio of boys also is less than 100 per cent (see Appendix III, Table 4). The same scarcities and constraints which are responsible for the low enrolment ratios of boys are also partly responsible for the low enrolment ratios of girls. The challenge to increase the access of girls to schooling and to provide increased opportunities for them to continue to the higher levels is therefore part of a broader challenge to provide increased educational opportunities as such, for both girls and boys. There is a link, therefore, to the prospects of development in general.

This link is perhaps most vividly apparent in the continuing struggle against illiteracy. It has been observed before by UNESCO that 'illiteracy and poverty not only go hand in hand, but shoulder to shoulder, each supporting the other'. It is the world's poor who are illiterate. If they live in want today and in fear of tomorrow, if they have neither a stake in society nor a hope in the future, what would prompt them each to allocate several hundred hours, needed in a harsh struggle for survival, to the arduous task of mastering an alphabet? To become literate, people must be motivated to learn and this will occur only when they perceive the possibility of transforming the existential conditions of their lives. Womens' lives, for the most part. The global struggle against illiteracy, therefore, is also, and at the same time, a struggle for development, justice, greater equality and recognition of the human dignity of all and of the claims of each to a responsible economic, social and political role in society, and to the fruits which derive therefrom.

3
Challenges
to pedagogy

As the number of countries which are able to ensure a broad measure of equality of access for the two sexes to the different levels of formal education gradually increases, the question of equal opportunity for access to the different fields of study within education has become more salient at both national and international levels. The increasing participation of women in the labour market in most countries has probably been a crucial factor in directing national and international attention to this aspect of equal opportunity, because of the connection between fields of study and women's employment prospects.

The idea that women should have equal opportunities for access to the same types of education or fields of study as those available to men has probably encountered more resistance historically than any other aspect of women's education. Before the advent of mass education in the last century, philosophies of education in the western as much as in other civilizations stressed the separate and distinct nature of women's education, in so far as they acknowledged that women should be educated at all. It has only been in the present century, and especially since the Second World War, that the principle of equal opportunity for men and women to have access to the same types of education has become widely accepted. The experience of implementing a common elementary or basic education for the two sexes possibly was decisive in this development. At the younger ages, in most countries today, girls and boys learn pretty much the same things, usually in a co-educational setting.

It is at the secondary level that significant differences in the types of education received by the two sexes usually begin to appear, and they tend to become more pronounced at the post-secondary and higher levels. Such differences, especially the widespread tendency for girls to participate less than boys in technical and science-related studies, are the main concern of this chapter. The final point of reference for the chapter – hence its title – is the individual teacher: what (if anything) can he or she do about these differences?

First, the norms of equal opportunity and treatment laid down by existing international conventions are briefly recalled, as well as certain of the philosophical and psycho-pedagogical assumptions which traditionally have underpinned the idea of a separate and distinct education for women. In subsequent sections, several global patterns and trends in the types of education received by the two sexes at the secondary and tertiary levels of education are considered, having regard in particular to the changing context of post-school employment opportunities, the findings of cross-national studies of girls' and boys' learning achievement (especially in science and mathematics), and recent developments in thinking in some countries concerning appropriate and effective pedagogies for both girls and boys.

Equal opportunity and treatment

There exist several international conventions which have a bearing on the types of education offered to the two sexes. In the background is the *Universal Declaration of Human Rights* (1948), which requires that education 'shall be directed to the full development of the human personality and to the strengthening of respect for human rights and fundamental freedoms' (Article 26); this precludes any *a priori* judgements concerning the types of education that men and women should receive.

The first international convention to lay down specifically the terms of equal opportunity in education was UNESCO's *Convention against Discrimination in Education* (1960), now ratified by eighty-four states. (Key Articles from this convention were reproduced in Boxes 3.4 and 3.5 of the *World Education Report 1993*.) 'Discrimination' is defined as 'any distinction, exclusion, limitation or preference which, being based on race, colour, sex, language, religion, political or other opinion, national or social origin, economic condition or birth, has the purpose or effect of nullifying or impairing equality of treatment in education' (Article 1). The 'establishment or maintenance of separate educational systems or institutions for the pupils of the two sexes' is not deemed to constitute discrimination (Article 2), but the convention requires that in all substantive respects the educational opportunities available to the two sexes should be the same.

Nearly twenty years later, the United Nations *Convention on the Elimination of All Forms of Discrimination against Women* (1979), in its Article 10 concerning education, added several important details to the requirements of the UNESCO convention, particularly as regards the process and content of education. In the United

Nations convention there is specific mention of career and vocational guidance, curricula and examinations, and stereotyping of the roles of men and women in textbooks, school programmes and teaching methods; also mentioned are scholarships and other study grants, continuing education (including adult and functional literacy programmes), sports and physical education, and educational information to help to ensure the health and well-being of families (Box 3.1).

The UNESCO *Convention on Technical and Vocational Education* (1989) reaffirmed the injunctions against discrimination already contained in the earlier UNESCO and United Nations conventions: 'The Contracting States shall guarantee that no individual who has attained the educational level for admission into technical and vocational education shall be discriminated

---

Box 3.1
The State's responsibility to 'take all appropriate measures'
to eliminate discrimination against women in the field of education

States parties shall take all appropriate measures to eliminate discrimination against women in order to ensure to them equal rights with men in the field of education and in particular to ensure, on a basis of equality of men and women:

(a) The same conditions for career and vocational guidance, for access to studies and for the achievement of diplomas in educational establishments of all categories in rural as well as in urban areas; this equality shall be ensured in pre-school, general, technical, professional and higher technical education, as well as in all types of vocational training;

(b) Access to the same curricula, the same examinations, teaching staff with qualifications of the same standard and school premises and equipment of the same quality;

(c) The elimination of any stereotyped concept of the roles of men and women at all levels and in all forms of education by encouraging coeducation and other types of education which will help to achieve this aim and, in particular, by the revision

of textbooks and school programmes and the adaptation of teaching methods;

(d) The same opportunities to benefit from scholarships and other study grants;

(e) The same opportunities for access to programmes of continuing education, including adult and functional literacy programmes, particularly those aimed at reducing, at the earliest possible time, any gap in education existing between men and women;

(f) The reduction of female student drop-out rates and the organization of programmes for girls and women who have left school prematurely;

(g) The same opportunities to participate actively in sports and physical education;

(h) Access to specific educational information to help to ensure the health and well-being of families, including information and advice on family planning.

Source: Convention on the Elimination of All Forms of Discrimination against Women, Article 10, New York, United Nations, 1979. (As of 31 December 1994, this Convention had been ratified by 135 states.)

against on grounds of race, colour, sex, language, religion, national or social origin, political or other opinions, economic status, birth, or on any other grounds' (Article 2). It also affirmed that, 'The Contracting States shall work towards the right to equal access to technical and vocational education and towards equality of opportunity to study throughout the educational process'. Such equality of opportunity doubtless was intended to mean equal opportunity for access to the different types of curricula or study programmes within technical and vocational education; this certainly is the sense of the *Convention against Discrimination in Education* and also of the *Convention on the Elimination of All Forms of Discrimination against Women,* both of which insist not just on equal opportunity for access to education in general but also to its different components.

None of the conventions, though, precludes the possibility that males and females might choose to participate in different curricula or study programmes. They require only that the two sexes should have equal opportunity to choose, and should be treated equally.

Choice and purpose

Before considering the empirical patterns and trends in female participation in the various types of education or fields of study in different countries and regions of the world, it may be useful to acknowledge the difficulty of knowing whether these patterns and trends reflect constrained or unconstrained choices by the populations concerned.

The exercise of choice, even under the most favourable circumstances when it is not constrained by discrimination, opens up the possibility of specialization by the sexes among types of education or fields of study. Specialization in itself does not necessarily signify discrimination. It does, however, indicate that some kind of constraint is present, which in many cases may well

be a restriction of opportunities for access to particular fields of study, although in other cases it may amount to nothing more than social convention. Probably in most cases it is a combination of both factors, since social conventions which are deeply entrenched will often be reflected in real restrictions or limitations of opportunity for choice.

It is not unreasonable to suggest that in most societies up to now social convention has favoured specialization by the sexes among types of education or fields of study, and it is probably true historically, at least in the Western civilization, that educational philosophies which have emphasized specialization have rooted their arguments in assumptions concerning the division of labour between men and women in the family and household. This was the case of the eighteenth century French philosopher Rousseau, for example, but already at that time (which was not long before the advent of mass education in Europe), in the counter-arguments of his English feminist critic Mary Wollstonecraft, different assumptions were beginning to appear, including the possibilities of women 'being enabled to earn their own subsistence' (Box 3.2).

Some modern feminist critics have suggested that the basic idea of a social and even biological necessity for different types of education for the two sexes has never really disappeared from Western and other civilizations' educational thinking. It prevails in the common educational assumptions of most societies concerning differences in girls' and boys' abilities and motivations. In conjunction with assumptions about future employment possibilities and household responsibilities, it has probably in most countries served to constrain socially, if not legally, the range of choices available to girls and young women among the various curricula and programmes of study at the secondary and higher levels of education.

The instruments available to national educational policy- and decision-makers for counter-

Box 3.2
An eighteenth century philosophical dispute: arguments for and against the provision of different education for men and women

For ... *(Jean-Jacques Rousseau, 1712–1778)*

But for her sex, a woman is a man; she has the same organs, the same needs, the same faculties. The machine is the same in its construction; its parts, its working, and its appearance are similar. Regard it as you will the difference is only in degree.

Yet where sex is concerned man and woman are unlike; each is the complement of the other; the difficulty in comparing them lies in our inability to decide, in either case, what is a matter of sex, and what is not. [...]

These resemblances and differences must have an influence on the moral nature; this inference is obvious, and it is confirmed by experience; it shows the vanity of the disputes as to the superiority or the equality of the sexes; as if each sex, pursuing the path marked out for it by nature, were not more perfect in that very divergence than if it more closely resembled the other. A perfect man and a perfect woman should no more be alike in mind than in face, and perfection admits of neither less nor more.

[...]

When once it is proved that men and women are and ought to be unlike in constitution and in temperament, it follows that their education must be different. Nature teaches us that they should work together, but that each has its own share of the work; the end is the same, but the means are different, as are also the feelings which direct them.

Source: Jean-Jacques Rousseau, *Emile*, pp. 384–91, London, J. M. Dent (Everyman), 1993.

Against ... *(Mary Wollstonecraft, 1759–1797)*

If marriage be the cement of society, mankind should all be educated after the same model, or the intercourse of the sexes will never deserve the name of fellowship, nor will women ever fulfil the peculiar duties of their sex, till they become enlightened citizens, till they become free by being enabled to earn their own subsistence, independent of men; in the same manner, I mean, to prevent misconstruction, as one man is independent of another. Nay, marriage will never be held sacred till women, by being brought up with men, are prepared to be their companions rather than their mistresses; for the mean doublings of cunning will ever render them contemptible, whilst oppression renders them timid. So convinced am I of this truth, that I will venture to predict that virtue will never prevail in society till the virtues of both sexes are founded on reason; and, till the affections common to both are allowed to gain their due strength by the discharge of mutual duties.

Were boys and girls permitted to pursue the same studies together, those graceful decencies might early be inculcated which produce modesty without those sexual distinctions that taint the mind.

Source: Mary Wollstonecraft, *A Vindication of the Rights of Woman*, pp. 289–90, London, Penguin Books, 1992.

ing conventional attitudes in the society towards girls' choices of fields of study are quite limited. The 'policy dilemma' reaches down to the most basic level in the classroom: if, say, a 14-year-old girl who is capable in most school subjects does not want to pursue science studies into upper secondary and higher education, notwithstanding national policies to try to encourage more girls to take up science, what (if anything) can or should her teachers do about it? (On the reverse side of

this coin of course is the boy who is perfectly able, but does not wish, to study, say, literature or history.)

If it is believed generally that girls cannot be taught technical subjects or science and mathematics as successfully as boys, because they are thought to be less able and/or less motivated than boys to learn these subjects, then the 14-year-old girl above is unlikely to receive much encouragement to take up science. Pedagogical challenges, and behind them questions concerning girls' and boys' abilities and motivations, therefore are coming to be recognized as central to the management of opportunities for the two sexes in the types of education they receive; they will be considered later in this chapter.

There ultimately are links to the purposes of education. Starting points are crucial. If the formulation of policy or pedagogy begins with a search for what distinguishes or separates men and women, then the conclusion – like Rousseau's or the modern economic theory of the household –

will be a theory of comparative advantage and specialization. If it begins with a search – like Mary Wollstonecraft's – for what binds men and women (indeed society) together, the conclusion will be quite different.

Specialization or discrimination?

In most countries there is some form of specialization among fields of study at the secondary level, if only because at this level students are normally

Table 3.1

Percentage of female enrolment in selected fields of study in second-level vocational education in selected countries,[1] 1980 and 1992[2]

	Commerce and service trades		Craft, Industry and engineering			Commerce and service trades		Craft, Industry and engineering	
	1980	1992	1980	1992		1980	1992	1980	1992
Sub-Saharan Africa					*Asia/Oceania*				
Burundi	89.3	80.0	3.9	3.1	Bangladesh	4.8	14.3	0.8	6.7
Comoros	58.3	38.9	–	19.4	Cyprus	56.3	17.0	9.1	10.7
Guinea[3]	97.1	61.6	13.7	2.8	Indonesia	54.9	67.7	2.3	2.3
Mozambique	34.1	49.6	9.8	12.6	Iran, Islamic				
Rwanda	49.4	47.3	62.3	40.9	Republic of	15.0	14.0	0.1	10.3
Togo	35.5	32.0	–	2.5	Israel	99.3	85.8	20.6	12.2
					Japan	69.6	70.1	4.1	6.3
Arab States					Lao People's				
Algeria	48.1	48.6	11.3	25.7	Democratic Republic	18.8	21.7	19.6	7.9
Bahrain	55.2	51.8	–	3.8	Malaysia	87.6	80.1	11.9	7.0
Egypt	54.2	69.9	11.5	25.1	New Zealand	94.7	68.5	17.6	12.6
Iraq	78.9	76.4	6.3	3.8	Republic of				
Jordan	45.1	57.2	–	–	Korea	69.3	78.9	12.2	6.4
Lebanon	60.5	55.9	5.9	5.7	Turkey	39.0	50.3	36.3	28.2
Morocco	32.1	57.7	3.7	10.1					
Sudan	36.3	41.1	–	–	*Europe*				
Syrian Arab Republic	52.7	51.5	5.6	3.7	Albania	72.6	67.8	32.5	24.3
					Austria	63.3	63.4	13.5	13.2
Latin America /Caribbean					Bulgaria	89.9	80.1	35.0	34.3
Argentina[4]	61.3	57.1	23.1	20.7	Denmark	66.4	62.4	12.4	20.9
Chile	71.9	75.9	3.7	5.0	Finland	75.8	69.4	16.7	16.5
Costa Rica	74.7	67.8	30.2	29.4	Hungary	80.0	75.1	20.7	23.4
El Salvador	55.5	62.6	5.0	5.0	Italy	62.9	61.3	7.4	11.7
Nicaragua	66.7	77.9	16.2	16.4	Netherlands	49.3	53.0	5.6	10.5
Panama	77.3	73.4	4.9	4.2	Norway	67.3	59.1	16.4	10.7
Trinidad and Tobago[4]	90.1	76.6	11.7	15.6	Poland	94.6	87.4	25.4	21.9
Uruguay[5]	79.5	76.0	17.2	38.8	Sweden	65.8	56.6	8.3	14.5
Venezuela	81.8	74.9	14.9	18.8	Switzerland	66.3	65.0	9.6	13.1

– Magnitude nil.
1. Countries for which the relevant data are available to UNESCO.
2. Or nearest year available.

3. Data shown for 1980 refer to 1985.
4. Data shown for 1992 refer to 1988.
5. Data shown for 1980 refer to public schools only.

allowed a certain amount of choice among optional subjects in the secondary curriculum, which can mean either choosing to study a new subject, e.g. a second foreign language or technical drawing, or choosing to study an existing subject, e.g. science, in greater depth. In probably a majority of countries there are different types of schools at the secondary level; usually the largest group is general secondary schools providing scope for a certain amount of choice as above, while the others typically are various kinds of vocational or technical schools. The general secondary schools in many countries often have vocational or technical 'tracks', and in the higher grades the academic track – which tends to be a preparation for admission to tertiary level education – is often differentiated into science and arts/humanities tracks or 'streams'.

The data available to UNESCO on enrolment in second-level vocational and technical education are at best only indicative, because of differences between countries in their definitions (and reporting) of vocational, technical and general education at this level. Caution is required, therefore, in making inter-country comparisons. Nevertheless, it is clear that females generally account for significantly higher percentages of enrolment in courses of study and training oriented towards commercial and service trades or occupations than in courses oriented towards craft, industrial and engineering trades or occupations (Table 3.1). There was little change in this pattern between 1980 and 1992. It is not necessarily the case, though, that females are disadvantaged by this pattern, because in most countries employment in commerce and especially services has been growing faster than in other sectors. Nevertheless, there probably is more potential for female participation in technical fields than has yet been realized; at least, this was one of the conclusions of the International Expert Meeting on the Promotion of Equal Access of Girls and Women to Technical and Vocational Education which was recently held in Seoul (July, 1995) in the context

of UNESCO's International Project on Technical and Vocational Education (UNEVOC).

It would be of interest to have more information on patterns and trends in male-female participation by field of study within general education, which in any case accounts for the largest proportion of enrolment at the second level in most countries, but systematic data are not available. In probably a majority of countries the general secondary curriculum includes one or two subjects specifically intended for girls or boys as such (e.g.home economics, woodwork), but these subjects typically are not critical for future access to higher education or employment. It is in the core academic subjects which are determinant for access to higher education that secondary education plays a key role.

The breakdown of students by gender and broad field of study in third-level education in over 100 countries in 1992 is shown in Appendix III, Table 9. In most countries there probably is some relationship between the pattern of student enrolments in third-level education and the student enrolments and curricula in second-level education, particularly at the upper stage of the latter, but in the absence of comprehensive cross-country data on second-level education the nature of this relationship can only be surmised. Nonetheless, the third-level breakdown is of considerable interest in itself.

Several points may be noted. First, there is substantial global variation among countries in the percentage of female students in all fields taken together. With one or two exceptions, the low percentages tend to be found in sub-Saharan Africa and to a lesser extent in Southern Asia.

Second, in every country for which the data are available to UNESCO the female share of enrolment in the natural sciences, engineering and agriculture is less than the female share of total enrolment in all fields (Figure 3.1). The opposite tendency is apparent in the humanities. The proportions are broadly balanced in law and social sciences. In both education and medical sciences

Figure 3.1
Female share of enrolment in different fields of study in third-level education, 1992

Humanities

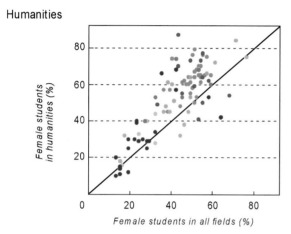

Law and social sciences

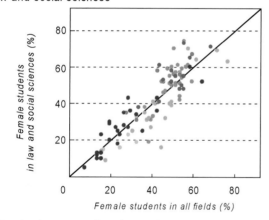

Natural sciences, engineering and agriculture

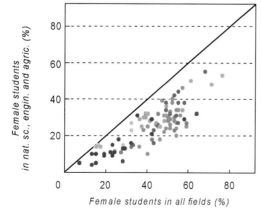

●Sub-Saharan Africa ●Arab States ●Latin America/Caribbean
●Eastern Asia/Oceania ●Southern Asia ●Developed countries

– which are not shown in Figure 3.1 – the female share of enrolment tends to be somewhat higher (except possibly in regard to medical sciences in Africa) than the female share of enrolment in all fields.

This partitioning of the sexes among fields of study, in particular the apparently universal under-representation of females in the natural sciences, engineering and agriculture, is so well defined empirically – every region of the world, industrial and developing countries alike – that it would seem virtually to constitute an 'iron law' of education. What does it mean?

The interpretation depends on the starting point, as was noted at the end of the previous section. If a difference between males and females is assumed to be important from the start, then specialization can be attributed to comparative advantage. If the difference cannot be specified, the argument of comparative advantage becomes circular and cannot serve as an explanation of the phenomenon observed.

It may be argued instead that the specialization simply reflects students' choices, but even in this case circularity cannot be avoided because any observed partitioning of the students could just as well be attributed to discrimination by the fields between the students. For example, if all third-level students had an equal chance of entering a given field, and if there were no 'bias' in the field's selection of students, then the proportions, respectively, of all third-level female and male students which are enrolled in that field would be equal. Yet this is not the case. Either the humanities, law and social sciences are more 'welcoming' to females, or females tend to prefer these fields (Figure 3.2). An equally inconclusive observation can be made of males in the natural sciences, engineering and agriculture (Figure 3.3). Clearly, the explanation of gender partitioning among fields of study cannot be ascertained just from an examination of the partitioning itself; some kind of causal sequence has to be postulated, whereby males and females are either

Figure 3.2
**Gender 'bias' of selection into humanities,
law and social sciences, 1992**

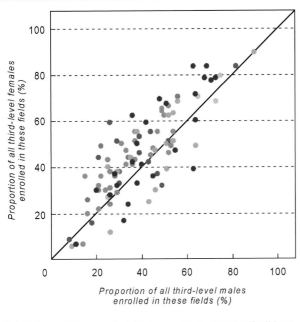

- Sub-Saharan Africa   • Arab States   • Latin America/Caribbean
- Eastern Asia/Oceania   • Southern Asia   • Developed countries

The truth of the matter (specialization or discrimination?) presumably lies somewhere in between, with its exact position varying from country to country. The mix of social and institutional pressures on males and females to try to enter certain fields rather than others is not the same in every country, nor is the pattern of places available among the different fields. Yet it would be unreasonable to suggest that social and institutional pressures and the availability of places are the whole story, and that young women (and men) the world over rarely are comfortable with their choices. What would the 'ideal' distribution of the sexes among the fields be, anyway? The measure which at first sight seems to be the most plausible – considered below – yields unexpected results.

'pushed' or 'pulled' (or both), by their own choices and those of others, into the various fields of study.

Most explanations which have been offered by commentators and analysts to date have not been general enough, tending to focus either on only one aspect of gender representation, e.g. females in science and engineering, or on only one kind of causal sequence, e.g. the 'pull' of science and engineering in favour of males. Probably, also, the tendency of a majority of explanations has been to focus on the female rather than the male specialization because it is females whose choices are considered to be more constrained. Certainly, as many feminist critics have pointed out, females often do not have much say in running the fields: even in countries where they constitute a majority of the students, they constitute only a minority of the teaching staff (Figure 3.4).

Figure 3.3
**Gender 'bias' of selection into natural sciences,
engineering and agriculture, 1992**

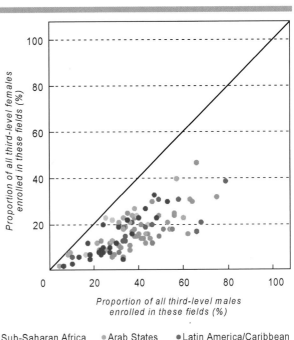

- Sub-Saharan Africa   • Arab States   • Latin America/Caribbean
- Eastern Asia/Oceania   • Southern Asia   • Developed countries

Figure 3.4
Gender distribution of national higher-education staff in Sweden, by occupation, 1992

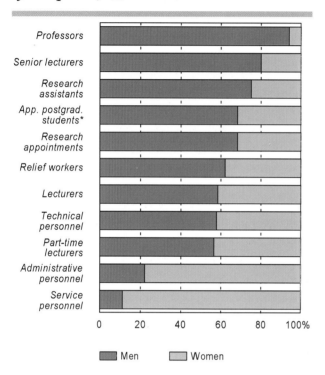

* Postgraduate students holding academic appointments.

Source: Education in Sweden 1994, p. 58, Stockholm, Statistics Sweden, 1994.

Gender segregation index

If a sufficient number of females and males in the different fields in a given country were willing and able to change places, a 'balanced' distribution of the sexes among the fields could be achieved, that is to say, one where the ratio of females to males is the same in all fields. The percentage of persons who would need to change fields for this to happen therefore can be understood as an index of gender segregation, with low percentages indicating a low degree of segregation (specialization) of the sexes and high percentages indicating a high degree of segregation.

The application of this index can be illustrated

with reference to two culturally very different countries: Bangladesh and Finland for example. In Bangladesh, 1 per cent of the enrolment in third-level education would need to change fields of study, whereas in Finland the corresponding figure is 23 per cent (Table 3.2). On this index, therefore, there is very much less gender segregation among fields of study in higher education in Bangladesh than in Finland. The reasons deserve close scrutiny. The basic reason is that in Bangladesh, in those fields of study where the largest numbers of students of both sexes are enrolled, the percentages which are female are very close (15–16 per cent) to the overall percentage of females in the total enrolment in all fields (16 per cent), whereas in Finland this is not the case. It remains, though, that the overall percentage of females in the total enrolment in Finland (53 per cent) is much higher than in Bangladesh. In which education system are the females better off? In Bangladesh there are proportionately fewer females in the total higher education enrolment than in Finland, but in Finland the females

Table 3.2
Gender segregation by field of study in third-level education in Bangladesh and Finland, 1992

Field of study	Bangladesh		Finland	
	Distribution of all students by field (%)	Per cent female	Distribution of all students by field (%)	Per cent female
Education	1	35	11	76
Humanities	30	16	14	70
Law and social sciences	42	15	19	57
Natural sciences, engineering and agriculture	25	15	38	23
Medical sciences	2	27	18	84
Other	0	0	0	0
Total (all fields)	100	16	100	53
Gender segregation index (%)[1]	1		23	

1. See Appendix I, p. 98.

Figure 3.5
Percentage of female students
in third-level education
and gender segregation by field of study,[1] 1992

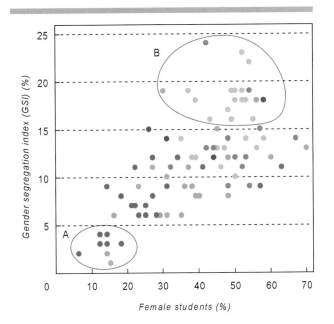

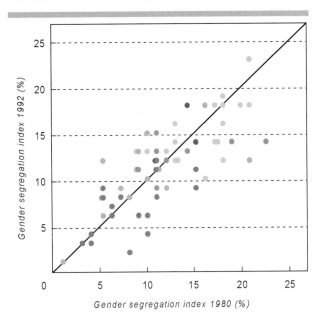

segregation by field of study increases as the overall percentage of females in higher education increases (Figure 3.5), although it should also be recognized that among countries with a high percentage of females in total enrolment there is much variation in the gender segregation index.

There was little change in the overall pattern between 1980 and 1992: out of sixty-two countries for which the relevant data for both dates are available to UNESCO, the gender segregation index improved in twenty-eight countries, remained the same in ten and deteriorated in twenty-four (Figure 3.6).

In so far as the gender segregation index points at least to the possibility of discrimination, there emerges from all this a certain ground for caution against hastily assuming that problems of gender discrimination are mostly confined to poor developing countries.

- Sub-Saharan Africa   - Arab States   - Latin America/Caribbean
- Eastern Asia/Oceania   - Southern Asia   - Developed countries

Group A (GSI < 5)

Benin	(13, 3)	Guinea	(7, 2)
Bangladesh	(16, 1)	Mauritania	(15, 2)
Comoros	(15, 3)	Niger	(15, 4)
Congo	(19, 3)	Togo	(13, 4)

Group B (GSI > 15)

Afghanistan	(31, 19)	Guyana	(43, 24)
Australia	(53, 18)	Hungary	(51, 18)
Azerbaijan	(38, 19)	Japan	(40, 18)
Bahrain	(57, 18)	Philippines	(59, 18)
Belarus	(50, 19)	Poland	(56, 16)
Czech Republic	(44, 16)	Russian Federation	(55, 22)
Denmark	(53, 19)	Saint Kitts and Nevis	(55, 19)
Estonia	(51, 19)	Slovakia	(49, 17)
Finland	(53, 23)	Sweden	(54, 18)
Greece	(50, 16)		

1. See Appendix I, p. 98. See also Appendix III, 'Explanatory notes', p. 116.

Figure 3.6
Overall gender segregation
in third-level education, 1980 and 1992

- Sub-Saharan Africa   - Arab States   - Latin America/Caribbean
- Eastern Asia/Oceania   - Southern Asia   - Developed countries

are under-represented in certain fields, e.g., the natural sciences, engineering and agriculture.

In a global perspective, at least in regard to the countries for which the relevant data are available to UNESCO, it is generally the case that gender

Figure 3.7
**Labour force participation rates of females
in the United States, by age and birthyear cohort**

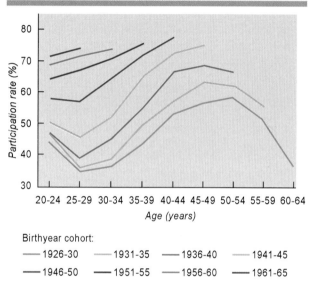

Birthyear cohort:

——— 1926-30 ——— 1931-35 ——— 1936-40 ——— 1941-45
——— 1946-50 ——— 1951-55 ——— 1956-60 ——— 1961-65

Source: Kathryn Shaw, 'The Persistence of Female Labor Supply', *Journal of Human Resources*, Vol. XXIX, No. 2, 1995, p. 351.

Whether any index can be formulated that would capture an 'ideal' distribution of the sexes among fields of study must, however, remain extremely doubtful. What normative advantage can there possibly be for a country in having an equi-proportional representation of the sexes among fields of study? And if equi-proportionality is not to be the goal, what alternative proportions are better? Who (if anyone) should decide?

One further aspect of gender segregation in third-level education that could be considered is the partitioning of the sexes among the different categories of third-level education, i.e., short courses not leading to a first university degree, courses leading to a first university degree or equivalent, and courses leading to a second or higher university degree, corresponding respectively to ISCED (International Standard Classification of Education) categories 5, 6 and 7 (see Appendix III, 'Explanatory notes', p. 116). However, there is such a large variation among countries in their definitions (and reporting) of enrolment in the ISCED categories, especially in regard to whether a particular course leads to a qualification 'equivalent' to a university degree, that little plausibility would attach to a gender segregation index calculated on the basis of these categories. For example, countries as varied as Honduras, India, Italy, Mauritania, Morocco and Spain all report to UNESCO that only 1 per cent of their third-level enrolment is in ISCED category 5, while countries such as France (23 per cent), Japan (19 per cent), Jordan (36 per cent), Paraguay (17 per cent), Switzerland (40 per cent), Thailand (20 per cent) and Zimbabwe (76 per cent) all report much higher percentages (see Appendix III, Table 8). UNESCO is currently revising the definitions of the ISCED categories in order to ensure greater inter-country consistency in the reporting of enrolment.

Employment perspectives

It is possible, even likely, that the whole question of gender specialization by field of study in secondary and higher education is ultimately connected with future employment prospects and the links that exist between fields of study and types of occupations and careers. In any case, the conditions of admission to higher education are not the only consideration influencing girls' choices during secondary schooling. In the majority of countries most girls leave the education system altogether after the first cycle or stage of secondary schooling. Whether or not admission to higher education is envisaged, employment and career expectations generally, in conjunction with perceptions of future marriage, child-raising and household responsibilities, are probably critical in girls' attitudes and motivations towards different fields of study in school.

The difficulty is to account for the consistency in gender specialization by field of study across both industrial and developing countries, given

Table 3.3
Labour force participation and part-time employment in OECD countries (percentages), 1979 and 1992

	Labour force participation rate[1]				Part-time employment as a proportion of total employment		Women's share in part-time employment		Part-time employment as a proportion of employment[2]			
	Men		Women						Men		Women	
	1979	1992	1979	1992	1979	1992	1979	1992	1979	1992	1979	1992
Australia	87.6	85.8	50.3	62.5	15.9	24.5	78.7	75.0	5.2	10.6	35.2	43.3
Austria	81.6	80.7	49.1	58.0	7.6	9.1	87.8	89.1	1.5	1.6	18.0	20.5
Belgium	79.3	72.6	46.3	54.1	6.0	12.4	88.9	89.7	1.0	2.1	16.5	28.1
Canada	86.3	78.9	55.5	65.1	12.5	16.8	72.1	70.0	5.7	9.3	23.3	25.9
Denmark	89.6	...	69.9	...	22.7	22.5	86.9	75.8	5.2	10.1	46.3	36.7
Finland	82.2	78.5	68.9	70.7	6.7	7.9	74.7	64.3	3.2	5.5	10.6	10.4
France	82.6	74.7	54.2	58.7	8.2	12.7	82.2	83.7	2.4	3.6	16.9	24.5
Germany	84.9	78.9	52.2	58.6	11.4	14.1	91.6	91.0	1.5	2.2	27.6	30.7
Greece	79.0	...	32.8	...	...	4.8	...	61.3	...	2.8	...	8.4
Ireland	88.7	...	35.2	...	5.1	...	71.2	...	2.1	...	13.1	...
Italy	82.6	79.1	38.7	46.5	5.3	5.9	61.4	68.5	3.0	2.9	10.6	11.5
Japan	89.2	89.7	54.7	62.0	15.4	20.5	70.1	69.3	7.5	10.6	27.8	34.8
Luxembourg	88.9	...	39.8	...	5.8	6.9	87.5	88.5	1.0	1.3	17.1	16.5
Netherlands	79.0	80.8	33.4	55.5	16.6	32.8	76.4	75.0	5.5	13.4	44.0	62.9
New Zealand	87.3	82.2	45.0	63.2	13.9	21.6	77.7	73.3	4.9	10.3	29.1	35.9
Norway	89.2	82.6	61.7	70.9	25.3	26.9	83.0	80.1	7.3	9.8	50.9	47.1
Portugal	90.9	83.1	57.3	61.9	7.8	7.2	80.4	67.4	2.5	4.2	16.5	11.0
Spain	83.1	74.8	32.6	42.0	...	5.9	...	76.8	...	2.0	...	13.7
Sweden	87.9	83.2	72.8	79.1	23.6	24.3	87.5	82.3	5.4	8.4	46.0	41.3
Switzerland	94.6	93.7	53.0	58.5	...	...	...	...	...	...	...	...
United Kingdom	90.5	84.5	58.0	64.8	16.4	23.2	92.8	85.2	1.9	6.3	39.0	45.0
United States	85.7	84.8	58.9	68.9	16.4	17.5	68.0	66.4	9.0	10.8	26.7	25.4

... Data not available
1. Total labour force divided by the population of working age (15–64).
2. Men or women employed part-time divided by the total men or women employed.

Source: OECD, *Employment Outlook, July 1994,* pp. 198–202, Paris, OECD, 1994.

the tremendous changes over the last fifty years in women's participation in the labour force, especially in the industrial countries (Figure 3.7). Women in the industrial countries today are far more likely – at any age – to seek employment than they were before the Second World War, and they also are much less likely to withdraw temporarily from the labour force during their childbearing years. It might therefore be concluded that young women's employment and career expectations today, in the industrial countries at least, would be unlikely to bias them against particular fields of study. From where, then, does the bias come?

Notwithstanding their increasing participation in the labour force, women in industrial countries generally still retain primary responsibility for child care and household management, and this has had an influence on both the kinds of employment they are willing to accept and the kinds they are likely to be offered. Some observers have pointed particularly to the role of women in part-time employment, which has been increasing as a proportion of total employment in virtually all the OECD countries (Table 3.3). While a majority of part-time jobs are believed to be just a means for employers to reduce labour costs, an increasing number, especially in the service sector, e.g.

health care, law and business information services, are thought to be 'real' jobs (often self-employed) favoured by men and women who want to manage their own time without permanent contractual ties to one employer. In that connection, it is of interest that polls of employed women in Western Europe apparently have found a strong desire for increased opportunities for part-time work so as to allow more time for family-related activities, and there is a scattered evidence of similar preferences in Russia and some of the 'transition' economies of Eastern Europe. In Japan, a new law was passed in 1993 with the aim of strengthening the social rights of part-time workers. Significantly, too, there appears to have been a levelling off in the growth of enrolment in pre-primary education in the industrial (developed) countries in recent years (Appendix II, Table 5); past growth has sometimes been thought to have been driven by the desire of women for full-time work outside the home.

While all this does not amount to a bias against traditional science-based occupations, it does suggest that the nature of the job, as much as its content, is probably an important consideration for women in their employment preferences, especially in the context of family-time constraints.

In the developing regions of the world, employment trends are notoriously difficult to analyse because of the very large agriculture and informal sectors, but there are signs that women are steadily increasing their share of non-agricultural employment (Table 3.4). In many cases they are regarded as cheap labour and tend to be concentrated in unskilled jobs with few if any social rights, but the evidence which is available regarding employment in professional, technical, administrative and managerial occupations shows that women in many developing countries have as much access to such occupations as their counterparts in the industrial countries (Figure 3.8).

In the Latin America and Caribbean Region, which has progressed further than the other developing regions towards equal educational

Table 3.4
Percentage share of women
in non-agricultural employment
in selected developing countries,[1] 1975–1992

Country/Territory	1975	1980	1985	1990	1992
Africa					
Botswana	19	24	30	33	36
Gambia	10	12	15	...	...
Kenya	16	17	20	21	22
Malawi	7	9	16	11	...
Mauritius	20	26	34	37	38
Niger	4	4	7	11	9
Swaziland	22	26	31	...	...
United Rep. of Tanzania	12	17	17	...	...
Zimbabwe	13	13	16	15	16
Latin America/Caribbean					
Barbados	41	43	44	46	48
Bermuda	...	43	46	49	50
Bolivia	32	31	35	35	...
Brazil	33	35	38	40	...
Chile	...	34	36	36	36
Colombia	37	39	38	40	42
Cuba	...	36	41	42	...
Honduras	...	...	43	48	47
Jamaica	46	48	48	49	...
Panama	38	39	43	42	45
Paraguay	39	41	44	42	41
Puerto Rico	35	38	39	40	41
Trinidad and Tobago	28	31	34	34	36
Venezuela	32	32	32	34	36
Asia					
Cyprus	30	33	35	38	39
Hong Kong	...	35	37	36	36
India	10	11	12	13	...
Indonesia	37	34	38	38	38
Jordan	14	17	22	23	24
Malaysia	...	30	33	36	...
Pakistan	...	...	5	7	8
Philippines	47	46	48	46	46
Republic of Korea	33	35	38	40	39
Singapore	30	35	36	39	40
Sri Lanka	18	18	24	39	39
Syrian Arab Republic	8	9	9	11	11
Thailand	42	42	44	45	45

1. Countries for which data are available (nearest year) with no break in series.

Source: International Labour Office database, 1994.

opportunities for the two sexes, a series of studies recently carried out by the World Bank has shown that women generally are paid less even when they have the same education and length of work experience as men: a sign that they either still tend – as happens in most industrial countries – to hold jobs that are of lower value to employers than those filled by men, or simply are exploited.

In Africa and Asia especially, because of the pervasiveness of family-based economic enterprises, occupations often cannot be meaningfully distinguished from family roles in the production and processing of food and participation in small scale trade and commerce. In these regions, however, what may be more significant for women than occupation as such is control over money income; at least, some economists have suggested that obtaining a job for wages – which education facilitates – contributes to women's control over the returns to their labour and hence alters their relative power in the allocation of household economic resources. In consequence, it is claimed, they are likely to invest more in the health and education of fewer but 'better quality' children. While there can hardly be agreement that countries with low birth rates have 'better quality' children than elsewhere, there is little doubt that acceptance of paid employment outside the home profoundly alters women's child-rearing parameters. This suggests again (as in the industrial countries) that expectations and preferences concerning the nature of future employment are likely to influence girls' motivations in school.

The question of 'ability'

Although the recent emphasis of economists on a logic of comparative advantage and rational choice to account for gender differences in employment, changing patterns of household consumption and investment, and trends in fertility has turned the spotlight away from discrimination and on to motivation as the critical factor in women's and girls' educational experiences, there is a more popular tradition, rooted in educational psychology and social-psychology, that tends to

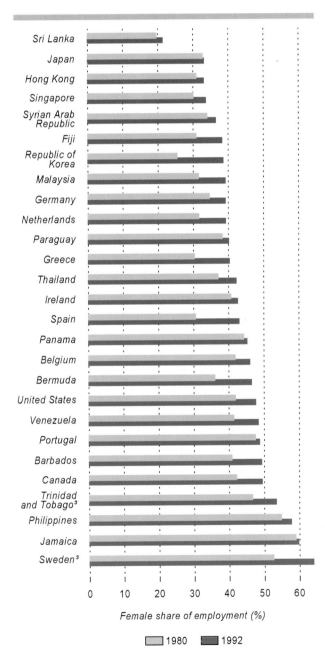

Figure 3.8
Female share of employment in professional, technical, administrative and managerial occupations in selected countries,[1] 1980 and 1992[2]

Female share of employment (%)

1980   1992

1. Countries for which data are available for both dates.
2. Or nearest year available.
3. Administrative and managerial workers are not included.

Source: International Labour Office database, 1994.

Figure 3.9
Reading literacy scores of boys and girls in thirty-two countries, 1990–1991[1]

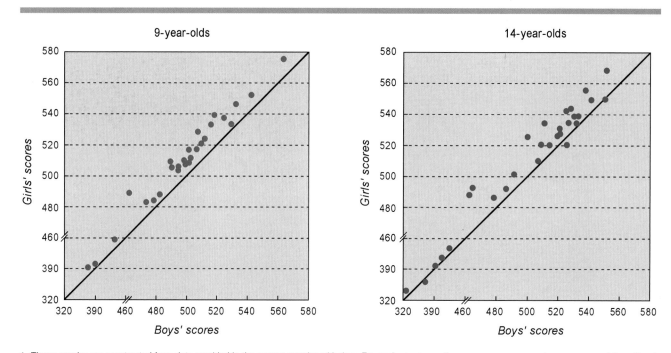

1. These graphs are constructed from data provided in the source mentioned below. For each age-group the scores are measured on a common international scale chosen in such a way that the international mean score (giving each participating country equal weight) is 500 and the standard deviation is 100. Thirty-two countries altogether participated in the study: twenty-six of them surveyed both 9-year-olds and 14-year-olds; one country surveyed only the 9-year-olds; another five countries surveyed only the 14-year-olds.

Source: Warwick B. Elley (ed.), *The IEA Study of Reading Literacy: Achievement and Instruction in Thirty-two School Systems,* pp. 105–6, Oxford, Pergamon, 1994.

look for differences in female and male abilities. The latter, as much as motivation – not to speak of discrimination – have often been thought to influence girls and boys in their school subject choices and women and men eventually in their observed employment and career paths.

The idea that girls might be less able than boys to learn science and mathematics has been the focus of a great deal of research and critical analysis over the last three decades. One important consequence has been the gradual opening up – demystification even – of the whole question of 'ability', its meaning and measurement as well as its status within the educational process. Scepticism towards 'ability' as an explanation of gender differences in school subject choices and learning

performances has grown with the realization that it would seem to preclude the possibility that any of the parties involved – the school authorities, teachers, parents and the pupils themselves – can ever do anything effective to counter such differences.

Thus, the long-standing difficulty which educational psychology has had in distinguishing between an 'ability' and performance of the task or tasks designed to measure it, is being pulled into the open. Unless such a distinction can be made (how?), a difference in 'ability' cannot (without circularity) explain or account for an observed difference in performance. Since this has not always been recognized, performance differences between girls and boys – and indeed between other groups too – have very often tended simply to confirm existing prejudices about abilities rather than stimulate further inquiry into the reasons for the differences.

Much recent research has focused on gender differences in early socialization and upbringing. The least plausible explanations – certainly the most controversial – have been chemical and neuro-psychological ones relating to differences between the sexes in hormones and brain structures. These explanations, critics have observed, are unable to account for the fact that male and female test performances so often overlap.

Moreover, the whole issue of gender bias in test instruments themselves, despite much attention from psychometricians and others, is still not fully resolved because of the difficulty of establishing test validity, i.e. that the test measures the arbitrarily defined 'construct' it is intended to measure, for example, verbal ability as distinct from problem-solving ability. If agreement cannot be reached that a test is valid, there will be difficulty in deciding whether it is fair. In a general history test, for example, should a question about Cleopatra be substituted for one about Napoleon in order to make the test more relevant to girls? Not if it reduces the test's validity. But how is that to be determined?

In a global perspective, the main drawbacks of the research which has been carried out on gender differences in performance are its restricted cultural setting (chiefly North America and Europe) and the limited scale of so many of the individual studies, the majority of which have little credibility as valid national samples of the relevant age-cohorts. There is a dearth of soundly conducted large-scale international comparative studies that could help support a richer international debate about girls' and boys' learning experiences and achievements. Only a handfull of such studies have been conducted up to now, chiefly under the auspices of the International Association for the Evaluation of Educational Achievement (IEA) and the International Assess-

ment of Educational Progress (IAEP), and even they have not always been immune from problems of sampling and test instrument design (see the *World Education Report 1993,* Chapter 4). Still, they at least have helped to bring a cross-cultural perspective into discussion of learning achievement, for example, in the area of reading literacy (Figure 3.9). The most recent IAEP Mathematics and Science Study (Figure 3.10) provides some startling cross-cultural contrasts: compare the science performances of 9-year-olds in Scotland and Ireland, which are cultural neighbours, with those in the Republic of Korea several thousand kilometers away (Figure 3.11); there would seem to be more in common between the 9-year-olds in Ireland and the Republic of Korea than between those in Ireland and Scotland.

Moreover, the Scottish (and Hungarian and American) 9-year-olds exhibit no significant gender differences in regard to either mathematics or science. Why? If whisky (not applicable to Hungary) and brain weight (different in the two sexes) cannot explain this result, what can? More seriously, it appears that the significant challenge for educational psychology is not really to explain why the learning performances of males and females are often different – correlates are easily found – but to accept that they are sometimes (in fact often) the same. Indeed, the possibility cannot be excluded that under certain circumstances (different social pressures? fairer tests? more effective pedagogies?) the performances will as often be the same as different.

It remains that the overall pattern of boys' and girls' performances in IAEP's 1991 study is broadly consistent with the results of previous international studies carried out by both IAEP and IEA, as well as with those of a large number of national studies, including a series recently sponsored jointly by UNESCO and UNICEF, focused mainly on basic education in developing countries. Generally speaking, the differences between girls and boys in the performances in science and mathematics tend to be less marked at the younger

Figure 3.10
Gender effect size[1] and total score[2] in mathematics and science for 9-year-olds and 13-year-olds in selected countries[3]

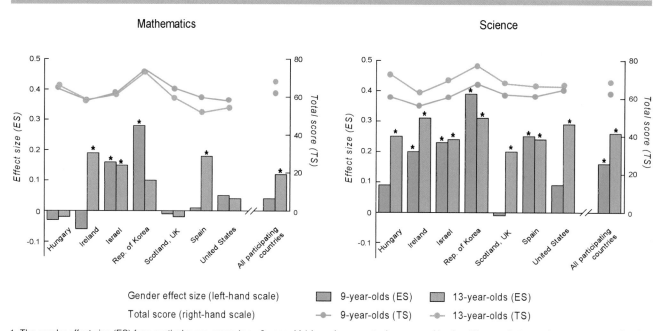

1. The gender effect size (ES) for a particular age-group (e.g., 9-year-olds) in a given country is measured by the difference between the mean scores of males and females divided by the standard deviation computed across the two groups (males and females). A positive effect size (ES > 0) indicates superior performance by males, while a negative effect size (ES < 0) indicates superior performance by females. The gender effect size is indicated in the diagrams by the vertical bars, which are referred to the left-hand scale. The asterisk (∗) indicates that the gender effect is statistically significant ($\alpha < 0.05$). The significance of the differences between boys and girls was tested using jacknifed standard errors.
2. Total score (TS) on a common scale of 0 to 100. The total score is indicated in the diagrams by the lines joining the total score points, which are referred to the right-hand scale.
3. Fourteen countries altogether participated in the testing of 9-year-olds and twenty countries in the testing of 13-year-olds. The seven selected countries shown in this figure were those which had comprehensive samples (i.e., representative of the countries). In the case of Spain: all Spanish-speaking schools except those in the Catalan autonomous community.

Source: Michal Beller and Naomi Gafni, *International Perspectives on the Schooling and Learning Achievement of Girls and Boys, as Revealed in the 1991 International Assessment of Educational Progress (IAEP)*, Jerusalem, National Institute for Testing and Evaluation, 1995. (Mimeo. Report commissioned by UNESCO from the International Association for Educational Assessment.)

than at the older ages, and possibly less marked in mathematics than in science. This has been found in countries in all regions of the world ranging from China and Russia to Europe, south and east Asia, Africa and the Americas. Another common finding – as noted in Figure 3.9 earlier – is that girls tend to perform better than boys in reading. Some observers have noted that this 'deficiency' in boys has never attracted quite the same attention from educational psychologists as girls' apparent 'deficiency' in science. Radical critics have charged that this is due to the reluctance of the reigning paradigm to accept the possibility of a male 'inferiority': boys are arbitrarily assumed to be the standard.

It has been suggested that the more recent international studies of performances in mathematics and science tend to show less marked gender differences than earlier studies carried out twenty or thirty years ago. Several explanations have been offered, ranging from a greater awareness among test constructors today of possible sources of bias in test items (questions) and formats (multiple-choice versus open-ended), to greater efforts today by education systems to encourage girls to pursue their mathematics and science studies in school and not to withdraw so readily as used to be the case in the past.

As regards test formats, it has sometimes been thought that multiple-choice formats tend to favour boys because of an allegedly greater propensity compared to girls in 'risk-taking' and hence a more confident completion of test items, but this effect was not found among the open-ended and multiple-choice formats built into IAEP's 1991 mathematics study.

The question of self-confidence, in particular girls' alleged lack of it, has been the focus of a great deal of recent debate in some Western industrial countries. Yet in a cross-cultural perspective, girls' lack of self-confidence hardly seems to matter in terms of performance: in IAEP's 1991 science study, girls in the Republic of Korea who considered themselves as not good at science scored just as well as American boys who considered themselves to be good (Figure 3.12).

Clearly, the whole subject of gender differences in performance and/or ability is extremely complex, and widely open to prejudice and misunderstanding. The difficulty of reaching any firm conclusions is especially apparent in a cross-cultural context. It is also clear that 'ability' can hardly contain a complete explanation of gender differences in school subject bias. The actual process or mechanism of school subject choice also needs to be taken into consideration, but this has not been given the attention which it merits in international and most national research relating to girls' and boys' learning experiences and performances in school. What exactly happens to the world's youngsters between, say, 9 years old when there apparently is not much difference between girls and boys – except possibly in reading, since the differences in mathematics and science are either less pronounced or less universally applicable – and 18 years old when those girls and boys who are still in the education system tend to go separate ways? If ability were the only thing that mat-

Figure 3.11

Gender effect size in science content areas[1] for 9-year-olds and 13-year-olds[2] in Ireland, the Republic of Korea and Scotland

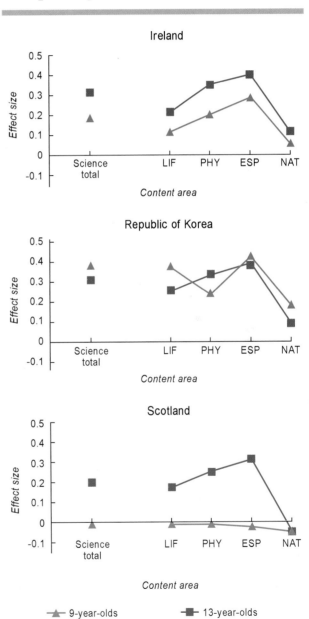

1. Content area: LIF: life sciences; PHY: physical sciences; ESP: earth and space sciences; NAT: nature of science.
2. All gender effect sizes (see Note 1 in Figure 3.10) shown in the present figure are statistically significant except for Ireland (9-year-olds) LIF and NAT, and (13-year-olds) NAT; Republic of Korea (9-year-olds) NAT; Scotland (9-year-olds) Science total, LIF, PHY, ESP and NAT, and (13-year-olds) NAT.

Source: M. Beller and N. Gafni, op. cit.

Figure 3.12
*Self-confidence expressed by 13-year-old boys
and girls in their science performance[1]
in the Republic of Korea and the United States*

ages of 9 and 18 would stress interest (and motivation) at least as much as ability, and would consider the nature and content of both in-school and out-of-school experiences during these years.

Towards effective pedagogies

The current national and international concern to ensure equal educational opportunities for girls possibly represents the most formidable challenge to thinking about pedagogy that has emerged since universal education became a global possibility. Feminist critics have charged – with some justification – that both received pedagogical theory and much of actual practice in many countries (if not most) is largely based on the needs and behaviour of the boy-pupil.

To bring in the term 'pedagogy' (literally, 'the science of teaching') is to recognize explicitly what schools are supposed to do. For the purposes of this report, the pedagogy which is adopted in any particular instance is understood to refer broadly to the way in which the teacher organizes and implements the teaching-learning task, whether for an individual pupil or for a whole class of pupils. From this standpoint, pedagogy is an applied science almost like engineering, except that the girls and boys, say, unlike roads and bridges, are not inert and are at least partly responsible themselves for the final outcome. It is also understood that any pedagogy is itself embedded in a larger educational framework consisting of curricular goals and subject matter, institutional forms and structures, technology, financing, and so on.

Bringing in 'pedagogy' recognizes the crucial role of teachers. It is their responsibility to ensure that the pupils in their charge have equal opportunities to participate fully in the teaching/learning process. If the girls and boys have different as well as overlapping interests, the pedagogical challenge is to treat these interests equally – in the spirit of the *Convention against Discrimination in*

I am good at science

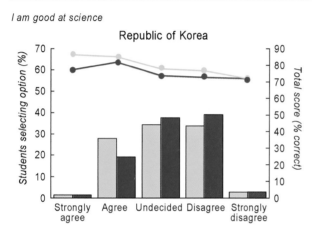

I am good at science

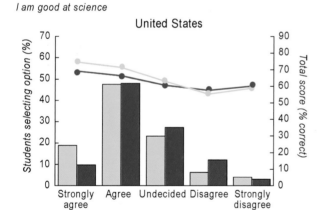

Students who select the option (%)
(left-hand scale)

Total score (% correct)
(right-hand scale)

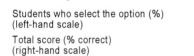

1. Each student was asked to select one of the options ('strongly agree', 'agree', etc.) which best expressed his/her feeling about the statement 'I am good at science'. Thus, for example, nearly 50 per cent of American boys agreed with this statement, and their average score was around 70 per cent correct on the science test.

Source: M. Beller and N. Gafni, op. cit.

tered, there would be a mystery about what schools are for – other than to administer tests – since any outcomes could be put down to 'comparative advantage'. Therefore a prudent account of what happens to young people between the

Box 3.3
Questions concerning co-education in Austria

Increased efforts are also being undertaken with regard to the problem of 'vocational orientation for girls'. Girls, on the basis of their socialization, still opt for traditional training courses and occupations. This one-sided choice of school and occupation on the part of girls frequently results, later on, in difficulties in finding suitable jobs, in lower pay, and fewer career possibilities. Therefore, the attempts of the Federal Ministry of Education and the Arts have concentrated, on the one hand, on the support of, and cooperation with, various initiatives and associations in this field concerned with vocational orientation for girls, and on the other hand, on measures ensuring better cooperation and exchange of information between schools and enterprises.

A point of emphasis, which researchers increasingly consider a problem, is *coeducation,* i.e. the joint education of girls and boys.

It has become apparent that this form of instruction may discriminate against girls particularly in the technological-scientific subjects. For this reason, attempts are being made to develop forms of instruction catering more to the specific needs of girls. Thus, a recent study on 'Computers in Education' (COMPED) revealed that girls enjoy computer work far less, try to avoid the optional subject 'information technology', etc., which may be a negative effect of coeducation. Another study ('Selection of a mathematical-scientific-technological study course and type of school attended') showed that an above-average number of female students in scientific-technological study courses previously attended (private) schools for girls only.

A problem that is connected with coeducation is that of *violence* (in different forms) *at school,* which particularly affects girls (but also female teachers).

Source: Austria: Development of Education, 1992–1994, pp. 90–1, Vienna, Federal Ministry of Education and the Arts in co-operation with the Federal Ministry of Science and Research, 1994. (National report presented at the 44th session of the International Conference on Education, Geneva, 1994.)

education became widespread at the post-elementary level in the industrial countries, it was generally thought that this type of education would ensure that girls and boys would be treated equally, but experience in many countries has shown that this does not necessarily happen (e.g., Box 3.3). In particular, there is now a great deal of evidence that during secondary education especially, boys 'lay claim' to science and computers – sometimes even physically so, for example, by grabbing the equipment first in the laboratory – while the girls withdraw. (The 'machismo' of much computer software is another story.)

During the early movement towards co-education in the 1920s and 1930s a few lone voices among the educational psychologists – the great Russian psychologist, L. S. Vygotsky (1896–1934), was one – tried to insist that there were important implications for pedagogical theory and practice, but they were drowned out. In Vygotsky's words, the question of co-education was usually treated 'as if the teenager himself/herself doesn't exist'. This was a mistake, it is now realized. Action-oriented pedagogical research today has begun to look closely at what teenage girls and boys really are like in alternative educational settings (e.g., Box 3.4).

With hindsight, it is apparent that the original proponents of co-education did not foresee the extent to which the various subjects or areas of the curriculum would get to be partitioned between the sexes. Yet with the increasing participation of women in the labour force in most countries, especially after the Second World War, it was perhaps inevitable that many women would eventually question the educational processes which seem to limit the range of occupations open to women in the wider economy and society. Some educators in a number of countries are looking again at single-sex schooling as a possible solution, although these schools often are private and highly selective in regard to their student intakes. Others, as seen in Box 3.4, are exploring

Education noted earlier – and not to give more importance to one sex than the other.

'Equal treatment' has always been difficult to ensure. After the Second World War, when co-

---

Box 3.4
'Teaching an all boys' class is a different matter from teaching an all girls' class'

Although teachers often have problems controlling boys' behaviour, they usually have a positive view of boys. But teachers – female as well as male – are often ambivalent in their opinions of girls. There are different reasons for this. For example, some teachers do not find girls as exciting or as interesting as boys; they do not approve of and do not understand the intimate friendship relations of girls, their ways of communicating, or their conflicts. Somehow, they do not approve of either girls who are too conventional, nice and adaptable or the opposite, too noisy, too demanding, too rebellious, too challenging. In this way, we are all carriers of society's double conceptualisation of women. [...] Furthermore, teaching girls is not easy for teachers who, for more than a generation, have been used to the fact that 'pupils' are synonymous with 'boys'.

An interesting illustrative example is Haarup School where 14 to 15 year old girls and boys from one class were segregated during four lessons a week in their eighth and ninth year at school. They were separated in German, English, mathematics and physics. This was initiated by Grethe Biil, a feminist teacher, who as their 'form-teacher' was responsible for the social welfare of the pupils. She also taught them Danish and German. I observed both in the class and the single-sex settings and interviewed all involved. Grethe Biil enjoyed being alone with the girls. But she also discovered that it can be enjoyable to work with boys on their own. This experience has been confirmed by other women teachers, including myself. It reduces the reproach heaped on boys for being too dominating. Teachers feel that at least now the boys are not suppressing the girls, and this can bring relaxation and greater openness towards them. But teaching an all boys' class is a different matter from teaching an all girls' class. Even lessons that have the same text or content or result in the same homework go through processes that are very different. In the two eighth to ninth grade settings Grethe Biil experienced the following differences:

The girls-only setting:
1. The girls work in a concentrated way. The subject matter is worked through in half the time used by boys.
2. The girls are well prepared.
3. The girls keep strictly to the subject.
4. The girls see the lesson as a shared venture.

5. The girls listen and show respect when others speak. They laugh in a caring way: 'Aren't we having a nice time together?'
6. The girls are helpful to each other.

The boys-only setting:
1. The boys are active in an anarchistic way.
2. The boys have a low degree of preparation.
3. The boys broaden the subject and include new angles and points of view.
4. They see the lesson as an individual matter.
5. The boys constantly interrupt each other with funny or ironical remarks. They are tough with each other, use swear words and bad language.
6. The boys compete with each other and in getting the teacher's attention.

In the girls-only setting Grethe Biil rarely scolded. Each girl became visible, and appeared as an individual with certain characteristics. In the boys-only setting she often told the boys off and lessons were often interrupted, especially when changing from one discipline to another. Also the quiet boys became more visible, and the power structures within the boys' group became more obvious.

When the girls had concentrated on the subject matter and on finishing their school-work, they wanted to talk; talk about vital things in their lives, and share reflections about their futures, about which they felt insecure. Thus many a German lesson became the place where the girls bettered their German qualifications and additionally gained the attention and support of a committed feminist teacher on other vital matters.

The very different ways in which the pupils interacted forced Grethe Biil to change her teaching style completely when in the girls' or in the boys' setting. At first she herself reacted spontaneously, but gradually she became aware of the need to develop different teaching strategies and to set different goals for each of the two groups.

Source: Anne-Mette Kruse, *Single-sex Settings and the Development of a Pedagogy for Girls and a Pedagogy for Boys in Danish schools,* pp. 4–5. (Mimeo. Paper presented at the UNESCO/Institute of Education Colloquium, 'Is There a Pedagogy for Girls?', London, Institute of Education, London University, 10–12 January 1995.).

Box 3.5
What assumptions, beliefs and knowledge do children bring with them when they start school?

Psychology and education have witnessed a theoretical sea change in the last twenty-five years. Until relatively recently, almost everyone accepted the empiricist's thesis that human infants start with mental blank slates, upon which the records of experience are gradually impressed. The common assumption was that newborns cannot hear, see or smell, that they spend their first year of life in a blooming-buzzing confusion and that they lack the ability to form complex ideas about the world. True, babies certainly are born with notably limited response abilities and spend much of their early life sleeping. Still, they are not simply passive receivers of data that wash over their sensoria.

In fact, healthy infants will use whatever limited response abilities they have to explore – and even control – their environments as soon as they come into the world.

[...]

From a very early point in their lives, children are motivated to persist with a task – seemingly on their own and without external reinforcement – until they have mastered some game, problem or area of knowledge. A famous example of this active involvement in learning comes from Piaget, who tells of his infant daughter's attempt to push a toy she was holding horizontally through the vertical bars of her crib. The opening was not wide enough, but she continued to try until, eventually, she began to rotate the toy. Soon thereafter she rotated it enough for it to pass through the bars.

Further examples of children actively engaging in cognitive activities on their own are seen everywhere now that we are paying attention to them.

[...]

The shift from the model of learner-as-depository of inputs to a model of learner-as-active-interpreter of inputs has important implications for education; in particular, we can no longer assume that children start school with little if any knowledge of the topics we propose to teach. Children start building organized representations of their social and non-social worlds early in development. What they have already learned, usually in informal and implicit ways, is used to interpret what they encounter in the classroom and in other settings in their lives. This means that what we teach is interpreted, not just absorbed, even at the beginning of school. Therefore, we need to consider what assumptions, beliefs and knowledge children bring with them when they start school.

S*ource:* Rochel Gelman and Meredith Gattis Lee, 'Trends and Developments in Educational Psychology in the United States', *Recent Trends and Developments in Educational Psychology: Chinese and American Perspectives*, pp. 24–6, Paris, UNESCO, 1994. (Educational Studies and Documents, 61.)

single-sex variants within co-education. Still others are re-examining the psychological and other premises which have underpinned existing pedagogical theory and practice in co-education.

Short of an educational revolution leading to the return of mainly single-sex schooling, as existed a hundred years ago, it seems that solutions need to be found within the pedagogy of co-education itself. The starting point, some researchers have urged, must be a more thorough understanding of the characteristic learning styles of girls and boys, and of their interaction in a co-educational setting. In that connection, it has been noted that the trend in educational psychology since the 1970s away from a behaviourist model,

towards a 'constructivist' theory of learning and cognition (Box 3.5), brings into sharper focus the early psychological and cognitive development and socialization experienced by girls and boys before they first enter school.

While there always were some psychologists, e.g., the Belgian Ovide Decroly (1871–1932) at the beginning of this century, who stressed the importance of the child's first 5–6 years for later learning, in the behaviourist or 'empiricist' model that dominated much pedagogical thinking until very recently, children coming into school were in effect regarded as 'blank slates', whence the question of sex differences in early psychological and cognitive development and socialization did not arise. Such differences, it is now argued, need to be taken into account in developing effective pedagogies of co-education. Most of the published research, though, has been carried out in Western industrial countries, and thus some of the experiments would need appropriate modification if they were to be replicated in other cultures: the toys in the 'actor baby' experiment (Box 3.6), for example, would need to be replaced, and an alternative to Freudian psychoanalysis (Box 3.7) might need to be formulated.

Box 3.6
'Maternal Behavior
and Perceived Sex of Infant'

Summary: Mothers of 32 firstborn infants aged 5–10 months were videotaped playing with a 6-month old 'actor baby'. 2 female infants and 2 males appeared equally often as actor babies in sex-appropriate and cross-sex clothes and names. [The mothers were told the study was concerned with analyzing play and asked to play with an actor baby for 10 min. The actor baby was presented by its own mother, who offered the name appropriate to the infant's clothing. The actor baby's mother then left the room and observed through a one-way mirror. After each session the subject mother was interviewed and debriefed.] Sex-typed and sex-neutral toys were available. [The toys rated as masculine were a squeaky hammer and a stuffed rabbit wearing trousers and bow tie; the feminine toys were a doll and a squeaky bambi; a squeaky pig, a plush ball, and an hour-glass-shaped rattle were rated as neutral.] Initial toy choice varied with perceived sex of infant. Perceived boys were verbally encouraged to gross motor activity more often than perceived girls, but there were no significant differences in overall physical stimulation. However, mothers responded to the gross motor behavior of perceived boys with gross motor activity significantly more often. Results suggest early socialization in the direction of a masculine stereotype of activity and physical prowess.

Source: Caroline Smith and Barbara Lloyd, 'Maternal Behavior and Perceived Sex of Infant', *Child Development,* Vol. 49, 1978, pp. 1263–5.

Box 3.7
'The Reproduction of Mothering'

This book is a contribution to the feminist effort. It analyzes the reproduction of mothering as a central and constituting element in the social organization and reproduction of gender. In what follows, I argue that the contemporary reproduction of mothering occurs through social structurally induced psychological processes. It is neither a product of biology nor of intentional role-training. I draw on the psychoanalytic account of female and male personality development to demonstrate that women's mothering reproduces itself cyclically. Women, as mothers, produce daughters with mothering capacities and the desire to mother. These capacities and needs are built into and grow out of the mother-daughter relationship itself. By contrast, women as mothers (and men as not-mothers) produce sons whose nurturant capacities and needs have been systematically curtailed and repressed. This prepares men for their less affective later family role, and for primary participation in the impersonal extra-familial world of work and public life. The sexual and familial division of labor in which women mother and are more involved in interpersonal, affective relationships than men produces in daughters and sons a division of psychological capacities which leads them to reproduce this sexual and familial division of labor.

I attempt to provide a theoretical account of what has unquestionably been true – that women have had primary responsibility for child care in families and outside of them; that women by and large want to mother, and get gratification from their mothering; and finally, that, with all the conflicts and contradictions, women have succeeded at mothering.

Source: Nancy Chodorow, *The Reproduction of Mothering: Psychoanalysis and the Sociology of Gender,* p. 7, Berkeley, University of California Press, 1978.

Nevertheless, it is not unreasonable to suggest that there would be a wide measure of agreement in many countries today that pedagogy in a co-educational setting needs to be more sensitive than in the past to the dangers of taking the boy-pupil as the point of reference: witness the efforts being made in many countries to ensure that school textbooks are not biased against girls. In China, to take one example, an analysis of the twelve basic textbooks used in the six-year primary cycle at the end of the 1980s revealed that only eleven out of the ninety-six 'personalities' mentioned in the texts were female; this imbalance is now being corrected. Other countries are proceeding similarly. In some single-sex settings (e.g., Box 3.8), efforts have been made to counter gender-stereotyping of school subjects.

It is at the adolescent stage, as suggested by Vygotsky's remark quoted earlier, that the real challenge to co-education pedagogy arises, because of the changed nature of the emotional and affective interaction between the sexes, in particular the tendency for boys at this stage of their lives often to assert – indeed to exercise – a dominating mode of behaviour towards girls. So long as there was not much inclination for girls to 'trespass' into traditional boys' subjects or areas of the curriculum, boys' social behaviour in school could be handled by the teacher easily enough, even tolerated, but in today's context of increasing

---

Box 3.8
'Boys have fun in home economics'

A boy sings on one of my tape-recordings of a home economics lesson. In the transcript I have noted fourteen bursts of song and thirteen outbreaks of whistling, as well as boys talking in funny voices, jokes, laughter and somewhere a rhythm being played on a saucepan or lid. I have no other tape like this one. It records a fourth-year [of secondary education] practical 'Home Economics: Food' lesson in a boys' school, and confirms evidence from other sources about the important difference between boys' and girls' experiences. Boys have fun in home economics.

Frankie, the boy who sang the most, was in danger of having too much fun. At one point in the lesson the teacher rebuked him, although not in a very serious way:

TEACHER: Frankie, when you come to do a practical exam how are you going to learn to keep quiet? I think you should start practising ... You can smile, we like you looking happy, but try to control ...
FRANKIE: I'm only happy when I'm singing.
TEACHER: Then I'm afraid we're going to have to make sure you're sad.

The outstanding feature of this encounter is its rarity. Nothing remotely like this happened in any of the lessons I observed – the majority – where girls were present. Frankie's whole class appeared to share his mood. Girls sometimes told me they liked home economics, but no girl provided such evidence of enjoyment. The mood in other classes, as far as I could detect it, was usually serious and sometimes discontented, but never lighthearted. No girls sang. [...]

The quality of the relationship between the teacher in the class described above and her pupils must have owed much to her experience and skills, but the friendliness and lack of stress which make it, unhappily, so exceptional also have a lot to do with gender. The boys were quite clearly placed as children, not as almost-adults, in their relationship with the teacher, yet with no apparent resentment on their side. Their behaviour towards her was dependent, though not always compliant. They saw her as an expert but were also prepared to challenge her:

TEACHER: [to pupil putting spaghetti into pan of water] This is nowhere near boiling.
FRANKIE: [...] it doesn't matter.
TEACHER: Frankie, if it didn't matter it wouldn't say: Frankie, come here. You did boiling water and how to speed it up last term ...

The boy in this exchange was also the one who sang, and was in too good a mood to stop. Frankie could enjoy the lesson but at the same time make clear that its content didn't much matter. A girl of fourteen or fifteen who was so dismissive of criticism or cared so little for detail – let alone one who had to be told how to boil water – would be making a different kind of statement.

Source: Dena Attar, *Wasting Girls' Time: the History and Politics of Home Economics*, pp. 114–5, London, Virago Press, 1990.

Box 3.9
A science, technology and mathematics education (STME) clinic for girls in Ghana

The [Ghana Education Service] has instituted a programme to organise annual STME clinics to give girls in secondary schools the type of orientation that would help to remove the misconceptions about girls' participation in the study of Science and Mathematics in school and subsequently related careers. The Clinic has chosen to focus on girls in secondary schools because that is where the problem manifests itself the most.

The programme which has the support of UNESCO, the Commonwealth Secretariat as well as other public and private organisations, attracts girls from other West African countries.

With its follow-up activities the STME Clinic is now a year-round effort to enhance the effectiveness of the study of Science and Mathematics among girls in the secondary school.

The programme has the following objectives:

1. To make participants aware of the gender stereotypes that tend to inhibit girls/women from entering STME-based occupations and how they can overcome these inhibitions.
2. To encourage the girls to study the full range of science and mathematics-related subjects in secondary schools.
3. To make participants aware of the application of Science and Mathematics skills in various occupations and in the production of goods and services.
4. To provide opportunities for participants to explore Science and Mathematics-based careers through first-hand experiences.
5. To assure participants, through role models, that they can succeed in STME-based occupations and at the same time maintain normal marital life.
6. To create opportunities for participants to improve their skills in creativity and problem-solving.

Source: The Development of Education: National Report from Ghana, 1992–1994, pp. 14–5, Accra, Ministry of Education, 1994. (National report presented at the 44th session of the International Conference on Education, Geneva, 1994.)

female participation in the labour force, boys' behaviour towards girls in school, especially at the adolescent stage when school subject and career choices are being formed, has a more weighty dimension than just school harmony. Sensitive teachers are becoming more aware of this today.

That girls and boys generally behave differently in class, whether in single-sex settings (as illustrated for example in Box 3.4) or in co-educational ones, is now well established by researchers, at least in Western industrial countries. In co-educational settings, girls typically are observed to be less aggressive than boys in demanding the teacher's attention. One consequence of this, it has been suggested, is that teachers do not make enough allowance in science classes, for example, for the greater interest of girls, compared to boys, in the social dimensions of science.

Taking into account the need to respond to the interests of both girls and boys, as well as the need to ensure equal opportunities for access to all parts of the curriculum, some researchers have concluded that the pedagogy of co-education cannot be unidimensional, based on an idealized model of '*the* child' or '*the* learner', but must be multidimensional, based on the plurality of learners in the class or group, if it is to be effective. Good teachers will already have adopted such an approach.

At a UNESCO/Institute of Education (London University) international colloquium (January, 1995) on the topic, 'Is there a Pedagogy for Girls?', the suggested elements of a multidimensional 'gender-sensitive' pedagogical strategy for co-education included the following:

- using more co-operative and interactive modes of learning;
- linking mathematical and scientific content to societal issues;
- emphasizing discussion and collaboration as well as competition;
- having class discussion *and* quiet reflection;
- 'private' as well as public questioning and probing of the pupil by the teacher;

Box 3.10
'How Do We Get Educators to Teach Gender Equity?'

This project served 200 classroom teachers and administrators in grades 6-12 in math, science or computers in a trainer-of-trainers model. The project was funded primarily by the National Science Foundation, with additional funding from IBM, Hewlett Packard, Chevron, Intel, American Express, Xerox, and Westinghouse for a total of $1,054,000 over two and a half years. We had a full-time staff of three.

Participants (whom we called trainers) received an expense-paid six-day seminar taught by some of the foremost gender equity specialists in the United States, an expense-paid three-day follow-up meeting a year later, a stipend of $100 per participant, a grant of $150 to each trainer's school, and considerable publicity about their participation.

[...]

Follow-up contact over 18 months consisted of frequent mailings, two lengthy telephone interviews, a bi-monthly newsletter, an electronic network, and site visits to a small number of trainers.

Results cannot be simply summarized, since the 'presenting' problems and the strategies were so varied. However, by trainers' estimates they reached a combined total of over 77,000 girls with their strategies, and taught or otherwise involved 9,400 of their colleagues. Many of the trainers reported to us pre/post results such as the following.

- The ratio of boys to girls in the after-school computer lab of a New York middle school was 25:2 before the project, 1:1 after.
- In a Wyoming high school, girls' enrolment in Physics rose from 46% to 62%, and in Introduction to Calculus, from 45 to 71 per cent.
- An Oklahoma high school had no girls in the elective computer science class before the project, but 31% girls afterward.
- The math team in a Massachusetts middle school increased from less than 20% to 50% female
- The Advanced Placement Pascal course went from 0% to 50% girls in one year in a Virginia high school.
- In an Oregon high school, girls' enrolment in Advanced Math rose from 37% to 64%; in Advanced Chemistry it was 20% to 63%.
- In a Maine high school, girls signed up for Physics for the first time in 12 years.

Ninety-eight per cent of the trainers carried out the activities required by the project. Seventy-one per cent of the trainers gave equity presentations not required by the project.

Source: Jo Sanders, *How Do We Get Educators to Teach Gender Equity?,* pp. 5–7. (Mimeo. Paper presented at the UNESCO/Institute of Education Colloquium, 'Is there a Pedagogy for Girls?', London, Institute of Education, London University, 10–12 January 1995.)

- slowing the pace of a lesson and encouraging pupils to use the time to compose responses;
- giving feedback which balances criticism with precise guidance and praise, not the bland praise – for 'dutiful hard work' – which girls currently tend to receive;
- balancing the presence of male/female historical figure, scientist, activity, etc. in teaching material and computer software;
- using assessment that supports learning and reflection rather than relying just upon competition with others.

In an historical perspective, more time is probably still needed for the pedagogy of co-education to become truly comfortable for both girls and boys. The basic issues were evaded for too long, but they have now been forced into the open by changes in the wider economy and society beyond the school. Nevertheless, it would be unwise to attribute the widely observed 'biased' partitioning of the sexes among school subjects just to ineffective pedagogy. While there certainly is a need to counter any irrational fears, e.g. relating to ability, that girls might have about science, and there will still be a continuing need for specific projects designed to break down the 'science barrier' in both developing countries (e.g., Box 3.9) and advanced industrial ones (e.g., Box 3.10), much also depends on what happens outside the school, especially in industry, which is where science has mainly been applied up to now. If corporations on the 'technological frontier' such as IBM, Hewlett Packard, Chevron, Intel, American Express, Xerox and Westinghouse want to help release the latent mathematical and science skills of women (Box 3.10), could they not also try to rethink the existing industrial model in order to give women and their families a better chance?

It is here, perhaps, in the direct association of science with the dominant mode of production and organization of work, that deeper fears may be founded. Feminist critiques of the 'machismo' of modern science, and of the economics which goes with it, cannot be dismissed out of hand. The industrial model which has evolved over the last 200 years – removal of man from the home and his subordination to the machine, eight to eighteen hours a day – was in the beginning regarded by poets as essentially inhuman, and new doubts about its capacity to serve human needs surface as fast as old ones are allayed. Even as prospects brighten for bringing nuclear arms under control, the challenge to protect the environment looms.

In that perspective, science and technology pose no less of a dilemma for women than for men, and can hardly serve as final purposes for the education of either. What purposes can, if not the ideals of peace, respect for human rights and the practice of democracy? True ideals, which so many of the world's women still do not have 'full and equal opportunities' to help realize.

4
Education
for peace,
human rights
and democracy

'ALL human rights are universal, indivisible and interdependent and interrelated', the World Conference on Human Rights (Vienna, 1993) has affirmed. Progress towards equality of educational opportunity for women, accordingly, reinforces the capacity of education to strengthen respect for human rights.

The challenge of nurturing values and attitudes that are conducive to, and supportive of international understanding and peace, human rights and democracy – one of education's most essential missions – remains as pertinent today for humanity's future as fifty years ago when the United Nations was founded and UNESCO's Constitution was drawn up. In this last chapter, therefore, recent trends and developments which have brought this challenge to the forefront of national policy-makers' concerns in a growing number of countries are briefly reviewed, having regard in particular to the conclusions of the World Conference on Human Rights (Box 4.1), as well as the exchanges of experience relating to education for peace, human rights and democracy that took place at the 44th session of the International Conference on Education (Geneva, 1994).

Box 4.1
Human rights education

The World Conference on Human Rights considers human rights education, training and public information essential for the promotion and achievement of stable and harmonious relations among communities and for fostering mutual understanding, tolerance and peace.

States should strive to eradicate illiteracy and should direct education towards the full development of the human personality and to the strengthening of respect for human rights and fundamental freedoms. The World Conference on Human Rights calls on all States and institutions to include human rights, humanitarian law, democracy and rule of law as subjects in the curricula of all learning institutions in formal and non-formal settings.

Human rights education should include peace, democracy, development and social justice, as set forth in international and regional human rights instruments, in order to achieve common understanding and awareness with a view to strengthening universal commitment to human rights.

Taking into account the World Plan of Action on Education for Human Rights and Democracy, adopted in March 1993 by the International Congress on Education for Human Rights and Democracy of the United Nations Educational, Scientific and Cultural Organization, and other human rights instruments, the World Conference on Human Rights recommends that States develop specific programmes and strategies for ensuring the widest human rights education and the dissemination of public information, taking particular account of the human rights needs of women.

Governments, with the assistance of intergovernmental organizations, national institutions and non-governmental organizations, should promote an increased awareness of human rights and mutual tolerance. The World Conference on Human Rights underlines the importance of strengthening the World Public Information Campaign for Human Rights carried out by the United Nations. They should initiate and support education in human rights and undertake effective dissemination of public information in this field. The advisory services and technical assistance programmes of the United Nations system should be able to respond immediately to requests from States for educational and training activities in the field of human rights as well as for special education concerning standards as contained in international human rights instruments and in humanitarian law and their application to special groups such as military forces, law enforcement personnel, police and the health profession. The proclamation of a United nations decade for human rights education in order to promote, encourage and focus these educational activities should be considered.

Source: World Conference on Human Rights, Vienna, Austria, 14–25 June 1993, *The Vienna Declaration and Programme of Action,* para. 78–82, New York, United Nations, 1993.

Box 4.2
'Problems of education are at the epicentre of the entire reform process' (Russian Federation)

Modern Russia is facing radical changes in all sectors of the society. Public mentality is changing just before one's eyes, alongside with the system of values.

Under these conditions, problems of education are [at] the epicentre of the entire reform process. [...] Since students, educators, and those upgrading their professional level comprise one-third of the Russian population, the value of education and educational reforms can hardly be overrated.

[...]

Ideological shifts in the country and in the system of education have led to a greater accent on human values and personal educational demands. This, in turn, has resulted in greater differentiation of educational institutions and services, both accompanied by social diversification and catalyzed by it.

1. It has become evident that what the state and society most urgently need is the upbringing of Russian citizens who share democratic values and are capable of actively participating in the formation of a state based on law.

To meet these demands, the following aspects of the educational system should undergo a certain change:

- the content of education, with greater accent on the Humanities (this cycle is being developed practically anew);
- educational technologies which should be oriented towards the students' personal development, involve individual training, and offer a variety of choices to students and their parents; and
- management technologies at all levels of government which should promote teachers' creativity (as only a free and creative teacher is capable of bringing up free, creative and independent students) and the availability of educational information to the broad public.

2. The younger generation should be prepared for the market conditions. This means that students should possess the following characteristics:

- an adequate level of economic awareness;
- acquaintance with the courses in market economy and an ability to act in these social and economic conditions;
- knowledge of the basics of economics; and
- for high or vocational school students, a general professional qualification (this does not mean the receiving of a certain professional preparation for working at a certain position, i.e. the vocational training itself, but the career orientation and professional education in a broader sense).

3. Another task facing the modern system of education is to develop in students such qualities as civic spirit, independence, feeling of personal responsibility, understanding of the value of serving the society, and the ability to cooperate with others in building a democratic society.

To achieve the goals above, it is necessary to balance on the verge between meeting the demands of persons, social groups, regions, etc. and a need to ensure national security, the more so as both regions and schools are now free to choose their own ways. [...] Therefore, it is important:

- to avoid the kind of standardized institutional structure, conditions and means of education which [previously] were similar for all forms of learning and instruction; and
- to preserve the unity of Russia's educational space, along with a common ideology and [linkages between] curricula at different educational levels that will help promote horizontal and vertical mobility of students regardless of the place of education.

Source: The Development of Education: National Report of the Russian Federation, pp. 3–14, Moscow, Ministry of Education, 1994. (National report presented at the 44th session of the International Conference on Education, Geneva, 1994.)

New perspectives

Recent political and economic reforms in many countries have opened up new perspectives for education for international understanding and peace, human rights and democracy. In certain cases even, because of the need to root the reforms in people's values and attitudes, education is considered to be at the 'epicentre of the entire reform process' (e.g., Box 4.2).

Box 4.3
Responding to the revival of democracy in Benin

Since the 1990 socio-political changes, which were essentially concerned with the advent of a pluralistic 'revival of democracy' political regime, the Benin Government has paid close attention to issues concerning its population's education in the ideals of peace, democracy, solidarity and understanding among local communities and among all nations.

1. The teaching of human rights and democracy

Innovations in this sector concern:

1.1 Introduction of the basic concepts of: (i) children's rights and human rights, and (ii) democracy as part of the social education syllabus in primary schools.

1.2 Organization of meetings and/or seminar-workshops on the strategies of civic instruction at all teaching levels.

1.3 Preparation of a plan of action for the promotion of human rights teaching.

1.4 Establishment of a specialist technical commission to be responsible for civic instruction.

1.5 Partnership between the National Radio and Television Corporation of Benin and the National Institute for Training and Research in Education to develop human rights educational programmes for radio broadcasting. The information will be intended not only for students but for the population as a whole, and especially for learners in informal sectors.

2. Ethics and religious instruction

2.1 The teaching of ethics (still referred to as morals) forms part of the primary-school curriculum.

2.2 Religious instruction is not on the State school curriculum. It is optional and is generally taught in places of worship or by special arrangement in secondary schools as an elective course.

2.3 Religious instruction is organized more systematically in private religious schools.

3. Education for international understanding and peace

3.1 Recent curriculum reforms have focused on the interaction needed between educational content and its ultimate purpose, namely, contributing to tolerance, understanding and solidarity among the members of the same national community and of the same 'global village' with a view to lasting, peaceful coexistence.

3.2 Language and literature syllabuses (French, English, American, Spanish, German and Russian), together with history, geography and philosophy syllabuses contribute substantially to making this branch of education effective and efficient.

3.3 Other activities also merit mention:

  3.3.1 the organization of student field trips to other parts of Benin or to other African or even European countries;

  3.3.2 twinning between schools within the country or with foreign schools;

  3.3.3 dissemination of UNESCO ideals through the 'Associated Schools' project.

Source: Développement de l'éducation: Rapport national de la République du Bénin, pp. 5–6, Porto-Novo, Ministère de l'Éducation Nationale, Commission Nationale pour l'UNESCO, Institut National pour la Formation et la Recherche en Éducation, 1994. (National report presented at the 44th session of the International Conference on Education, Geneva, 1994.)

New perspectives have been opened up too by other more sombre events in different parts of the world, ranging from outbreaks of ethnic conflict and violence to manifestations of hatred and intolerance towards immigrants and cultural minorities, that have drawn attention to values and attitudes – those of aggression and exclusion – which negate human rights and democracy and undermine international understanding and peace.

In sum, after decades of international tension and the threat of nuclear terror, fundamental changes in political and economic structures and a growing concern over the prospects for human solidarity have prompted an increasing number of nations to a search for educational contents and methods that could strengthen respect for human rights and the practice of democracy, and contribute effectively to international understanding and peace.

Education has always been recognized in every society as a crucial means both of aiding the young to interpret and understand the civil and political environment and of preparing them to enter it as responsible adults and citizens. These functions – referred to in this report as 'civic education' or 'education for citizenship' – have now become a priority focus of interest for national educational policy-makers in many countries. Changes in the civil and political environment have in many cases required a complete rethinking of the whole area of civic education, its purposes and modalities.

In the Russian Federation and a number of other countries, especially in east and central Europe, Africa and Latin America, which have recently undertaken radical political and economic reforms, civic education has been redefined with reference to new purposes ranging from the upbringing of 'citizens who share democratic values and are capable of actively participating in the formation of a state based on law' (Box 4.2) to the education of the population 'in the ideals of peace, democracy, solidarity and understanding among local communities and among all nations' (Box 4.3). Central to these purposes in most cases has been a commitment to strengthening respect for human rights.

The global impact of these developments, however, is still uncertain. The extent to which people in different countries and regions of the world are actually aware of significant changes affecting human rights elsewhere is certainly limited: most of the world's population still live on the outskirts of the much-heralded global media and communications 'village' (Figure 4.1). Indeed, the proportion of the world's adult population who have ever heard of the Universal

Figure 4.1
Media and communication indicators, by region, 1992

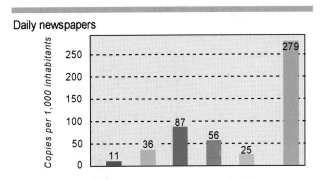

Daily newspapers

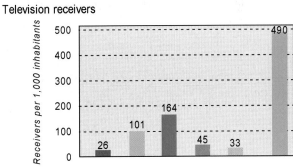

Radio receivers

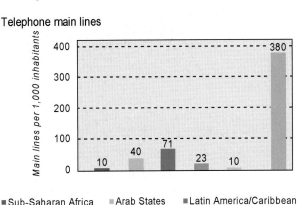

Television receivers

Telephone main lines

■ Sub-Saharan Africa   ■ Arab States   ■ Latin America/Caribbean
■ Eastern Asia/Oceania   ■ Southern Asia   ■ Developed countries

Box 4.4
**The UNESCO Associated Schools Project
in Germany**

Over the years, the Associated Schools' Project of
UNESCO has developed into a network incorpor-
ating almost 90 schools of all levels and types in
all Länder of the Federal Republic of Germany.
The focus of their common work is no longer so
much to produce model concepts but rather to
encourage exchanges of experience and opinion
on the practical implementation of intercultural
learning in teaching and in other areas of school
life.

In order to pursue the objectives binding on all
the schools

• the achievement of human rights for all
• the defeat of poverty and suffering
• the protection and maintenance of the environment
• the acceptance of differences between people

the associated schools of UNESCO develop their
own profile defining their work in relation to the
conditions specific to the school and the area it is
in. The network system is reflected in the efforts
made to overcome the diverse barriers between
people and groups, schools and states by using
diverse methods to encourage contact and con-
nections.

The school partnerships and exchanges run by
the associated schools of UNESCO are based on
this foundation. The focus is moving increasingly
away from Western Europe towards Central and
Eastern Europe and also towards partnership projects with schools in those countries referred to as
the 'Third World'.

*Source: Bericht über die Entwicklung des Bildungswesens, 1992–
1994: Bestandsaufnahme und Perspektiven Internationaler Erzie-
hung/Report on the Development of Education, 1992–1994:
Appraisal and Perspectives of Education for International Understanding, p. 214, Bonn, Sekretariat der Ständigen Konferenz der
Kultusminister der Länder in der Bundesrepublik Deutschland/
Secretariat of the Standing Conference of the Ministers of Education and Cultural Affairs of the Länder in the Federal Republic
of Germany, 1994. (National report presented at the 44th session
of the International Conference on Education, Geneva, 1994.)*

Declaration of Human Rights is unlikely to be
higher – and is probably very much lower – than
the world's adult literacy rate.

Nonetheless, there unmistakably has been a

surge of interest, among countries at many different levels of development, in those purposes of
education which were very much in the minds of
the founders of the United Nations and of
UNESCO. There were few illusions then that
education alone can establish the conditions
needed for democracy and respect for human
rights, improved international understanding and
peace, or that there can be significant progress at
the global level without substantial international
efforts to deal with the poverty and despair
which are the sources of so much violence
and conflict in the world. There are even fewer
illusions today, fifty years on. But now, as then,
education has come to be seen as truly indispensable.

Prospects for international co-operation

In most of the countries where new democratic
institutions have been put in place, educators are
conscious of having entered uncharted territory.
While some are exhilarated, others (probably
the majority) are perplexed and unsure of how
educational contents and methods, school organization and procedures, and relationships with
parents and the community can best help to con-
solidate the new democratic institutions of the
wider society. There is a great deal of interest in
how things are done in other countries.

The need is to increase the possibilities for
educators in each country to exchange experience on methods and procedures in the area of
education for human rights, democracy, international understanding and peace with other
countries of choice. In an ideal world, there
would be frequent such exchanges among neighbouring countries (Table 4.1).

The only worldwide network of exchange and
partnership among educational institutions in
this area is UNESCO's Associated Schools Project
(Box 4.4). Launched in 1953 with 33 secondary
schools in 15 countries aiming to experiment in

Table 4.1
'Neighbours': countries with six or more land borders

1. CHINA (14)	Afghanistan, Bhutan, Democratic People's Republic of Korea, India, Kazakstan, Kyrgyzstan, Lao People's Democratic Republic, Mongolia, Myanmar, Nepal, Pakistan, Russian Federation, Tajikistan, Viet Nam	15. SAUDI ARABIA (7)	Iraq, Jordan, Kuwait, Oman, Qatar, United Arab Emirates, Yemen
		16. UKRAINE (7)	Belarus, Hungary, Poland, Republic of Moldova, Romania, Russian Federation, Slovakia
2. RUSSIAN FEDERATION (14)	Azerbaijan, Belarus, China, Democratic People's Republic of Korea, Estonia, Finland, Georgia, Kazakstan, Latvia, Lithuania, Mongolia, Norway, Poland, Ukraine	17. UNITED REPUBLIC OF TANZANIA (7)	Burundi, Kenya, Malawi, Mozambique, Rwanda, Uganda, Zambia
		18. YUGOSLAVIA (7)	Albania, Bosnia and Herzegovina, Bulgaria, Croatia, Hungary, Romania, The former Yugoslav Republic of Macedonia
3. BRAZIL (10)	Argentina, Bolivia, Colombia, French Guiana, Guyana, Paraguay, Peru, Suriname, Uruguay, Venezuela	19. ZAMBIA (7)	Angola, Malawi, Mozambique, Namibia, United Republic of Tanzania, Zaire, Zimbabwe
4. GERMANY (9)	Austria, Belgium, Czech Republic, Denmark, France, Luxembourg, Netherlands, Poland, Switzerland	20. AFGHANISTAN (6)	China, Islamic Republic of Iran, Pakistan, Tajikistan, Turkmenistan, Uzbekistan
5. SUDAN (9)	Central African Republic, Chad, Egypt, Eritrea, Ethiopia, Kenya, Libyan Arab Jamahiriya, Uganda, Zaire	21. ALGERIA (6)	Libyan Arab Jamahiriya, Mali, Mauritania, Morocco, Niger, Tunisia
6. AUSTRIA (8)	Czech Republic, Germany, Hungary, Italy, Liechtenstein, Slovakia, Slovenia, Switzerland	22. BURKINA FASO (6)	Benin, Ghana, Côte d'Ivoire, Mali, Niger, Togo
7. FRANCE (8)	Andorra, Belgium, Germany, Italy, Luxembourg, Monaco, Spain, Switzerland	23. CAMEROON (6)	Central African Republic, Chad, Congo, Equatorial Guinea, Gabon, Nigeria
8. TURKEY (8)	Armenia, Azerbaijan, Bulgaria, Georgia Greece, Islamic Republic of Iran, Iraq, Syrian Arab Republic	24. CHAD (6)	Cameroon, Central African Republic, Libyan Arab Jamahiriya, Niger, Nigeria, Sudan
9. ZAIRE (8)	Angola, Burundi, Central African Republic, Congo, Rwanda, Sudan, Uganda, Zambia	25. GUINEA (6)	Côte d'Ivoire, Guinea-Bissau, Liberia, Mali, Senegal, Sierra Leone
10. HUNGARY (7)	Austria, Croatia, Romania, Slovakia, Slovenia, Ukraine, Yugoslavia	26. INDIA (6)	Bangladesh, Bhutan, China, Myanmar, Nepal, Pakistan
11. ISLAMIC REPUBLIC OF IRAN (7)	Afghanistan, Armenia, Azerbaijan, Iraq, Pakistan, Turkey, Turkmenistan	27. IRAQ (6)	Islamic Republic of Iran, Jordan, Kuwait, Saudi Arabia, Syrian Arab Republic, Turkey
12. MALI (7)	Algeria, Burkina Faso, Côte d'Ivoire, Guinea, Mauritania, Niger, Senegal	28. LIBYAN ARAB JAMAHIRIYA (6)	Algeria, Chad, Egypt, Niger, Sudan, Tunisia
13. NIGER (7)	Algeria, Benin, Burkina Faso, Chad, Libyan Arab Jamahiriya, Mali, Nigeria	29. MOZAMBIQUE (6)	Malawi, South Africa, Swaziland, United Republic of Tanzania, Zambia, Zimbabwe
14. POLAND (7)	Belarus, Czech Republic, Germany, Lithuania, Russian Federation, Slovakia, Ukraine	30. SOUTH AFRICA (6)	Botswana, Lesotho, Mozambique, Namibia, Swaziland, Zimbabwe

Figure 4.2
Teaching of foreign languages
during the period of compulsory education
in the European Community, 1994

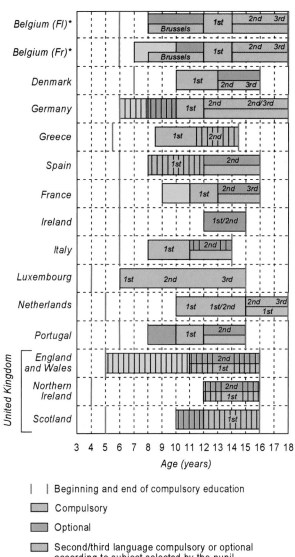

| | Beginning and end of compulsory education

◼ Compulsory

◼ Optional

◼ Second/third language compulsory or optional
according to subject selected by the pupil

◻ Experimentation in teaching at an early age

▥ Recently introduced, not yet generalized

* Fl: Flemish, Fr: French.

Note: 1st, 2nd, 3rd: these numbers refer, respectively, to first, second and third foreign language courses.

Source: Commission européenne, *Les chiffres clés de l'éducation dans l'Union européenne 94,* Brussels/Luxembourg, CECA-CE-CEEA, 1995, 120 pp. (Éducation, formation, jeunesse.)

new methods of teaching pupils about foreign countries and peoples, human rights and the activities of the United Nations, the Associated Schools Project now involves over 3,300 institutions (of which two-thirds are secondary schools) in 125 countries in all regions of the world. The activities of the Associated Schools are broadly focused on four main themes: global challenges and the role of the United Nations system; human rights; knowledge of other countries, respect for different cultures and the world heritage; and the environment.

The basic concept of human 'grass roots' exchanges that underlies the Associated Schools Project has been central to other educational exchange programmes, both bilateral and multilateral. It has been a major factor, for example, in the success of the European Union's exchange programmes with the new democracies of east and central Europe, although other factors such as an 'enabling' multilateral political environment (membership of the Council of Europe) have also been important. In the case of the Associated Schools Project, the 'enabling' environment is of course provided by UNESCO.

The impulse towards regional co-operation in education is likely to generate the majority of opportunities for cross-cultural exchange of experience in the area of education for international understanding and peace, human rights and democracy in coming years. There is little doubt that regional co-operation can have major implications for national education systems: witness the pressure to teach/ learn foreign languages from early ages in Western Europe (Figure 4.2). Most of the various regional and sub-regional forums and mechanisms which were originally established for reasons of political and economic co-operation in recent years have eventually tended towards educational co-operation. Besides the European Union and the long-standing educational co-operation within the Arab League and among the South East Asian countries, MERCOSUR involving Argentina,

Brazil, Paraguay and Uruguay is a more recent example (Box 4.5), and the Asia-Pacific Economic Co-operation Forum (APEC), as noted in the *World Education Report 1993*, is another. The recent initiative towards multilateral educational

---

Box 4.5
MERCOSUR's stimulus
to educational co-operation

One of the most significant actions taken in education matters within the MERCOSUR[1] framework is the 'Protocol for the Educational Integration and Validity of Certificates, Degrees and Elementary and Non Technical High [School] Studies' subscribed, in Buenos Aires, by the Ministries of Education of Argentina, Brazil, Paraguay and Uruguay, on August 4, 1994.

The Regional Coordinating Committee for Educational Matters within MERCOSUR has also made great progress in the area of technological and professional education by contributing with the preparation of a glossary containing unified terminology, system of equivalences for technical courses, integration of graduates and complementary modules.

As to Graduate Education, regional graduate studies are being conducted on how integration will impact on the farming activities of the countries in the region and also on university management. Efforts are being made toward acknowledgment of the validity of university degrees.

Basic subjects within History and Geography modules to be included in the curricula to be taught by schools in the four countries comprised in MERCOSUR are being defined and great progress has been made as to the teaching of Spanish and Portuguese as official languages of the region and to the outlining of Information Systems for Elementary and Non Technical High School Education.

1. MERCOSUR: Mercado Común del Sur.

Source: Educational Development in Argentina, 1993–1994, p. 21, Buenos Aires, Ministry of Culture and Education, 1994. (National report presented at the 44th session of the International Conference on Education, Geneva, 1994.)

Box 4.6
Educational co-operation
in the circumpolar north

To discuss matters of common concern and share experience regarding education in circumpolar jurisdictions several conferences have been organized since 1987. The states concerned are the Nordic countries, Greenland, Russia, Alaska and the northern provinces of Canada. The conference concentrates on issues regarding the indigenous populations of the circumpolar north. In 1992 Norway hosted the 5th conference on a theme relating to the cultural identity of the minorities of this region. It was then agreed to organize the conference on a regular basis, e.g. every second year.

Source: The Development of Education, 1992–94: National Report, p. 43, Oslo, Royal Ministry of Education, Research and Church Affairs, 1994. (National report presented at the 44th session of the International Conference on Education, Geneva, 1994.)

---

co-operation in the circumpolar region, however, is based on shared cultures and ways of life that have developed in response to a harsh environment (Box 4.6).

In all these cases, an important educational challenge for participating countries will be to not lose sight of the global dimension, that is to say, of values that can unite all peoples whether or not they live in (or come from) a particular region of the world.

Practice, contents and methods

Although the particularity of each country's civil and political – not to speak of cultural – life places limits on the extent to which co-operation and exchange between any two countries in the area of civic education can result in useful lessons for either party, there exists a basis for co-operation if there is a shared commitment by both parties to the values of the Universal

Box 4.7
Education for human rights and democracy, tolerance and peace in Egypt

First: Education for human rights and democracy

The aspect of education related to human rights and democracy is closely related to the issue of school curricula, especially as it concerns the modern methods and techniques that aim at heightening the effectiveness of this education. An analysis of the school curricula that directly copes with those concepts in Egypt during the past years reveals the following:

In the primary stage. The curricula of the first three grades of primary education inculcate concepts related to the rights of man, democracy and international understanding and peace both directly and indirectly. We find, for instance, the concepts of rights and duties of family members, the right of living creatures to life and growth, the rights of man regardless of his features (first grade); the concept of international communication and the necessity of peace, and conservation of the environment for man's welfare on earth (second grade); co-operation among communities and peoples, tourist exchange among the countries of the world, the citizen's duties towards societal institutions, and laws that contribute to discipline (third grade).
[...]

In the preparatory stage. The curricula for the three grades include concepts dealing with a study of the Arab League, the African Unity Organization, and the development of regional and international organizations, in addition to geographical concepts pertaining to the states of the Arab homeland and the various continents of the world, government systems and tourist and commercial exchange. These concepts help to develop democratic concepts through a study of systems of government; concepts of peace and international understanding through a study of the United Nations and the aims of regional organizations (the Arab League and the African Unity Organization).
[...]

In the secondary stage. In geography and history, the secondary stage curricula in Egypt include the study of man, environment, resources and geography of the Arab Homeland, then the geography of Egypt and the Nile Basin, while in history is included the ancient civilizations, the Islamic civilization and the history of modern Egypt. These curricula also include concepts of human civilizations, human activity, problems of population, resources and integration and the First and Second World Wars.
[...]

Secondly: Religions and ethical education for tolerance and peace

Religions and ethical education curricula applied now in the diverse education stages in Egypt stress a number of basic topics that call for deepening faith and the love of one's neighbours. All religions call for noble manners, and co-operation and compassion among all people; fraternal rights are needed not only in religion but at work, in the street and on all occasion and in misfortunes as well. Islam calls for tolerance with believers in other religions, the protection of life, property and honor of all people, the preservation of public property, repudiation of violence and fanaticism, and the confrontation of deviant behavior.

Religions and ethical education curricula, therefore, emphasize that Muslims and non-Muslims have a right to a dignified free life in a context of justice and equality where they enjoy stability and safety.

Source: Development of Education in the Arab Republic of Egypt 92/1993–93/1994, pp. 75–9, Cairo, National Centre for Educational Research and Development, 1994. (National report presented at the 44th session of the International Conference on Education, Geneva, 1994.)

Declaration of Human Rights. A simple test is whether the latter is taught in both countries' schools. The right to know of the Universal Declaration of Human Rights was specifically affirmed by the International Congress on Education for Human Rights and Democracy that was held in Montreal in 1993 in preparation for the World Conference on Human Rights.

In the area of education for international understanding and peace, human rights and democracy in general, it is clear from the information available to UNESCO (e.g., Box 4.7) that the variation among countries in practice, contents and methods is very wide, and is attributable at least as much to differences in objective factors relating to the polity and society outside of education, as it is to differences in the conception of the educational task as such.

In the first of these two categories, for example, can be placed factors ranging from the make-up of the country's political institutions to the country's size (surface, population), level of economic development, income distribution, ethnic composition, and the pattern and history of political, economic and cultural relations with neighbouring and other countries.

In the second category – relating to the educational task – are choices regarding various matters ranging from the education of migrant workers' children, of cultural minorities and different ethnic groups (especially in large multi-ethnic states), to school governance, the teaching of second/foreign languages, history, geography and social studies, the selection of teaching/ learning materials, classroom pedagogy, the teaching of ethics and values, religious education, extra-curricular activities and non-formal education.

If greater progress is to be made internationally towards the design and implementation of education that will contribute effectively to respect for human rights and democracy, international understanding and peace, it is also clear that the international community may need to adopt an approach not unlike that advocated by the great French mathematician and philosopher René Descartes (1596–1650) for the solution of complex mathematical and philosophical problems: to divide the difficulty 'into as many parts as might be possible and necessary in order best to solve it', and 'to make such complete enumerations and such general reviews [as to] be sure

---

Box 4.8
IBE's international project,
'What Education for What Citizenship?'

Aimed at coping with rapid changes and transitions which are intensifying misery, marginalization and violence in the world today, the IBE launched in 1994 the international research, experimentation and information project 'What Education for What Citizenship?' to obtain sound knowledge upon which efficient decision-making can be based with a view to preparing well-informed individuals who can tackle the problems of the world today. The project is devoted to *gathering new knowledge,* encouraging a better understanding of citizenship education practices in Member States and, correlatively, helping to *formulate educational policies* for citizenship education based upon relevant and reliable empirical evidence.

The research phase consists of a *nationally representative comparative survey* conducted in more than 40 countries and involving students, teachers and students' parents, and a series of case studies aimed at identifying country-specific innovations in the field. The research utilizes more than 15 different languages. More than 100 major national institutions in the fields of education curriculum, research, teacher training and planning are currently involved in the project activities. The *experimentation phase* in the participating countries is being initiated in 1995, with a view to evaluating the research findings and mobilizing national institutions to serve as a basis for educational reform, as well as for international and regional co-operation in the field of citizenship education. The *information phase* is developing, from 1995 onwards, a knowledge base which will put progressively the results of the research and the experimentation at the disposal of education sector decision-makers, researchers and practitioners, through conventional media and the worldwide network Internet.

Source: International Bureau of Education (IBE), Geneva, 1995.

---

to have omitted nothing'. This means, firstly, that the international community needs to have much more information than is now available on how educators in different countries conceive of

Box 4.9
'Global education' in Canada

'Global education' is a broad term for interdisciplinary programmes dealing with themes of social and economic development, sustainability, human rights, peace and security and the environment. Education methodologies stress cooperation, democratic decision-making, and innovative approaches to solving problems. Several federal departments and agencies provide schools and the general public with relevant information and educational material dealing with these issues. A variety of activities are funded during the International Environment Week in early June each year.

[...]

The global education programme is funded by CIDA[1] until 1995, and includes initiatives for pre- and in-service teacher training, curriculum development, and other more action-oriented activities. The broad objectives are to promote a prejudice-free world through understanding of global interdependence and solidarity between Canada and the Third World, and the encouragement of cultural enrichment through a better knowledge of other lifestyles and ways of thinking – to foster international understanding, tolerance, respect for the rights of others, and rejection of racism.

1. CIDA: Canadian International Development Agency.

Source: The Global Classroom: Appraisal and Perspectives on Education for International Understanding/Salle de classe ouverte sur le monde: bilan et perspectives de l'éducation pour la compréhension internationale, pp. 26–8, Toronto, Council of Ministers of Education/Conseil des Ministres de l'Éducation, 1994. (National report presented at the 44th session of the International Conference on Education, Geneva, 1994.)

the educational challenges in this area, and secondly, much more information on what practices, contents and methods are effective (Box 4.8, p. 87).

As for educators themselves, they need, above all, to have an 'enabling' international environment in which to work. Young people can be taught global solidarity (Box 4.9), but cannot be taught that the world is a more peaceful, tolerant and just place than it really is.

Epilogue

Nearly $800 billion was still being spent worldwide on armaments in 1994, a decline, certainly, from the estimated $1,200 billion of 1987, but still equivalent to around two-thirds of estimated world public expenditure on education (Appendix II, Table 11). Armed conflict is currently taking place in over forty countries, and there are over 20 million refugees and displaced persons

Box 4.10
'Three pillars of a global culture'

Ethnic, religious and cultural separatism threatens a return of some of the worst problems of the past: intolerance or antagonism toward other cultures; opposition to practices unlike one's own; and an inability to conduct productive dialogue across the global range of diverse cultures. When a culture walls itself off from others, the only outcome can be sterility and antagonism. The cause of co-operation and progress on a global scale cannot but be set back by this phenomenon.

Today, as Secretary-General, it is clear to me that only in a healthy flowering of many cultures, cherished for their rich diversity, can a truly global culture of peace – based on mutual respect and creative exchange – take shape.

This purpose is at the heart of the great historical enterprise that is the United Nations. The *raison d'être* of the United Nations is to foster the integrity of cultures and, upon this basis, to promote information, dialogue, understanding and co-operation among the peoples of all the world's diverse cultures. Upon this foundation, the United Nations can proceed toward the realization of the three pillars of a global culture:

A culture of peace
A culture of development
A culture of democracy

Source: Boutros Boutros-Ghali, Unity and Diversity: The Contemporary Challenge. Speech delivered at the Global Cultural Diversity Conference, Sydney (Australia), 26 April 1995. (United Nations Information Centre, Sydney, Press Release.)

in the world without proper shelter, not to speak of the 885 million illiterate adults and 129 million children of primary-school-age who are out of school, noted earlier in this report.

'What is new today', the Commission on Global Governance observed in its report, *Our Global Neighbourhood* (1995), 'is that the interdependence of nations is wider and deeper'. Yet there is a paradox: while technology and economics weave ever closer links between the different nations of the world, and awareness grows of the fragility of the biosphere that concerns them all, the sense of human solidarity, as much within as between nations, appears hardly to advance. Fifty years after its founding, the United Nations still have much work ahead (Box 4.10).

Appendices

I. Statistical notes

THE following notes provide explanations of several statistical measures referred to in the report.

School life and school survival expectancies

The definition of school life expectancy (SLE) that was given in the *World Education Report 1993* is retained: for a child of a certain age, the SLE is defined as the total number of years of schooling which the child can expect to receive in the future, assuming that the probability of his or her being enrolled in school at any particular future age is equal to the current enrolment ratio for that age.

Let it be supposed that the following enrolment ratios are observed in a given country:

| Age | Enrolment ratio (%) | |
	Male	Female
5	40	25
6	90	70
7	85	60
8	80	54
9	75	50
10	60	42
11	48	33
12	40	27
13	32	21
14	25	16
15	20	12
16	17	11
17	14	10
18	12	9
19–23	4	2

The SLE at age 5 for males is $[40+90+85+80+75+60+48+40+32+25+20+17+14+12+(4\times5)]/100 = 6.58$ years, and for females it is $[25+70+60+54+50+42+33+27+21+16+12+11+10+9+(2\times5)]/100 = 4.50$ years.

The school survival expectancy (SSE) for a child of a certain age (the 'reference' age) is defined as the number of years of schooling which a child of that age *who is already in school* can expect to receive in the future, assuming that the probability of his or her being enrolled in school at any future age is equal to the ratio of the current enrolment ratio at that age to the highest current enrolment ratio at any age from the refer-

ence age onwards. Normally, the highest current enrolment ratio at any age from the reference age onwards will be the current enrolment ratio at the reference age. However, in certain circumstances this will not be the case, especially where there is a mixture of ages at entry into school, which often produces a 'jump' in the observed enrolment ratios. For example, in the country represented by the table of enrolment ratios shown above, where it is assumed for the sake of argument that 6 is the 'official' age of school entry, 5-year-olds are allowed to enrol if they are ready and/or there are places available for them in their local school. If 5 is the reference age for the SSE, then for both males and females the highest current enrolment ratio at any age from the reference age onwards is actually at age 6, not 5.

The SSE at age 5 for males is $[40+90+85+80+75+60+48+40+32+25+20+17+14+12+(4\times5)]/90 = 7.31$ years, and for females it is $[25+70+60+54+50+42+33+27+21+16+12+11+10+9+(2\times5)]/70 = 6.43$ years.

The differences between the two measures can be summarized as follows.[1] Let E_i represent the proportion of the total population of age i that is enrolled in school, and let the reference age-range be 5–23. The SLE can be expressed as:

$$SLE = \sum_{i=5}^{23} E_i \qquad (1)$$

If the highest enrolment ratio occurs at age 6, then

$$SSE = \sum_{i=5}^{23} E_i / E_6 \qquad (2)$$

in other words,

$$SSE = SLE/E_6 \qquad (3)$$

If the subscripts m and f are understood to denote males and females respectively, and if for the sake of argument the highest enrolment ratios for both males and females occur at age 6, then

$$SSE_f/SSE_m = (SLE_f/SLE_m)(E_{6m}/E_{6f}) \qquad (4)$$

---

1. See Rati Ram, *Use of School Life Expectancies and School Survival Expectancies to Study Gender Gaps in Educational Opportunities,* Paris, UNESCO, 1995. (Mimeo. Background paper prepared for the *World Education Report 1995.)*

or alternatively,

$$SLE_f/SLE_m = (SSE_f/SSE_m)(E_{6f}/E_{6m}) \qquad (5)$$

The expression (5) shows clearly that the male-female 'disparity' represented by SLE_f/SLE_m is essentially made up of two components: a disparity in school survival expectancies and a disparity in access to schooling at age 6.

It may be seen that the SLE is in effect defined with reference to the total population from age 5 onwards, while the SSE is defined with reference only to the enrolled population.

A certain amount of caution should be exercised when utilizing the two measures in international comparisons. For example, it should be noted that neither the SLE nor the SSE necessarily represents the expected number of grades that will be completed, because of the possibility of repeating grades. Each represents simply the expected number of years that will be completed including years spent repeating one or more grades. Moreover, a year or grade completed in one country is not necessarily the same in terms of educational content or quality as a year or grade completed in another country. It should also be noted that both measures are essentially synthetic summary descriptions or indicators of the overall pattern of enrolment ratios at one particular point in time; they have no predictive value except in so far as it is believed that this pattern will remain unchanged into the future.

It was observed by UNESCO several years ago that comparisons between the SLE and SSE could provide useful insights into gender differences in educational enrolments.[1] In the example given above, the gap between the male SLE and the female SLE is $6.58 - 4.50 = 2.08$ years, while between the male SSE and female SSE it is $7.31 - 6.43 = 0.88$ years. The smaller gender gap in the SSEs compared to that for the SLEs is basically due to the fact that a larger proportion of males than females gets into school in the first place. Once the girls get into school their chances of 'survival' are only slightly less favourable than those for boys.

Indeed, in the example shown above, if the reference age is 15 instead of 5, the SSE for girls is actually slightly higher than that for boys. From a policy standpoint, therefore, the main challenge in this particular country is to ensure that girls have the same opportunity as boys in gaining access to school at age 6. Other examples could of course be formulated to illustrate the case where it is the differences between males and females in school survival or drop-out that constitute the main challenge for educational policy.

When comparing the SSEs for males and females the caution noted earlier concerning grade-repetition should be borne in mind. In countries where there is a significant difference between males and females in grade-repeating rates, the SSEs of males and females will not convey the same information regarding expected number of grades that will be completed. A similar caution applies to the SLEs. If data on male and female repeaters are available, then both the SSEs and the SLEs can be adjusted to show the expected number of grades that will be completed.

In a cross-national perspective, the male-female gap in the SLE is generally in favour of males when the values of the SLE are low (as in many developing countries), but is as often in favour of females as of males at the higher values of the SLE (as in many industrial countries).

Alternative measures of male-female disparities in literacy rates

The following table shows the adult literacy rates in selected countries as reported by the national censuses taken around 1950, as well as UNESCO's estimates of the adult literacy rates for these countries in 1995. The diagram shows scatter-plots of these rates with the lower point of each line corresponding to the year 1950 and the upper point corresponding to the year 1995. The letters signify the countries. The 45° line joining the lower left and upper right corners of the diagram represents all points where the male and female literacy rates are equal. Only in the case of Nicaragua are the female literacy rates higher (in both years) than the male literacy rates. In all the other selected countries the male literacy rate is higher than the female rate in both years, although in the case of the Philippines in

1. Isabelle Deblé, *The School Education of Girls: An International Comparative Study on School Wastage among Girls and Boys at the First and Second Levels of Education.* Paris, UNESCO, 1980.

***Alternative measures of disparity between male and female literacy rates
in selected countries, 1950 and 1995***

Country	1950 Literacy rate (%)[1]				1995 Literacy rate (%)[2]			
	Male (1)	Female (2)	M–F[3] (3)	F/M[4] (4)	Male (5)	Female (6)	M–F[3] (7)	F/M[4] (8)
Bolivia	42.4	32.8	9.6	0.77	90.5	76.0	14.5	0.84
Egypt	31.5	8.7	22.8	0.28	63.6	38.8	24.8	0.61
Guatemala	34.4	24.4	10.0	0.71	62.5	48.6	13.9	0.78
Haiti	12.8	8.5	4.3	0.66	48.0	42.2	5.8	0.88
Mozambique	5.2	1.4	3.8	0.27	57.7	33.3	24.4	0.58
Nicaragua	38.0	38.7	– 0.7	1.02	64.6	66.6	–2.0	1.03
Philippines	74.1	56.2	17.9	0.76	95.0	94.3	0.7	0.99
Singapore	64.7	32.5	32.2	0.50	95.9	86.3	9.6	0.90
Turkey	31.8	8.0	23.8	0.25	91.7	72.4	19.3	0.79

1. Percentage of literate adults aged 15 years and over, as reported by national censuses; 1947 censuses in the case of Egypt and the Philippines, and 1948
   census in the case of Singapore.
2. UNESCO's estimates of the percentage of literate adults aged 15 years and over.
3. Male literacy rate minus female literacy rate.
4. Female literacy rate divided by male literacy rate.

1995 the male and female rates are estimated to be very close. The length of the line for each country can be regarded as a measure of the overall amount of change in that country's literacy rates between the two dates.

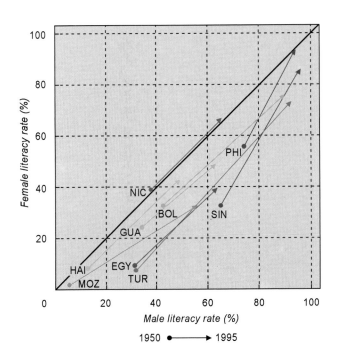

1950 ●———▶ 1995

The biggest change was in the case of Turkey and the smallest in Guatemala. The direction of the line is an indicator of whether the change in literacy rates was in favour of males (the line points away from the 45° line, for example Mozambique) or in favour of females (the line points towards the 45° line, for example Philippines). However, it cannot be unambiguously determined from the diagram itself whether the 'disparity' between the male and female literacy rates in a particular country in a particular year is greater or less than in another country; this depends on how the 'disparity' is measured.

Two alternative measures are proposed below. Each orders the countries somewhat differently.

Alternative 1: The 'gap' between the male and female literacy rates, as indicated in columns (3) and (7) of the table. In the diagram, this 'gap' is represented by the vertical distance of each country from the 45° line.

Alternative 2: The ratio of the female to the male literacy rate, as indicated in columns (4) and (8) of the table. In the diagram, this ratio is represented by the angle between the horizontal axis and the line which could be drawn from a given country to the origin of the diagram.

Clearly, neither of the two measures above is fully satisfactory on its own. At least, both of them need to be used in conjunction with other information about the literacy rates if a complete picture of the male-female differences is to be obtained. For example, under Alternative 1 the least disparity in 1950 was in Nicaragua, followed by Mozambique and Haiti, yet in both of the latter two countries the small size of the disparity is perhaps more a reflection of the fact that the overall literacy rates for both males and females are very low than it is of factors relating to the difference between male and female literacy as such. Similarly, under Alternative 2, in 1950 the ratio of the female literacy rate to the male literacy rate was lower in Singapore than in Haiti, notwithstanding that the literacy rates for both males and females were several times higher in Singapore than in Haiti.

Nevertheless, when taking into account the entire range of developing countries for which literacy estimates (1995) are available, the two measures are broadly correlated with each other ($r = -0.91$, $n = 107$) and each is correlated with the overall female literacy rate: in the case of the first measure (Alternative 1), $r = -0.84$, and in the case of the second measure (Alternative 2), $r = 0.96$. The higher correlation of the second measure (Alternative 2) with the overall female literacy rate, as well as its positive sign, make it more useful than the first measure for most analytic purposes.

Index of gender segregation by fields of study

The index of gender segregation by fields of study is defined as the percentage of all persons enrolled at a given level of education who would need to change their field of study if the ratio of females to males were to be the same in all fields of study, assuming that in each field of study there is no change in the total enrolment.

In effect, the index equalizes the gender compositions of enrolments in all fields of study on the basis of the gender composition of the total enrolment in all fields of study taken together. For example, let the enrolments at a given level of education with two fields of study A and B be as follows:

	Male	*Female*	*Total*
Field A	220	60	280
Field B	20	100	120
All fields	240	160	400

The gender composition of the total enrolment in all fields taken together (400) is 60 per cent male (240) and 40 per cent female (160). If the gender composition of the total enrolment in field A (280) were also to be 60 per cent male and 40 per cent female, then the enrolment in field A would need to be 168 males and 112 females. In other words, 52 males in field A would need to 'move' into field B, and 52 females in field B would need to 'move' into field A, giving a total of 104 persons who would need to change fields out of the grand total of 400 persons enrolled, which means that the gender segregation index would be $104/400 = 26$ per cent.

In general, the calculation of the number of persons who need to change field is based on the percentages of males and females in the total enrolment for all fields taken together, and on the differences between these percentages and the observed percentages of males and females in each field. Let m and f be respectively the percentages of males and females in the total enrolment for all fields taken together, and let M_s and F_s respectively represent the existing enrolments of males and females in field s, where $s = 1, 2, ..., n$. If T_s represents the total enrolment in field s, then

$$m = \left(\sum_{1}^{n}M_s / \sum_{1}^{n}T_s\right) \text{ and } f = \left(\sum_{1}^{n}F_s / \sum_{1}^{n}T_s\right)$$

The required changes in the numbers of males and females respectively in field s will be $m.T_s - M_s$ and $f.T_s - F_s$. Since it is a condition that there is no net change in the total enrolment in any particular field, it follows that $(m.T_s - M_s) + (f.T_s - F_s) = 0$. Whether it is males or females who are under- or over-represented in any particular field depends on the signs (− or +) of the expressions $(m.T_s - M_s)$ and $(f.T_s - F_s)$. For example, if $m.T_s < M_s$, then males are over-represented in field s, and some of them need to change to other fields. Conversely, if $m.T_s > M_s$, then males are under-represented in field s, and some males in other fields need to change to field s.

Since the total number of males who need to move out of their existing fields must equal the total number of females who need to move into these fields, and likewise the total number of females who need to move out of their existing fields must equal the total number of males who need to move into them, it follows that the total number of persons who need to change field is equal to both the total number of males who must either move out of, or into, an existing field, and the total number of females who must either move out of, or into, an existing field. In other words,

$$P = \sum_1^n \left| m.T_s - M_s \right| = \sum_1^n \left| f.T_s - F_s \right|$$

where P is the total number of persons who need to change field. The gender segregation index I, therefore, is given by the expression

$$I = 100 \left(P / \sum_1^n T_s \right)$$

The general idea of such an index is not new, but it typically has been applied to the study of gender segregation among occupations.[1]

Another index which has also been used in the study of gender segregation among occupations is the index of dissimilarity D (sometimes referred to as 'Duncan's index'[2]):

$$D = 100 \sum_1^n \left(\left| m_s - f_s \right| \right) / 2$$

where m_s and f_s are the proportions of total male and female enrolments respectively which are in field s. This index represents the percentage of persons of one sex that would need to change fields in order to have the same distribution among fields as persons of the other sex.

A certain amount of caution is required when using I, whether the focus is on fields of study, occupations, or other classifications. With reference to fields of study, it should be noted that the index is not a measure of the overall gender disparity in access to, or participation in, a particular level of education. In the numerical example given below, the value of I (10 per cent) is quite different from that in the earlier example given above (26 per cent), although the female share of total enrolment is the same in both cases (40 per cent).

	Male	Female	Total
Field A	100	25	125
Field B	200	175	375
All fields	300	200	500

Probably a more significant ground for caution in using the index is uncertainty concerning the comparability (consistency of classification criteria) among different countries as regards the various fields of study. Comparability is likely to be less when the number of fields is large than when it is small. In Appendix III, Table 9, the index is calculated for five fields of study in third-level education; breaking down any one of these fields further would probably erode inter-country comparability quite substantially. The 'ideal' number of fields, for the purposes of calculating the index, cannot be determined *a priori*.

Correlation analysis of male and female enrolment ratios and female teachers, literacy rates and GNP per capita

Several factors which possibly could help account for the observed variation among countries in the enrolment ratios of girls in first- or second-level education are considered in the correlation matrix overpage.

In regard to first-level education, it may be hypothesized that variation among countries in the male and female gross enrolment ratios is likely to be associated with variation in the percentage of female teachers in first-level education (e.g. less disparity between the male and female enrolment ratios when there is a high percentage of female teachers, and vice versa when the percentage of female teachers is low), as well as with variation in the male and female adult literacy rates and levels of overall income per capita. Similar hypotheses

1. See, for example, Francine D. Blau and Marianne A. Ferber, 'Women's Work, Women's Lives: A Comparative Economic Perspective', pp. 33–4, in Hilda Kahne and Janet Z. Giele (eds.), *Women's Work and Women's Lives,* Boulder, Colo., Westview Press, 1992.
2. See, for example, Victor R. Fuchs, 'Women's Quest for Economic Equality', *Journal of Economic Perspectives,* Vol. 3, No. 1, Winter 1989, pp. 25–41.

Correlation coefficients for several variables relating to enrolment in first- and second-level education in developing countries,[1] 1992

Variable[2]	GER1.M	GER1.F	GER1.F/M	FTEACH.1	GER2.M	GER2.F	GER2.F/M	FTEACH.2	LIT.M	LIT.F	LIT.F/M	GNP/CAP
GER1.M	1.00	0.91	0.52	0.38	0.57	0.52	0.35	0.46	0.62	0.55	0.49	0.13
GER1.F	0.91	1.00	0.81	0.64	0.62	0.67	0.65	0.67	0.79	0.77	0.73	0.23
GER1.F/M	0.52	0.81	1.00	0.77	0.47	0.63	0.84	0.70	0.80	0.83	0.82	0.30
FTEACH.1	0.38	0.64	0.77	1.00	0.55	0.74	0.85	0.89	0.66	0.78	0.82	0.42
GER2.M	0.57	0.62	0.47	0.55	1.00	0.94	0.40	0.66	0.60	0.65	0.61	0.57
GER2.F	0.52	0.67	0.63	0.74	0.94	1.00	0.65	0.81	0.68	0.78	0.77	0.63
GER2.F/M	0.35	0.65	0.84	0.85	0.40	0.65	1.00	0.79	0.65	0.75	0.80	0.33
FTEACH.2	0.46	0.67	0.70	0.89	0.66	0.81	0.79	1.00	0.72	0.83	0.85	0.46
LIT.M	0.62	0.79	0.80	0.66	0.60	0.68	0.65	0.72	1.00	0.94	0.85	0.29
LIT.F	0.55	0.77	0.83	0.78	0.65	0.78	0.75	0.83	0.94	1.00	0.96	0.40
LIT.F/M	0.49	0.73	0.82	0.82	0.61	0.77	0.80	0.85	0.85	0.96	1.00	0.44
GNP/CAP	0.13	0.23	0.30	0.42	0.57	0.63	0.33	0.46	0.29	0.40	0.44	1.00

1. 57 countries.
2. The variables are identified as follows:
   GER1.M: Gross enrolment ratio in first-level education, males.
   GER1.F: Gross enrolment ratio in first-level education, females.
   GER1.F/M: GER1.F/GER1.M.
   FTEACH.1: Percentage of female teachers in first-level education.
   GER2.M: Gross enrolment ratio in second-level education, males.

   GER2.F: Gross enrolment ratio in second-level education, females.
   GER2.F/M: GER2.F/GER2.M.
   FTEACH.2: Percentage of female teachers in second-level education.
   LIT.M: Adult literacy rate, males.
   LIT.F: Adult literacy rate, females.
   LIT.F/M: LIT.F/LIT.M.
   GNP/CAP: Gross national product per capita in US dollars.

may be posited in regard to second-level education; in addition, the possibility that the second-level male and female enrolment ratios are associated with variation in the corresponding ratios in first-level education may also be considered.

There are several points of interest in the correlations. In regard to first-level education, it may be noted that the female gross enrolment ratio (GER1.F) is more highly correlated than the male gross enrolment ratio (GER1.M) with the percentage of female teachers ($r = 0.64$ compared to $r = 0.38$); it also is more highly correlated than the male gross enrolment ratio with the levels of literacy in the adult population. The ratio of the female to the male gross enrolment ratio (GER1.F/M) is even more highly correlated with the

percentage of female teachers ($r = 0.77$) and with the adult literacy rates.

In regard to second-level education, the female gross enrolment ratio (GER2.F) is again more highly correlated than the male gross enrolment ratio (GER2.M) with the percentage of female teachers ($r = 0.81$ compared to $r = 0.66$) and likewise with the adult literacy rates. The ratio of the female to the male gross enrolment ratio (GER2.F/M) is highly correlated with the corresponding ratio at the first level (GER1.F/M), as well as with the percentage of female teachers at the second level and the adult literacy rates.

It is of interest that the correlations of the enrolment ratios with GNP per capita are more marked at the second level than at the first.

II. Regional tables

Two changes have been made in the classification of countries by region in this report compared to the previous report (1993): (i) South Africa is now included in sub-Saharan Africa, and hence also is included under 'Developing countries', and (ii) the states of the former USSR are now allocated as appropriate between Europe and Asia, and are retained under 'Developed countries'.

The overall system of classification, in particular the traditional dichotomy of 'developed' and 'developing' countries, is being reviewed taking into account the different practices of the various organizations of the United Nations system. The classification adopted in this report is as follows:[1]

Developing countries and territories

Sub-Saharan Africa comprises Angola, Benin, Botswana, Burkina Faso, Burundi, Cameroon, Cape Verde, Central African Republic, Chad, Comoros, Congo, Côte d'Ivoire, Djibouti, Equatorial Guinea, Eritrea, Ethiopia, Gabon, Gambia, Ghana, Guinea, Guinea-Bissau, Kenya, Lesotho, Liberia, Madagascar, Malawi, Mali, Mauritania, Mauritius, Mozambique, Namibia, Niger, Nigeria, Rwanda, Sao Tome and Principe, Senegal, Seychelles, Sierra Leone, Somalia, South Africa, Sudan, Swaziland, Togo, Uganda, United Republic of Tanzania, Zaire, Zambia and Zimbabwe.

Arab States comprises Algeria, Bahrain, Djibouti, Egypt, Iraq, Jordan, Kuwait, Lebanon, Libyan Arab Jamahiriya, Mauritania, Morocco, Oman, Palestine, Qatar, Saudi Arabia, Somalia, Sudan, Syrian Arab Republic, Tunisia, United Arab Emirates and Yemen.

Latin America and the Caribbean comprises Antigua and Barbuda, Argentina, Bahamas, Barbados, Belize, Bolivia, Brazil, British Virgin Islands, Chile, Colombia, Costa Rica, Cuba, Dominica, Dominican Republic, Ecuador, El Salvador, Grenada, Guatemala, Guyana, Haiti, Honduras, Jamaica, Mexico, Netherlands Antilles, Nicaragua, Panama, Paraguay, Peru, Saint Kitts and Nevis, Saint Lucia, Saint Vincent and the Grenadines, Suriname, Trinidad and Tobago, Uruguay and Venezuela.

Eastern Asia and Oceania comprises Brunei Darussalam, Cambodia, China, Democratic People's Republic of Korea, Fiji, Hong Kong, Indonesia, Kiribati, Lao People's Democratic Republic, Malaysia, Mongolia, Myanmar, Papua New Guinea, Philippines, Republic of Korea, Samoa, Singapore, Solomon Islands, Thailand, Tonga, Tuvalu, Vanuatu and Viet Nam.

Southern Asia comprises Afghanistan, Bangladesh, Bhutan, India, Islamic Republic of Iran, Maldives, Nepal, Pakistan and Sri Lanka.

Least developed countries comprises Afghanistan, Bangladesh, Benin, Bhutan, Burkina Faso, Burundi, Cambodia, Cape Verde, Central African Republic, Chad, Comoros, Djibouti, Equatorial Guinea, Eritrea, Ethiopia, Gambia, Guinea, Guinea-Bissau, Haiti, Kiribati, Lao People's Democratic Republic, Lesotho, Liberia, Madagascar, Malawi, Maldives, Mali, Mauritania, Mozambique, Myanmar, Nepal, Niger, Rwanda, Samoa, Sao Tome and Principe, Sierra Leone, Solomon Islands, Somalia, Sudan, Togo, Tuvalu, Uganda, United Republic of Tanzania, Vanuatu, Yemen, Zaire and Zambia.

Developed countries

Northern America comprises Canada and the United States of America.

Asia and Oceania comprises Armenia, Australia, Azerbaijan, Georgia, Israel, Japan, Kazakstan, Kyrgyzstan, New Zealand, Tajikistan, Turkmenistan and Uzbekistan.

Europe and Russian Federation comprises Albania, Austria, Belarus, Belgium, Bulgaria, Czech Republic, Denmark, Estonia, Finland, France, Germany, Greece, Hungary, Iceland, Ireland, Italy, Latvia, Lithuania, Luxembourg, Monaco, Netherlands, Norway, Poland, Portugal, Republic of Moldova, Romania, Russian Federation, San Marino, Slovakia, Spain, Sweden, Switzerland, Ukraine and United Kingdom.

1. As in previous editions of the *World Education Report*, the totals for 'Developing countries' include Cyprus, Malta, Turkey and the countries of the former Yugoslavia (Bosnia and Herzegovina, Croatia, Slovenia, The Former Yugoslav Republic of Macedonia and Yugoslavia). Also, Djibouti, Mauritania, Somalia and Sudan are included under both 'Sub-Saharan Africa' and 'Arab States'; however, in all graphs presented in the report where individual countries are shown, these countries are included under the 'Arab States' region only.

Table 1
Dependency ratios[1] and population aged 15–64, 1980–2000

	1980				1995				2000			
	Dependency ratio (percentage)			Population (millions)	Dependency ratio (percentage)			Population (millions)	Dependency ratio (percentage)			Population (millions)
	0–5	6–14	65+	15–64	0–5	6–14	65+	15–64	0–5	6–14	65+	15–64
WORLD TOTAL	24.7	35.1	10.0	2 616	21.5	29.4	10.5	3 540	20.2	28.5	10.8	3 857
Developing countries of which:	28.9	40.4	7.2	1 884	24.3	32.5	7.8	2 730	22.7	31.4	8.2	3 027
Sub-Saharan Africa	41.6	45.4	5.5	200	41.4	46.6	5.7	307	39.6	46.7	5.7	357
Arab States	38.4	44.5	6.5	89	31.8	41.3	6.1	142	29.4	38.7	6.2	166
Latin America/Caribbean	29.9	39.8	7.8	202	23.0	32.4	8.5	294	20.9	30.0	8.9	327
Eastern Asia/Oceania	23.4	39.5	7.5	837	17.7	25.9	8.5	1 176	16.3	25.1	9.2	1 262
of which: China	20.7	38.8	7.9	597	15.6	23.5	9.1	824	14.2	23.1	9.9	873
Southern Asia	31.6	40.1	6.8	532	27.2	36.1	7.2	778	25.0	34.0	7.4	881
of which: India	29.1	38.0	7.1	395	24.8	33.7	7.6	563	22.6	31.7	8.0	630
Least developed countries	40.6	46.3	5.9	203	38.0	43.9	5.6	308	36.2	43.1	5.6	358
Developed countries of which:	13.8	21.5	17.4	731	11.9	19.1	19.7	810	11.4	18.1	20.4	830
Northern America	13.1	20.9	16.7	167	14.0	19.5	19.2	192	13.1	19.7	18.8	202
Asia/Oceania	17.1	25.6	12.7	125	13.9	21.2	17.0	147	13.5	20.2	19.0	152
Europe/Russian Federation	13.2	20.6	19.0	439	10.4	18.2	20.7	471	9.9	16.6	21.6	476

1. Percentage ratio of the population in each age-group to the population aged 15–64.

Source: United Nations Population Division database (1994 revision).

Table 2
Estimated illiterate population (millions) aged 15 and over, 1980–2000

	1980			1995			2000		
	MF	F	%F	MF	F	%F	MF	F	%F
WORLD TOTAL	877.4	551.4	62.8	884.7	564.7	63.8	880.8	564.6	64.1
Developing countries of which:	848.4	530.6	62.5	871.8	556.7	63.9	870.0	558.1	64.2
Sub-Saharan Africa	125.9	76.2	60.5	140.5	87.1	62.0	143.4	89.3	62.3
Arab States	55.8	34.5	61.8	65.5	41.2	62.9	67.9	42.9	63.3
Latin America/Caribbean	44.1	24.7	56.1	42.9	23.4	54.7	42.1	22.7	54.0
Eastern Asia/Oceania	276.1	186.3	67.5	209.9	149.5	71.2	182.4	132.3	72.6
of which: China	218.8	147.9	67.6	166.2	119.5	71.9	143.5	105.7	73.7
Southern Asia	345.9	207.2	59.9	415.5	256.1	61.6	437.7	271.8	62.1
of which: India	250.6	152.7	60.9	290.7	182.7	62.8	300.8	190.5	63.3
Least developed countries	135.4	81.2	59.9	166.0	101.0	60.8	178.0	109.0	61.2
Developed countries	29.0	20.9	72.0	12.9	7.9	61.6	10.7	6.5	60.5

Table 3
Estimated adult literacy rates (percentages),[1] 1980–2000

	1980			1995			2000		
	MF	M	F	MF	M	F	MF	M	F
WORLD TOTAL	69.5	77.2	61.9	77.4	83.6	71.2	79.4	85.2	73.6
Developing countries of which:	58.0	68.9	46.8	70.4	78.9	61.7	73.4	81.2	65.5
Sub-Saharan Africa	40.2	51.8	29.2	56.8	66.6	47.3	62.0	70.9	53.3
Arab States	40.8	55.0	26.2	56.6	68.4	44.2	61.5	72.2	50.1
Latin America/Caribbean	79.7	82.1	77.5	86.6	87.7	85.5	88.2	89.0	87.4
Eastern Asia/Oceania	69.3	80.4	58.0	83.6	90.6	76.3	86.8	92.8	80.6
of which: China	66.0	78.6	52.7	81.5	89.9	72.7	85.0	92.3	77.4
Southern Asia	39.1	52.8	24.5	50.2	62.9	36.6	53.7	66.0	40.7
of which: India	40.8	55.3	25.3	52.0	65.5	37.7	55.8	68.6	42.1
Least developed countries	36.5	48.3	24.9	48.8	59.5	38.1	52.7	62.9	42.4
Developed countries	96.6	98.0	95.4	98.7	98.9	98.4	98.9	99.1	98.8

1. Percentage of literate adults in the population aged 15 years and over. The population data utilized are those of the United Nations Population Division database (1994 revision).

Table 4
Culture and communication indicators, 1985 and 1992

	Consumption of newsprint and other printing and writing paper (kgs per inhabitant)		Circulation of daily newspapers (copies per thousand inhabitants)		Radio receivers (per thousand inhabitants)		Television receivers (per thousand inhabitants)	
	1985	1992	1985	1992	1985	1992	1985	1992
WORLD TOTAL	17.0	19.0	95	96	345	350	142	153
Developing countries of which:	3.4	4.8	40	44	145	177	39	57
Sub-Saharan Africa	1.5	1.7	12	11	145	152	16	26
Arab States	3.3	3.2	33	36	216	248	81	101
Latin America/Caribbean	8.7	10.0	85	87	320	350	142	164
Eastern Asia/Oceania	3.8	6.6	46	56	141	197	23	45
of which: China	3.6	5.7	36	43	112	183	9	31
Southern Asia	1.4	1.8	22	25	72	86	14	33
of which: India	1.5	1.8	26	31	65	79	13	38
Least developed countries	0.4	0.3	5	6	87	97	5	9
Developed countries of which:	59.0	69.0	274	279	986	961	471	490
Northern America	125.0	127.0	257	233	1 978	2 006	772	797
Asia/Oceania	43.0	67.0	365	366	581	641	386	403
Europe/Russian Federation	39.0	46.0	351	271	723	639	388	395

Table 5
Enrolment (millions) and gross enrolment ratios in pre-primary education, 1985 and 1992

	Enrolment						Gross enrolment ratio (%)					
	1985			1992			1985			1992		
	MF	*F*	*%F*	*MF*	*F*	*%F*	*MF*	*M*	*F*	*MF*	*M*	*F*
WORLD TOTAL	70.7	34.1	48	88.4	42.4	48	26.0	26.3	25.6	28.1	28.4	27.8
Developing countries of which:	35.7	16.9	47	53.4	25.4	48	16.5	17.0	16.1	20.7	21.0	20.3
Sub-Saharan Africa	1.8	0.9	47	2.8	1.3	48	7.1	7.5	6.8	9.0	9.3	8.6
Arab States	1.6	0.6	38	2.2	0.9	41	14.9	18.2	11.5	16.4	19.1	13.7
Latin America/Caribbean	8.3	4.1	50	11.1	5.5	50	31.6	31.4	31.7	39.5	39.3	39.7
Eastern Asia/Oceania	19.7	9.4	48	31.5	15.1	48	20.1	20.3	19.9	26.3	26.3	26.4
of which: China	14.8	7.0	47	24.3	11.4	47	20.0	20.4	19.5	26.4	26.7	26.0
Southern Asia	4.1	1.7	43	5.6	2.4	44	7.5	8.3	6.7	8.8	9.7	8.0
of which: India	1.2	0.6	45	1.5	0.7	45	3.2	3.3	3.0	3.3	3.5	3.0
Least developed countries	2.3	1.0	45	3.5	1.6	46	8.8	9.6	8.0	11.1	12.0	10.2
Developed countries of which:	35.0	17.2	49	35.0	17.0	49	65.1	65.0	65.2	64.1	64.6	63.7
Northern America	6.7	3.3	49	7.5	3.6	48	60.7	60.1	61.3	60.6	61.4	59.8
Asia/Oceania	4.8	2.4	49	5.5	2.7	49	43.0	43.0	42.9	46.0	46.1	45.9
Europe/Russian Federation	23.5	11.5	49	22.0	10.7	49	72.3	72.3	72.3	70.7	71.0	70.3

Table 6
Enrolment (millions) and gross enrolment ratios in first-level education, 1985 and 1992

	Enrolment						Gross enrolment ratio (%)					
	1985			1992			1985			1992		
	MF	*F*	*%F*	*MF*	*F*	*%F*	*MF*	*M*	*F*	*MF*	*M*	*F*
WORLD TOTAL	563.7	254.8	45	610.8	281.9	46	98.6	105.5	91.4	98.6	103.8	93.2
Developing countries of which:	477.0	212.6	45	521.9	238.6	46	98.9	107.1	90.4	98.4	104.4	92.2
Sub-Saharan Africa	57.7	25.8	45	68.9	31.3	45	76.0	83.9	68.1	73.1	79.6	66.7
Arab States	26.1	11.1	42	31.7	14.0	44	87.8	99.1	76.0	89.2	97.9	80.2
Latin America/Caribbean	70.2	34.0	48	78.0	37.8	48	106.5	108.6	104.3	108.2	110.2	106.1
Eastern Asia/Oceania	203.1	93.2	46	195.4	92.2	47	116.4	122.9	109.6	114.5	117.1	111.6
of which: China	133.7	59.9	45	122.0	56.9	47	123.2	132.0	113.9	120.4	123.5	117.1
Southern Asia	113.6	45.4	40	142.3	60.5	43	84.7	97.6	70.6	91.2	101.4	80.2
of which: India	87.4	35.2	40	105.4	44.9	43	95.9	110.1	80.5	100.9	111.6	89.3
Least developed countries	44.8	18.7	42	56.3	24.6	44	65.6	75.2	55.6	68.7	76.5	60.8
Developed countries of which:	86.6	42.2	49	88.9	43.3	49	97.1	97.3	97.0	99.7	100.0	99.5
Northern America	22.5	10.9	49	25.7	12.5	48	100.9	101.2	100.7	106.3	107.0	105.5
Asia/Oceania	18.3	8.9	49	17.1	8.3	49	96.8	96.9	96.7	95.4	95.6	95.2
Europe/Russian Federation	45.9	22.4	49	46.1	22.5	49	95.5	95.7	95.3	98.0	98.0	98.0

Table 7
Enrolment (millions) and gross enrolment ratios in second-level education, 1985 and 1992

	Enrolment						Gross enrolment ratio (%)					
	1985			1992			1985			1992		
	MF	F	%F	MF	F	%F	MF	M	F	MF	M	F
WORLD TOTAL	293.9	128.0	44	333.7	149.2	45	48.7	53.6	43.6	54.1	58.3	49.6
Developing countries of which:	184.9	74.4	40	226.6	96.0	42	37.7	43.9	31.2	44.9	50.4	39.0
Sub-Saharan Africa	12.4	5.1	41	16.7	7.3	44	21.8	25.7	17.9	23.1	25.9	20.3
Arab States	11.6	4.6	40	15.9	6.8	43	45.7	53.9	37.2	53.8	60.1	47.1
Latin America/Caribbean	20.5	10.4	51	23.4	12.1	52	50.3	48.8	51.8	53.5	51.2	55.9
Eastern Asia/Oceania	79.2	33.5	42	84.3	37.7	45	40.4	45.5	35.1	50.1	54.0	45.9
of which: China	50.9	20.5	40	53.5	23.3	43	39.1	45.3	32.5	53.7	58.9	48.2
Southern Asia	56.4	18.9	34	80.4	29.7	37	34.0	43.4	23.7	43.0	52.2	33.1
of which: India	44.5	14.8	33	62.2	22.8	37	37.5	47.9	26.1	48.0	58.4	36.7
Least developed countries	10.1	3.4	34	12.7	4.7	37	16.5	21.7	11.3	17.6	21.8	13.2
Developed countries of which:	109.0	53.6	49	107.0	53.2	50	96.4	95.9	97.0	95.8	94.3	97.3
Northern America	22.9	11.2	49	22.5	11.1	49	97.7	97.5	97.8	96.5	95.8	97.3
Asia/Oceania	21.9	10.8	49	21.8	10.8	50	97.0	96.8	97.2	97.0	96.0	98.0
Europe/Russian Federation	64.2	31.6	49	62.7	31.3	50	95.8	95.0	96.6	95.1	93.2	97.1

Table 8
Enrolment (millions) and gross enrolment ratios in third-level education, 1985 and 1992

	Enrolment						Gross enrolment ratio (%)					
	1985			1992			1985			1992		
	MF	F	%F	MF	F	%F	MF	M	F	MF	M	F
WORLD TOTAL	58.6	26.5	45	73.7	33.8	46	12.5	13.4	11.6	14.6	15.4	13.7
Developing countries of which:	22.9	8.4	37	32.4	12.4	38	6.1	7.5	4.6	7.8	9.3	6.1
Sub-Saharan Africa	0.9	0.2	25	1.6	0.5	32	2.2	3.4	1.1	3.3	4.5	2.1
Arab States	2.0	0.7	35	2.8	1.0	38	11.5	14.7	8.1	13.0	15.8	10.1
Latin America/Caribbean	6.4	2.9	45	7.9	3.8	48	15.7	17.2	14.3	17.7	18.1	17.2
Eastern Asia/Oceania	7.3	2.8	38	9.7	4.0	41	4.3	5.2	3.3	5.5	6.2	4.6
of which: China	1.8	0.5	30	2.3	0.8	33	1.4	2.0	0.9	1.9	2.4	1.3
Southern Asia	5.5	1.6	29	9.3	2.6	28	5.3	7.3	3.2	7.7	10.7	4.5
of which: India	4.5	1.3	30	...	...	...	6.0	8.1	3.8	...	...	...
Least developed countries	1.0	0.3	26	1.5	0.4	26	2.6	3.8	1.3	3.1	4.5	1.6
Developed countries of which:	35.7	18.1	51	41.3	21.5	52	38.9	37.7	40.1	46.7	44.0	49.5
Northern America	13.9	7.3	53	16.4	8.9	54	61.7	57.4	66.1	82.0	73.2	91.3
Asia/Oceania	4.8	2.1	43	5.9	2.8	47	28.8	32.2	25.2	33.3	34.4	32.1
Europe/Russian Federation	17.0	8.7	51	19.0	9.7	51	32.3	31.1	33.6	37.4	35.7	39.1

Table 9

Number of teachers (millions), by level of education, 1985 and 1992

	1985					1992				
	Pre-primary	First level	Second level	Third level	All levels	Pre-primary	First level	Second level	Third level	All levels
WORLD TOTAL	3.94	20.62	16.89	4.28	45.73	4.77	23.40	19.87	5.19	53.22
Developing countries of which:	1.34	15.83	9.42	1.73	28.31	2.01	18.05	11.55	2.26	33.87
Sub-Saharan Africa	0.05	1.49	0.54	0.07	2.15	0.09	1.90	0.73	0.09	2.81
Arab States	0.07	0.98	0.62	0.11	1.79	0.09	1.36	0.94	0.14	2.53
Latin America/Caribbean	0.32	2.60	1.34	0.51	4.77	0.48	3.19	1.56	0.67	5.90
Eastern Asia/Oceania	0.75	7.88	4.34	0.64	13.61	1.16	8.29	5.31	0.77	15.52
of which: China	0.56	5.38	3.00	0.34	9.28	0.82	5.53	3.62	0.39	10.36
Southern Asia	0.11	2.65	2.33	0.36	5.44	0.15	3.09	2.71	0.53	6.48
of which: India	0.02	1.87	1.72	0.30	3.91	0.02	2.22	1.95	0.42	4.61
Least developed countries	0.07	1.07	0.41	0.05	1.60	0.10	1.32	0.54	0.08	2.05
Developed countries of which:	2.61	4.79	7.48	2.55	17.42	2.76	5.35	8.32	2.92	19.35
Northern America	0.28	1.56	1.44	0.75	4.03	0.30	1.76	1.50	0.90	4.46
Asia/Oceania	0.48	0.79	1.34	0.42	3.05	0.63	0.87	1.64	0.50	3.64
Europe/Russian Federation	1.85	2.44	4.69	1.37	10.35	1.83	2.72	5.18	1.52	11.25

Table 10

Number of teachers (all levels) per thousand population in the age-group 15–64 and percentage of female teachers by level of education, 1985 and 1992

	Number of teachers (all levels)[1] per thousand population in the age-group 15–64		Percentage of female teachers					
			1985			1992		
	1985	1992	Pre-primary	First level	Second level	Pre-primary	First level	Second level
WORLD TOTAL	16	16	94.6	54.3	43.6	94.6	57.1	46.6
Developing countries of which:	13	13	89.9	46.8	35.0	90.4	50.2	38.6
Sub-Saharan Africa	9	10	87.0	38.0	33.3	88.6	41.6	33.3
Arab States	17	19	50.0	47.8	35.0	62.6	52.2	39.6
Latin America/Caribbean	21	22	97.2	76.9	47.9	97.7	77.2	48.4
Eastern Asia/Oceania	14	14	96.1	44.1	32.9	95.1	48.6	37.9
of which: China	13	13	94.2	39.6	28.0	94.5	45.2	33.7
Southern Asia	9	9	46.7	29.7	30.8	45.8	31.2	34.5
of which: India	9	9	94.2	27.3	30.8	93.3	27.9	34.4
Least developed countries	7	7	36.9	29.6	24.8	36.3	34.1	23.9
Developed countries of which:	23	24	97.1	79.0	54.4	97.8	80.2	57.6
Northern America	23	24	94.6	81.6	53.5	94.7	82.7	53.9
Asia/Oceania	23	25	97.3	68.4	48.6	98.9	71.8	52.7
Europe/Russian Federation	23	24	97.5	80.7	56.4	97.9	81.3	60.2

1. Including third level.

Table 11
Public expenditure on education, 1980 – 1992

	US$ (billions)				Percentage of GNP			
	1980	*1985*	*1990*	*1992*	*1980*	*1985*	*1990*	*1992*
WORLD TOTAL[1]	526.7	566.2	1 017.0	1 196.8	4.9	4.9	4.9	5.1
Developing countries	102.2	101.2	163.4	209.5	3.8	4.0	4.0	4.2
of which:								
Sub-Saharan Africa	15.8	11.3	15.2	16.0	5.1	4.8	5.3	5.7
Arab States	18.0	23.6	24.7	26.0	4.1	5.8	5.2	5.6
Latin America/Caribbean	34.2	28.9	47.1	56.8	3.9	4.0	4.1	4.4
Eastern Asia/Oceania	16.0	20.1	31.8	41.4	2.8	3.2	3.0	3.1
of which: China	7.6	7.7	9.1	9.8	2.5	2.6	2.3	2.0
Southern Asia	12.8	14.7	35.8	60.4	4.1	3.3	3.9	4.4
of which: India	4.8	7.1	11.9	10.0	2.8	3.4	4.0	3.7
Least developed countries	3.1	2.7	4.2	4.1	2.7	2.8	2.9	2.8
Developed countries[1]	424.5	465.0	853.6	987.3	5.2	5.1	5.1	5.3
of which:								
Northern America	155.1	221.6	330.2	369.7	5.2	5.1	5.4	5.7
Asia/Oceania[1]	73.0	79.3	160.8	225.5	5.8	5.1	4.8	4.8
Europe[1]	196.3	164.2	362.6	419.3	5.1	5.1	5.0	5.2

1. Excluding countries of the former USSR.

Table 12
Public current expenditure per pupil, by level of education, 1985 and 1992

	Number of countries		All levels		Pre-primary + first level		Second level		Pre-primary + first + second levels		Third level	
			US$	% of GNP per capita	US$	% of GNP per capita	US$	% of GNP per capita	US$	% of GNP per capita	US$	% of GNP per capita
Developing countries	76	1985	106	16.4	...	...	...	...	73	11.3	633	98.1
		1992	218	18.0	...	...	...	...	158	13.0	1 031	84.9
of which:												
Sub-Saharan Africa	26	1985	74	23.5	44	14.0	131	42.0	56	18.0	1 324	423.7
		1992	81	27.9	44	15.1	156	53.7	61	20.9	1 477	507.8
Arab States	9	1985	241	23.6	...	...	...	...	176	17.2	1 177	115.1
		1992	203	18.8	...	...	...	...	161	15.0	816	75.7
Latin America/Caribbean	26	1985	238	12.2	122	6.3	247	12.7	147	7.6	847	43.5
		1992	433	14.2	252	8.2	394	12.9	281	9.2	1 485	48.6
Eastern Asia/Oceania	8	1985	58	14.3	31	7.6	74	18.1	42	10.4	527	129.2
		1992	113	14.4	65	8.2	149	18.9	88	11.2	706	90.1
Southern Asia	5	1985	76	18.3	46	10.9	76	18.2	55	13.2	334	79.8
		1992	220	19.6	120	10.7	257	22.9	168	14.9	857	76.3
Least developed countries	22	1985	38	18.3	22	10.6	58	27.9	29	13.7	325	155.3
		1992	38	18.1	21	10.1	69	32.3	29	13.9	302	142.8
Developed countries[1]	27	1985	2 218	20.7	...	...	...	...	1 796	16.8	3 656	34.1
		1992	4 270	21.4	...	...	...	...	3 525	17.7	5 865	29.4

1. Excluding countries of the former USSR.

Table 13

Foreign students by host region and region of origin, 1992

Host region[1]	WORLD	Region of origin								
		Developing countries	Sub-Saharan Africa	Arab States	Latin America/ Caribbean	Eastern Asia/ Oceania	Southern Asia	Least developed countries	Developed countries	Un-specified
WORLD	1 233 237	729 373	89 490	148 060	69 806	284 500	96 292	67 475	480 395	23 469
Developing countries of which:	89 502	69 099	11 778	39 333	2 018	8 324	4 916	15 572	14 439	5 964
Sub-Saharan Africa	1 952	1 896	1 653	510	3	7	1	1 279	56	–
Arab States	44 185	39 447	5 269	35 518	50	1 062	1 168	10 540	642	4 096
Latin America/ Caribbean	5 516	5 417	3 012	600	1 725	55	64	1 214	54	45
Eastern Asia/ Oceania	22 436	11 097	1 223	911	213	7 116	1 835	1 682	10 831	508
Southern Asia	...	...	...	...	...	...	...	...	...	...
Developed countries	1 143 735	660 274	77 712	108 727	67 788	276 176	91 376	51 903	465 956	17 505

1. Refers to 50 major host countries for which data are available and does not include major host countries such as Brazil, India, Lebanon and Sweden due to lack of recent data.

III. World education indicators

THIS Appendix contains eleven tables of statistical indicators relating to selected aspects of education and its demographic, socio-economic, cultural and communications setting in 188 countries.

The particular selection of indicators shown in this and previous editions of the *World Education Report* basically represents a compromise between the demands of a wide range of users on the one hand and the availability of data on the other. The majority of the indicators are repeated in each edition of the report; a minority are new, being selected for their particular relevance to the themes of the report, or, in a few cases, because new data have become available. An important consideration in selecting any particular indicator is that the relevant data should be available for a number of countries belonging to all major regions of the world, and not just for countries in only one or two regions. This means that certain types of data which are only available for the OECD countries, for example, are not included in the World Education Indicators; they can of course be consulted in OECD publications (e.g., *Education at a Glance: OECD Indicators,* Paris, OECD, 1995).

Improvement of the comparability, scope and depth of coverage of the World Education Indicators, and of international educational statistics generally, is a long term task; the main constraints were evoked in the *World Education Report 1993* (pp. 108–9).

During the current biennium (1994–1995), the Organization took several steps towards strengthening international co-operation in education statistics. These steps included a preliminary revision and updating of the International Standard Classification of Education (ISCED), the commissioning of a comprehensive study and review, by the United States' National Academy of Sciences, of the long-term needs for development of international education statistics generally, and the establishment of co-operative networks for the development of education indicators at the regional level in Asia, the Caribbean and Latin America. In addition, assistance to African countries for the development of their education statistics was strengthened with the support and co-operation of the Association for the Development of African Education (DAE) Working Group on Education Statistics.

Explanatory notes

General notes

The indicators are finalized at the end of the first quarter in the year in which the *World Education Report* is published, one quarter ahead of the corresponding statistics in *UNESCO's Statistical Yearbook*. In the few cases where there is a difference between particular figures given in the two publications, the yearbook's figure should be regarded as superseding the report's figure.

Data refer to the year indicated or to the nearest year for which data are available. For educational indicators the year indicated is that in which the school year begins; e.g. 1992 refers to the school year 1992/93. Expenditure indicators refer to the financial year.

Certain indicators such as enrolment ratios, dependency ratios and illiteracy rates were not calculated for some countries because of inconsistencies between enrolment and population data and/or the unavailability of population data by age.

Data presented for Jordan, with the exception of data on population in Table 1, refer to the East Bank only.

Data for Federal Republic of Germany refer to the territory of the Federal Republic of Germany prior to 3 October 1990.

Enrolment data for Cyprus do not include Turkish schools.

Data provided for Former Yugoslavia refer to the Socialist Federal Republic of Yugoslavia which was composed of six republics.

The following symbols are used:

–	Magnitude nil.
0 or 0.0	Magnitude less than half the unit employed.
*	Estimated data.
...	Data not available.
·	Category not applicable.
♦	The explanation of this symbol is given below for each specific indicator.
./.	Data included elsewhere with another category.

Table notes

Table 1. Population and GNP

Total population. Estimates of 1992 population, in thousands.

Population growth rate. Average annual percentage growth rate of total population between 1980 and 1992.

Dependency ratios. Populations in the age-groups 0–14 and 65 years and over, expressed as percentages of the population in the age-group 15–64.

Urban population. Number of persons living in urban areas, expressed as a percentage of the total population. 'Urban areas' are defined according to national criteria, which affects the comparability between countries.

Life expectancy at birth. The average number of years a newborn infant would live if prevailing patterns of mortality at the time of its birth were to stay the same throughout its life.

Total fertility rate. The average number of children that would be born alive to a woman during her lifetime if she were to bear children at each age in accord with prevailing age-specific fertility rates.

Infant mortality rate. The number of deaths of infants under 1 year of age per 1,000 live births in a given year. More specifically, the probability of dying between birth and exactly 1 year of age times 1,000.

GNP per capita. Gross National Product per capita in 1992 US dollars, the average annual growth rate of GNP per capita between 1980 and 1992 in constant prices, and estimates of GNP per capita based on purchasing power parities (PPP). The figures are extracted from the World Bank database.

Table 2. Literacy, culture and communication

Estimated number of adult illiterates. Estimated number of adult illiterates (15 years and over), in thousands, and the percentage of female illiterates, 1980 and 1995.

Estimated adult illiteracy rate, 1995. Estimated number of adult illiterates (15 years and over) expressed as a percentage of the population in the corresponding age-group.

Number of volumes in public libraries. Number of books and bound periodicals in public libraries per 1,000 inhabitants.

Daily newspapers. Estimated circulation of daily newspapers, expressed in number of copies per 1,000 inhabitants.

Radio and television receivers. Number of radio and television receivers per 1,000 inhabitants. The indicators are based on estimates of the number of receivers in use.

Main telephone lines. Number of telephone lines per 1,000 inhabitants connecting a customer's equipment to the switched network and which have a dedicated port on a telephone exchange.

Table 3. Enrolment in pre-primary education and access to schooling

Age-group in pre-primary education. Population age-group that according to the national regulations can be enrolled at this level of education.

The symbol ♦ is shown when there has been a change in the duration of pre-primary school between 1980 and 1992.

Gross enrolment ratio, pre-primary. Total enrolment in education preceding the first level, regardless of age, expressed as a percentage of the population age-group corresponding to the national regulations for this level of education.

Apparent intake rate, first level. Number of new entrants into first grade, first level, regardless of age, expressed as a percentage of the population of official admission age to the first level of education.

The symbol ♦ is shown when enrolment data including repeaters are used instead of new entrants.

School life expectancy. The school life expectancy, or expected number of years of formal education, is the number of years a child is expected to remain at school, or university, including years spent on repetition. It is the sum of the age-specific enrolment ratios for first-, second- and third-level education.

Table 4. First-level education: duration, population and enrolment ratios

Duration of compulsory education. Number of years of compulsory education, according to the regulations in force in each country.

Duration of first-level education. Number of grades (years) in primary education, according to the education system in force in each country in 1992.

The symbol ♦ is shown when there has been a change in the duration between 1980 and 1992.

School-age population. Population, in thousands, of the age-group which officially corresponds to primary schooling.

Gross enrolment ratio/Net enrolment ratio. The gross enrolment ratio is the total enrolment in first-level education, regardless of age, divided by the population of the age-group which officially corresponds to primary schooling. The net enrolment ratio only includes enrolment for the age-group corresponding to the official school age of first-level education. All ratios are expressed as percentages.

The symbol ♦ is shown when the gross and net enrolment ratios do not refer to the same year.

Table 5. First-level education: internal efficiency

Percentage of repeaters. Total number of pupils who are enrolled in the same grade as the previous year, expressed as a percentage of the total enrolment at the first level.

Percentage of a cohort reaching Grade 2 and Grade 5. Percentage of children starting primary school who eventually attain Grade 2 or Grade 5 (Grade 4, if the duration of primary education is four years). The estimate is based on the Reconstructed Cohort Method, which uses data on enrolment and repeaters for two consecutive years. (See Birger Fredriksen, *Statistics of Education in Developing Countries: An Introduction to their Collection and Analysis,* Paris, UNESCO, 1983. (Training Seminars on Education Statistics, Basic Background Material, Book 3.)(Document ST-83/WS/1.))

The symbol ♦ is shown when data on repeaters are missing for the year shown and the Apparent Cohort Method was used for estimating survival. When repetition rates are relatively high and vary between grades this method may overestimate or underestimate the survival rate.

Table 6. Second-level education: duration, population and enrolment ratios

Duration of second-level general education, first and second stages. Number of grades (years) in secondary general education, first stage and second stage, according to the education system in force in each country in 1992.

The symbol ♦ is shown when there has been a change in the duration between 1980 and 1992.

School-age population. Population, in thousands, of the age-group which officially corresponds to second-level general education.

Gross enrolment ratio/Net enrolment ratio. The gross enrolment ratio is the total enrolment in second-level education, regardless of age, divided by the population of the age-group which officially corresponds to secondary schooling. The net enrolment ratio only includes enrolment for the age-group corresponding to the official school age of second-level education. All ratios are expressed as percentages.

The symbol ♦ is shown when the gross and net enrolment ratios do not refer to the same year.

Table 7. Teaching staff in pre-primary, first- and second-level education

Pupil-teacher ratio. This ratio represents the average number of pupils per teacher at the level of education specified. Since teaching staff includes in principle both full- and part-time teachers, comparability of these ratios may be affected as the proportion of part-time teachers varies from one country to another. For secondary education the ratio refers to general education only.

Percentage of female teachers. The number of female teachers, at the level specified, expressed as a percentage of the total number of teachers at the same level. For secondary education, the data refer to general education only.

Table 8. Third-level education: enrolment ratios and breakdown by ISCED level

Number of students per 100,000 inhabitants. Number of students enrolled at the third level of education (or higher education) per 100,000 inhabitants.

Percentage of students by ISCED level. Enrolment in higher education at each ISCED level as a percentage of total enrolment.

Percentage of female students in each ISCED level. Female enrolment as a percentage of total (male and female) enrolment at the level specified.

Definitions of ISCED level categories within higher education:

Level 5: education at the third level, first stage, of the type that leads to an award not equivalent to a first university degree.

Level 6: education at the third level, second stage, of the type that leads to a first university degree or equivalent.

Level 7: education at the third level, second stage, of the type that leads to a postgraduate degree or equivalent.

Table 9. Third-level education: students and graduates by broad field of study, 1992

Percentage of students and graduates by field of study. Enrolment at the third level, in the broad field of study specified, expressed as a percentage of the total enrolment at the third level. The total may not add to 100 per cent due to 'other' or 'unspecified'. Figures in parentheses refer to graduates.

Percentage of female students in each field of study. Number of female students in each broad field of study, expressed as a percentage of the total (male and female) enrolment in the field specified.

Gender segregation index. This index is explained in Appendix I. It is defined as the percentage of all persons enrolled in third-level education who would need to change their field of study if the ratio of females to males were to be the same in all fields of study, assuming that in each field of study there is no change in the total enrolment. The index shown

in this table is calculated on the basis of enrolments in the five broad fields of study mentioned below, plus the residual field 'other'. The index is calculated only for countries where the percentage of students in 'other' is less than 10 per cent.

ISCED fields of study are grouped into the following broad fields of study:

Education: education science and teacher training. When the symbol ♦ is shown, education also includes humanities.

Humanities: humanities; fine and applied arts; religion and theology. When the symbol ♦ is shown, humanities also include part of social sciences.

Law and social sciences: law; social and behavioural sciences; commercial and business administration; home economics; mass communication and documentation; service trades.

Natural sciences, engineering and agriculture: natural sciences; engineering; mathematics and computer sciences; architecture and town planning; transport and communications; trade, craft and industrial programmes; agriculture, forestry and fisheries.

Medical sciences: medical and health related sciences.

Table 10. Private enrolment and public expenditure on education

Private enrolment as percentage of total enrolment. Enrolment in private schools, at the level specified, expressed as a percentage of the total enrolment at the same level. Government-aided schools are considered as private if they are privately managed. For second level, data refer to general education only.

Public expenditure on education as percentage of GNP. Total public expenditure on education expressed as a percentage of the Gross National Product (for Cuba as a percentage of Global Social Product).

The symbol ♦ is shown when total public expenditure on education refers to expenditure of the Ministry of Education only.

Public expenditure on education as percentage of government expenditure. Total public expenditure on education expressed as a percentage of total government expenditure.

The symbol ♦ is shown when total public expenditure on education refers to expenditure of the Ministry of Education only.

Average annual growth rate of public expenditure on education. The average annual growth rate between 1980 and 1992 refers to the growth of total public expenditure on education in constant prices (data are deflated by using the implicit Gross Domestic Product (GDP) deflator); it has been computed by fitting a trend line to the logarithmic values of the expenditure data for each year of the period.

Current expenditure as percentage of total. Public current expenditure on education, expressed as a percentage of total public expenditure on education.

Table 11. Public current expenditure on education

Teachers' emoluments as percentage of total current expenditure. Expenditure on emoluments of teaching staff expressed as a percentage of total public current expenditure on education.

The symbol ♦ is shown when the indicator refers to the emoluments of total personnel (administrative staff, teaching staff and other personnel).

Percentage distribution of current expenditure by level. Public current expenditure by level, expressed as a percentage of total public current expenditure on education. The total may not add to 100 due to

expenditure on 'other types of education' and/or expenditure not distributed by level of education.

When the symbol ♦ is shown, the indicator for pre-primary and first-level also includes second-level education.

Current expenditure per pupil as a percentage of GNP per capita. Public current expenditure per pupil, at each level of education, expressed as a percentage of GNP per capita.

When the symbol ♦ is shown, the indicator for pre-primary and first-level also includes second-level education.

Data sources

Population and demographic indicators: United Nations Population Division database (1994 revision).

GNP and GNP per capita: World Bank, World Tables 1994 and World Development Report 1994.

Illiteracy: Estimates and projections by the UNESCO Division of Statistics based on actual country data supplied by the United Nations Statistical Division or drawn from national publications.

Education, culture and communication: UNESCO Division of Statistics.

Main telephone lines: International Telecommunication Union database.

World education report

Table 1
Population and GNP

Country or territory	Population										GNP per capita		
	Total (000)	Average annual growth rate (%)	Dependency ratio				Percentage urban	Life expectancy at birth (years)	Total fertility rate (births per woman)	Infant mortality rate (per 1,000 live births)	Average annual growth		PPP (International dollars)
			Age 0-14		Age 65 and over						US$	rate (%)	
	1992	1980-92	1980	1992	1980	1992	1992	1992	1992	1992	1992	1980-92	1992
Africa													
Algeria	26 127	2.8	94	73	8	6	53	67	3.9	55	1 830	– 0.5	5 740
Angola	9 888	2.9	85	95	6	6	30	46	7.2	124	...	...	...
Benin	4 930	3.0	89	94	6	6	30	48	7.1	86	410	– 0.7	1 500
Botswana	1 359	3.4	99	83	4	4	25	65	4.8	43	2 790	6.1	5 190
Burkina Faso	9 502	2.6	82	85	5	6	21	47	6.5	130	290	1.0	730
Burundi	5 847	2.9	86	90	7	6	7	50	6.8	102	210	1.3	750
Cameroon	12 184	2.9	85	85	7	7	42	56	5.7	63	820	– 1.5	2 300
Cape Verde	360	1.8	96	82	13	9	48	65	4.3	50	850	3.0	...
Central African Republic	3 077	2.4	77	80	7	8	38	49	5.7	102	410	– 1.5	1 040
Chad	5 846	2.2	77	82	7	7	21	48	5.9	122	220	3.4	710
Comoros	585	3.6	97	99	5	5	29	56	7.1	89	510	– 1.3	...
Congo	2 371	3.0	88	89	7	7	56	51	6.3	84	1 030	– 0.8	2 450
Côte d'Ivoire	12 860	3.8	91	100	5	5	42	51	7.4	92	670	– 4.7	1 640
Djibouti	546	5.7	82	78	5	5	82	48	5.8	115	...	...	...
Egypt	58 988	2.5	70	69	7	7	44	64	3.9	67	630	1.8	3 670
Equatorial Guinea	369	4.5	75	80	8	8	38	48	5.9	117	330	...	...
Eritrea	3 255	2.6	83	83	5	5	16	50	5.8	105	...	...	...
Ethiopia	50 329	2.7	90	90	5	6	13	47	7.0	119	110	– 1.9	340
Gabon	1 213	3.5	53	67	10	10	47	54	5.3	94	4 450	– 3.7	...
Gambia	1 002	3.8	78	75	5	5	24	45	5.6	132	390	– 0.4	...
Ghana	15 959	3.4	86	88	5	6	35	56	6.0	81	450	– 0.1	1 890
Guinea	6 116	2.7	89	93	5	5	27	45	7.0	134	510	...	...
Guinea-Bissau	1 006	2.0	68	76	7	8	21	44	5.8	140	210	1.6	690
Kenya	25 431	3.6	108	100	7	6	25	56	6.3	69	330	0.2	1 360
Lesotho	1 891	2.9	77	80	7	7	21	60	5.2	79	590	– 0.5	1 770
Liberia	2 751	3.2	85	90	7	7	43	55	6.8	126	...	...	...
Libyan Arab Jamahiriya	4 876	4.0	91	88	4	5	84	63	6.4	68	...	...	...
Madagascar	13 417	3.3	86	91	6	6	25	56	6.1	93	230	– 2.4	720
Malawi	10 163	4.2	95	93	4	5	12	46	7.2	143	210	– 0.1	730
Mali	9 816	3.0	92	94	5	5	25	46	7.1	159	300	– 2.7	500
Mauritania	2 107	2.6	82	83	6	6	49	51	5.4	101	530	– 0.8	1 380
Mauritius	1 079	0.9	59	44	6	9	41	70	2.4	18	2 700	5.6	11 390
Morocco	25 402	2.3	82	65	8	7	47	63	3.8	68	1 040	1.4	3 270
Mozambique	14 735	1.7	81	85	6	6	30	46	6.5	148	60	– 3.6	570
Namibia	1 423	2.7	81	79	7	7	34	59	5.3	60	1 610	– 1.0	3 040
Niger	8 264	3.3	92	97	5	5	16	47	7.4	124	300	– 4.3	740
Nigeria	102 129	3.0	84	88	5	5	37	50	6.4	84	320	– 0.4	1 440
Rwanda	7 363	3.0	100	93	5	5	6	47	6.6	110	250	– 0.6	770
Sao Tome and Principe	124	2.3	...	...	...	...	44	...	...	...	370	3.0	...
Senegal	7 709	2.8	87	87	5	6	41	49	6.1	68	780	0.1	1 750
Seychelles	71	1.0	...	...	...	...	52	...	...	...	5 480	3.2	...
Sierra Leone	4 194	2.2	80	83	6	6	34	39	6.5	167	170	– 1.4	770
Somalia	8 865	2.3	90	94	6	6	25	47	7.0	122	...	...	...
South Africa	38 778	2.4	72	65	7	7	50	63	4.1	53	2 670	0.1	...
Sudan	25 940	2.8	86	84	5	5	23	53	5.7	78	...	...	...
Swaziland	787	2.9	90	83	6	5	28	58	4.9	75	1 080	1.6	...
Togo	3 763	3.1	85	89	6	6	29	55	6.6	85	400	– 1.8	1 100
Tunisia	8 407	2.3	76	62	7	7	56	68	3.1	43	1 740	1.3	5 130
Uganda	19 261	3.3	96	99	5	5	12	45	7.3	115	170	...	1 070
United Rep. of Tanzania	27 204	3.2	95	90	5	5	22	52	5.9	85	110	0.0	630

Country or territory	Population Total (000) 1992	Average annual growth rate (%) 1980–92	Dependency ratio Age 0–14 1980	Age 0–14 1992	Age 65 and over 1980	Age 65 and over 1992	Percentage urban 1992	Life expectancy at birth (years) 1992	Total fertility rate (births per woman) 1992	Infant mortality rate (per 1,000 live births) 1992	GNP per capita US$ 1992	Average annual growth rate (%) 1980–92	PPP (International dollars) 1992
Zaire	39 939	3.3	90	96	6	6	29	52	6.7	93	...	...	...
Zambia	8 674	3.5	102	96	5	5	42	49	6.0	104	290	...	...
Zimbabwe	10 469	3.3	97	83	5	5	30	54	5.0	67	570	− 0.9	1 970
America, North													
Antigua and Barbuda	65	0.5	...	...	...	...	36	...	...	...	4 870	5.0	...
Bahamas	264	1.9	67	48	7	7	85	73	2.0	23	12 020	1.0	...
Barbados	259	0.3	50	37	18	19	46	76	1.8	9	6 530	1.0	...
Belize	199	2.6	97	84	9	8	47	74	4.2	33	2 210	2.6	...
British Virgin Islands	17	3.0	...	...	...	...	...	...	...	...	...	...	...
Canada	28 487	1.2	33	31	14	17	77	77	1.9	7	20 320	1.8	19 720
Costa Rica	3 192	2.8	68	60	6	7	48	76	3.1	14	2 000	0.8	5 550
Cuba	10 786	0.9	53	33	13	12	75	75	1.8	12	...	...	...
Dominica	71	− 0.3	...	...	...	...	...	...	...	...	2 520	4.6	...
Dominican Republic	7 400	2.2	77	60	6	6	62	70	3.1	42	1 040	− 0.5	3 360
El Salvador	5 396	1.5	90	79	6	7	44	66	4.0	46	1 170	0.0	2 230
Grenada	91	0.2	...	...	...	...	...	...	...	...	2 310	...	...
Guatemala	9 745	2.9	90	87	6	6	40	65	5.4	49	980	− 1.5	3 370
Haiti	6 755	2.0	74	72	8	7	30	57	4.8	86	...	...	...
Honduras	5 180	3.2	94	86	5	6	42	68	4.9	43	580	− 0.3	1 930
Jamaica	2 394	1.0	76	53	13	11	52	74	2.4	14	1 340	0.2	3 770
Mexico	88 187	2.3	85	63	7	7	74	71	3.2	36	3 470	− 0.2	7 490
Netherlands Antilles	193	0.9	47	39	10	10	69	73	2.1	19	...	...	...
Nicaragua	3 955	2.9	95	95	5	6	61	67	5.0	52	410	− 5.3	2 160
Panama	2 491	2.1	74	57	8	8	52	73	2.9	25	2 440	− 1.2	5 440
Saint Kitts and Nevis	42	− 0.5	...	...	...	...	41	...	...	...	3 990	5.7	...
Saint Lucia	137	1.5	...	...	...	...	47	...	...	...	2 900	...	...
Saint Vincent and the Grenadines	109	0.9	...	...	...	...	43	...	...	...	1 990	5.0	...
Trinidad and Tobago	1 265	1.3	57	55	9	9	70	72	2.4	18	3 940	− 2.6	8 410
United States	255 191	1.0	34	33	17	19	76	76	2.1	9	23 120	1.7	23 120
America, South													
Argentina	33 377	1.4	50	49	13	15	87	72	2.8	24	6 050	− 0.9	6 080
Bolivia	6 893	2.1	79	74	7	7	58	59	4.8	75	680	− 1.5	2 270
Brazil	153 821	2.0	65	55	7	8	76	66	2.9	58	2 770	0.4	5 250
Chile	13 600	1.7	55	47	9	10	84	74	2.5	16	2 730	3.7	8 090
Colombia	33 424	1.9	71	56	7	7	71	69	2.7	37	1 290	1.4	5 760
Ecuador	10 741	2.5	80	66	8	7	56	69	3.5	50	1 070	− 0.3	4 380
Guyana	808	0.5	74	52	7	6	35	65	2.5	48	330	− 5.6	...
Paraguay	4 573	3.2	77	73	6	7	50	70	4.3	38	1 340	− 0.7	3 510
Peru	22 447	2.2	77	62	7	7	71	66	3.4	64	950	− 2.8	3 080
Suriname	410	1.2	72	58	8	8	49	70	2.7	28	3 700	− 3.6	...
Uruguay	3 130	0.6	43	40	17	19	89	72	2.3	20	3 340	− 1.0	7 450
Venezuela	20 446	2.6	73	64	6	6	91	72	3.3	23	2 900	− 0.8	8 790
Asia													
Afghanistan	16 624	0.3	79	78	5	5	19	43	6.9	163	...	...	...
Armenia	3 441	1.0	48	48	9	10	68	73	2.6	21	780	...	2 500
Azerbaijan	7 296	1.4	58	53	9	8	55	71	2.5	28	870	...	2 650
Bahrain	520	3.4	55	49	3	4	89	72	3.8	18	...	...	...
Bangladesh	112 709	2.1	91	73	7	5	17	56	4.4	108	220	1.8	1 230
Bhutan	1 582	2.1	71	73	6	6	6	51	5.9	124	180	6.3	630

Table 1 (continued)

Country or territory	Population											GNP per capita		
	Total (000)	Average annual growth rate (%)	Dependency ratio				Per-centage urban	Life expect-ancy at birth (years)	Total fertility rate (births per woman)	Infant mortality rate (per 1,000 live births)		US$	Average annual growth rate (%)	PPP (Inter-national dollars)
			Age 0–14		Age 65 and over									
	1992	1980–92	1980	1992	1980	1992	1992	1992	1992	1992		1992	1980–92	1992
Brunei Darussalam	269	2.8	66	57	5	5	58	74	3.1	8		...	...	...
Cambodia	9 399	3.1	83	82	5	5	19	52	5.3	116		...	...	...
China	1 183 617	1.4	59	40	8	9	28	68	1.9	45		380	7.6	1 910
Cyprus	718	1.1	37	41	16	16	52	77	2.5	9		9 820	5.0	...
Dem. People's Rep. of Korea	22 615	1.8	72	42	6	6	60	71	2.4	24		...	...	...
Georgia	5 442	0.6	40	37	14	15	57	73	2.1	19		850	...	2 470
Hong Kong	5 777	1.1	38	29	9	13	94	79	1.2	7		15 380	5.5	20 050
India	884 425	2.1	67	60	7	7	26	60	3.7	82		310	3.1	1 210
Indonesia	188 740	1.9	74	56	6	7	32	63	2.9	58		670	4.0	2 970
Iran, Islamic Rep. of	62 507	4.0	87	86	6	7	57	67	5.0	36		2 190	– 1.4	5 280
Iraq	19 011	3.2	90	83	5	5	73	66	5.7	58		...	...	...
Israel	5 036	2.2	57	50	15	15	90	77	2.9	9		13 230	1.9	14 600
Japan	124 243	0.5	35	25	13	18	77	79	1.5	4		28 220	3.6	20 160
Jordan	4 675	4.0	104	82	7	5	69	68	5.6	36		1 120	– 5.4	4 220
Kazakstan	16 877	1.0	53	49	10	10	58	70	2.5	30		1 680	...	4 780
Kuwait	1 938	2.9	69	62	2	2	96	75	3.1	18		...	...	...
Kyrgyzstan	4 513	1.9	65	66	10	9	38	69	3.7	35		810	...	2 820
Lao People's Dem. Rep.	4 469	2.8	76	84	5	6	20	51	6.7	97		250	...	1 930
Lebanon	2 698	0.1	74	57	10	9	85	69	3.1	34		...	...	...
Malaysia	18 796	2.6	69	66	6	7	51	71	3.6	13		2 790	3.2	8 050
Maldives	231	3.2	81	94	8	7	26	62	6.8	60		500	6.8	...
Mongolia	2 273	2.6	80	70	5	6	59	64	3.6	60		...	...	...
Myanmar	43 652	2.1	70	65	7	7	25	58	4.2	84		...	...	...
Nepal	20 276	2.6	81	79	5	6	12	54	5.4	99		170	2.0	1 100
Oman	1 909	4.7	86	95	5	5	12	70	7.2	30		6 490	4.1	9 630
Pakistan	129 314	3.5	84	84	5	6	33	62	6.2	91		410	3.1	2 130
Palestine														
Gaza Strip	687	3.8	...	...	...	...	94	...	...	...		...	...	...
West Bank	...	...	...	...	...	...	...	...	...	...		...	...	...
Philippines	63 427	2.3	76	68	5	6	51	66	3.9	44		770	– 1.0	2 480
Qatar	517	7.0	49	39	2	2	91	71	4.3	20		16 240	– 11.2	...
Republic of Korea	43 703	1.1	55	35	6	7	77	71	1.7	11		6 790	8.5	8 950
Saudi Arabia	16 825	4.8	84	75	5	5	78	70	6.4	29		7 940	– 3.3	11 170
Singapore	2 764	1.1	40	32	7	9	100	75	1.7	6		15 750	5.3	16 720
Sri Lanka	17 671	1.5	58	51	7	9	22	72	2.5	18		540	2.6	2 810
Syrian Arab Republic	13 234	3.6	100	97	7	5	51	67	5.9	39		...	...	...
Tajikistan	5 604	2.9	82	82	9	8	32	70	4.9	48		480	...	2 000
Thailand	56 972	1.7	71	47	6	7	19	69	2.1	37		1 840	6.0	5 890
Turkey	58 426	2.3	70	56	8	7	64	66	3.4	65		1 950	2.9	5 170
Turkmenistan	3 833	2.5	76	72	8	7	45	65	4.0	58		1 270	...	3 950
United Arab Emirates	1 770	4.7	41	46	2	2	82	74	4.2	19		22 220	– 4.3	...
Uzbekistan	21 376	2.5	76	74	9	8	41	69	3.9	41		860	...	2 600
Viet Nam	69 737	2.2	81	67	9	9	20	65	3.9	42		...	...	...
Yemen	12 510	3.6	106	95	5	5	31	50	7.6	120		...	...	...
Former Dem. Yemen	.	.	.	.	.	.	.	.	.	.		.	.	.
Former Yemen Arab Rep.	.	.	.	.	.	.	.	.	.	.		.	.	.
Europe														
Albania	3 364	1.9	61	52	9	9	36	72	2.9	30		...	...	...
Austria	7 807	0.3	32	26	24	22	55	76	1.5	7		22 110	2.0	18 350
Belarus	10 210	0.5	34	34	16	17	68	70	1.6	17		2 910	...	6 840
Belgium	10 012	0.1	31	27	22	23	97	76	1.6	6		20 880	2.0	18 160

Country or territory	Population							Life expect- ancy at birth (years)	Total fertility rate (births per woman)	Infant mortality rate (per 1,000 live births)	GNP per capita		
	Total (000)	Average annual growth rate (%)	Dependency ratio				Per- centage urban				US$	Average annual growth rate (%)	PPP (Inter- national dollars)
			Age 0–14		Age 65 and over								
	1992	1980–92	1980	1992	1980	1992	1992	1992	1992	1992	1992	1980–92	1992
Bosnia and Herzegovina	3 944	0.1	41	33	9	9	46	72	1.6	15	...	...	...
Bulgaria	8 920	0.1	34	29	18	20	69	71	1.5	14	1 330	1.2	5 130
Croatia	4 516	0.3	31	29	17	17	62	71	1.6	9	...	...	...
Czech Republic	10 299	0.0	37	31	21	19	65	71	1.8	9	2 440	...	7 160
Former Czechoslovakia	.	.	.	.	.	.	.	.	.	.	.	.	.
Denmark	5 156	0.1	32	25	22	23	85	75	1.7	7	25 930	2.1	18 650
Estonia	1 563	0.5	33	33	19	18	72	69	1.6	16	2 750	– 2.3	6 320
Finland	5 033	0.4	30	29	18	20	62	76	1.9	5	22 980	2.0	15 970
France	57 260	0.5	35	30	22	22	73	77	1.7	7	22 300	1.7	19 200
Germany	80 365	0.2	28	24	24	22	86	76	1.3	6	23 030	...	.
Former German Dem. Rep.	.	.	.	.	.	.	.	.	.	.	.	.	.
Germany, Federal Rep. of	.	.	.	.	.	.	.	.	.	.	.	.	.
Greece	10 335	0.6	36	27	21	22	64	78	1.4	10	7 180	1.0	8 010
Hungary	10 262	– 0.4	34	29	21	20	63	69	1.7	15	3 010	0.2	5 740
Iceland	260	1.1	44	38	16	17	91	78	2.2	5	23 670	1.5	...
Ireland	3 511	0.3	52	42	18	18	57	75	2.1	7	12 100	3.4	12 070
Italy	57 096	0.1	34	23	20	22	67	77	1.3	8	20 510	2.2	17 730
Latvia	2 638	0.3	31	32	20	19	72	69	1.6	14	1 930	0.2	4 690
Lithuania	3 717	0.7	36	34	17	17	70	70	1.8	13	1 310	– 1.0	3 710
Luxembourg	390	0.6	28	25	20	20	87	76	1.6	7	35 260	3.3	...
Malta	359	0.8	34	35	15	16	88	76	2.1	9	...	...	...
Monaco	31	1.2	...	...	...	...	100	...	...	...	...	...	...
Netherlands	15 172	0.6	34	26	17	19	89	77	1.6	7	20 590	1.7	17 560
Norway	4 280	0.4	35	29	23	25	73	77	1.9	8	25 800	2.2	18 040
Poland	38 263	0.6	37	37	15	16	63	71	1.9	15	1 960	0.1	4 880
Portugal	9 847	0.1	41	30	16	20	34	75	1.6	10	7 450	3.1	10 120
Republic of Moldova	4 396	0.8	41	43	12	14	49	68	2.1	25	1 260	...	3 870
Romania	23 120	0.3	42	34	16	16	54	70	1.5	23	1 090	– 1.1	2 750
Russian Federation	148 064	0.6	32	34	15	16	75	68	1.5	21	2 680	...	6 220
San Marino	24	1.1	...	...	...	...	93	...	...	...	...	...	...
Slovakia	5 295	0.5	41	37	16	16	57	71	1.9	12	1 920	...	5 620
Slovenia	1 931	0.4	36	29	17	17	61	73	1.5	8	6 330	...	...
Spain	39 452	0.4	42	27	17	21	76	78	1.2	7	14 020	2.9	13 170
Sweden	8 650	0.3	31	29	25	28	83	78	2.1	5	26 780	1.5	17 610
Switzerland	6 980	0.8	30	25	21	21	60	78	1.6	6	36 230	1.4	22 100
The FYR of Macedonia	2 095	1.3	44	38	11	11	59	72	2.0	27	...	...	...
Ukraine	51 620	0.3	32	32	18	20	69	69	1.6	16	1 670	...	5 010
United Kingdom	57 755	0.2	33	30	24	24	89	76	1.8	7	17 760	2.4	16 730
Yugoslavia	10 454	0.8	36	34	15	15	54	72	2.0	20	...	...	...
Former Yugoslavia	.	.	.	.	.	.	.	.	.	.	.	.	.
Oceania													
Australia	17 377	1.5	39	32	15	17	85	78	1.9	7	17 070	1.6	17 350
Fiji	746	1.4	67	62	5	6	40	71	3.0	23	2 010	0.3	...
Kiribati	75	1.7	...	...	...	...	35	...	...	...	700	...	...
New Zealand	3 439	0.8	42	36	16	17	85	76	2.2	9	12 060	0.6	14 400
Papua New Guinea	4 017	2.2	77	70	3	5	15	56	5.1	68	950	0.0	2 020
Samoa	165	0.3	102	95	6	7	21	68	4.5	64	940	...	...
Solomon Islands	343	3.5	96	87	6	5	16	70	5.4	27	710	3.3	...
Tonga	97	0.4	...	...	...	...	37	...	...	...	1 350	...	...
Tuvalu	9	1.0	...	...	...	...	43	...	...	...	...	...	...
Vanuatu	157	2.5	87	83	6	7	19	65	4.7	47	1 220	...	...

Table 2
Literacy, culture and communication

Country or territory	Estimated number of adult illiterates				Estimated adult illiteracy rate (%)			Culture and communication										
	1980		1995		1995			Number of volumes in public libraries (per 1,000 inhabitants)		Daily newspapers (number of copies per 1,000 inhabitants)		Radio receivers (per 1,000 inhabitants)		Television receivers (per 1,000 inhabitants)		Main telephone lines (per 1,000 inhabitants)	
	Total (000)	%F	Total (000)	%F	Total	Male	Female	1980	1992	1980	1992	1980	1992	1980	1992	1980	1992
Africa																	
Algeria	6 103	64	6 582	66	38.4	26.1	51.0	...	...	24	38	197	236	52	77	17	37
Angola	...	...	...	...	...	...	...	...	...	20	12	21	29	4	6	5	5
Benin	1 532	57	1 792	60	63.0	51.3	74.2	...	6	0	2	66	90	1	5	2	3
Botswana	207	70	255	69	30.2	19.5	40.1	119	...	21	29	83	118	–	16	9	27
Burkina Faso	3 458	55	4 597	57	80.8	70.5	90.8	...	...	0	0	18	27	3	5	...	2
Burundi	1 740	62	2 221	62	64.7	50.7	77.5	...	...	0	3	39	62	–	1	...	2
Cameroon	2 695	64	2 712	67	36.6	25.0	47.9	...	...	8	4	88	146	–	24	...	4
Cape Verde	79	70	64	71	28.4	18.6	36.2	...	...	–	–	142	175	–	3	5	29
Central African Republic	956	60	760	63	40.0	31.5	47.6	...	...	–	1	52	71	0	5	1	2
Chad	1 751	62	1 868	64	51.9	37.9	65.3	...	...	0	0	168	244	–	1	...	1
Comoros	89	59	143	58	42.7	35.8	49.6	...	...	–	–	120	128	–	0	3	8
Congo	444	65	354	68	25.1	16.9	32.8	...	7	2	8	60	114	2	6	5	7
Côte d'Ivoire	3 309	55	4 339	57	59.9	50.1	70.0	3	...	10	7	122	143	38	59	5	7
Djibouti	108	61	181	64	53.8	39.7	67.3	...	...	–	–	75	75	18	46	9	12
Egypt	15 946	62	18 954	62	48.6	36.4	61.2	30	35	39	41	137	305	32	110	...	39
Equatorial Guinea	51	72	49	76	21.5	10.4	31.9	...	...	7	3	401	420	5	9	...	3
Eritrea	...	...	...	...	...	...	...	...	...	...	...	...	...	...	...	...	...
Ethiopia	15 117	57	19 052	57	64.5	54.5	74.7	...	...	1	1	82	197	1	3	2	2
Gabon	321	62	295	65	36.8	26.3	46.7	...	...	19	16	130	146	12	38	...	23
Gambia	278	59	403	62	61.4	47.2	75.1	105	94	–	2	114	155	–	–	...	14
Ghana	3 286	64	3 387	67	35.5	24.1	46.5	...	108	47	18	158	269	5	16	4	3
Guinea	1 877	58	2 272	61	64.1	50.1	78.1	...	...	–	–	30	42	1	7	...	2
Guinea-Bissau	295	63	282	65	45.1	32.0	57.5	...	...	8	6	31	40	–	–	...	8
Kenya	3 479	67	3 237	69	21.9	13.7	30.0	31	...	13	14	39	87	4	10	5	8
Lesotho	334	68	340	68	28.7	18.9	37.7	...	14	33	7	25	32	–	6	3	6
Liberia	787	58	1 014	62	61.7	46.1	77.6	...	...	6	13	179	226	11	18	...	2
Libyan Arab Jamahiriya	749	68	702	73	23.8	12.1	37.0	...	...	18	15	66	226	61	99	...	48
Madagascar	...	...	...	...	...	...	...	5	...	6	4	177	191	5	19	2	3
Malawi	1 789	69	2 587	69	43.6	28.1	58.2	...	23	3	2	42	225	–	...	2	3
Mali	3 135	55	3 917	57	69.0	60.6	76.9	...	...	1	4	15	44	–	1	1	1
Mauritania	613	59	806	60	62.3	50.4	73.7	...	...	–	0	97	147	–	24	2	3
Mauritius	163	66	138	62	17.1	12.9	21.2	...	...	83	74	269	366	95	222	24	72
Morocco	7 824	60	9 730	62	56.3	43.4	69.0	...	...	14	13	155	218	46	77	9	25
Mozambique	4 558	64	5 298	65	59.9	42.3	76.7	...	...	4	5	21	48	0	3	...	4
Namibia	...	...	...	...	...	...	...	...	...	26	147	...	137	5	22	...	40
Niger	2 730	54	4 081	55	86.4	79.1	93.4	...	...	1	1	45	61	1	5	1	1
Nigeria	26 229	60	26 075	63	42.9	32.7	52.7	7	12	15	18	97	196	8	37	...	3
Rwanda	1 534	62	1 695	63	39.5	30.2	48.4	...	...	0	0	34	66	–	–	1	2
Sao Tome and Principe	...	...	...	...	...	...	...	...	...	–	–	245	269	–	–	...	19
Senegal	2 376	56	3 084	58	66.9	57.0	76.8	...	...	6	6	65	115	1	37	3	7
Seychelles	...	...	...	...	...	...	...	397	600	48	45	333	479	–	87	55	146
Sierra Leone	1 494	58	1 727	61	68.6	54.6	81.8	...	...	3	2	139	234	6	11	4	3
Somalia	...	...	...	...	...	...	...	...	...	1	1	17	39	–	13	...	2
South Africa	4 234	53	4 731	51	18.2	18.1	18.3	...	...	48	32	274	312	69	101	55	89
Sudan	7 216	60	8 507	61	53.9	42.3	65.4	...	...	6	24	187	257	43	79	2	2
Swaziland	120	56	114	56	23.3	22.0	24.4	...	...	15	15	145	164	2	20	9	18
Togo	967	63	1 085	67	48.3	33.0	63.0	...	18	6	3	203	211	4	6	2	4
Tunisia	1 974	64	1 930	68	33.3	21.4	45.4	137	297	43	49	157	200	47	80	18	45
Uganda	3 669	65	4 172	66	38.2	26.3	49.8	6	4	2	4	30	106	5	10	2	2
United Rep. of Tanzania	4 912	67	5 171	69	32.2	20.6	43.2	22	...	11	8	16	25	0	2	2	3

Country or territory	Estimated number of adult illiterates				Estimated adult illiteracy rate (%)			Culture and communication										
	1980		1995		1995			Number of volumes in public libraries (per 1,000 inhabitants)		Daily newspapers (number of copies per 1,000 inhabitants)		Radio receivers (per 1,000 inhabitants)		Television receivers (per 1,000 inhabitants)		Main telephone lines (per 1,000 inhabitants)	
	Total (000)	%F	Total (000)	%F	Total	Male	Female	1980	1992	1980	1992	1980	1992	1980	1992	1980	1992
Zaire	5 931	70	5 184	73	22.7	13.4	32.3	...	...	2	3	56	97	0	1	1	1
Zambia	1 308	64	1 082	68	21.8	14.4	28.7	...	...	19	8	24	81	10	26	6	9
Zimbabwe	919	66	940	68	14.9	9.6	20.1	...	108	19	19	34	85	10	27	14	12
America, North																	
Antigua and Barbuda	...	...	...	...	...	...	...	...	...	98	–	279	423	262	361	...	255
Bahamas	4	63	3	60	1.8	1.5	2.0	...	...	157	133	486	542	148	225	148	303
Barbados	9	68	5	65	2.6	2.0	3.2	696	676	156	160	542	876	209	280	180	309
Belize	...	...	...	...	...	...	...	...	679	21	–	486	578	–	164	26	125
British Virgin Islands	...	...	...	...	...	...	...	2 417	3 200	–	–	458	502	167	221	153	235
Canada	...	...	...	...	...	...	...	1 854	2 193	221	215	721	990	432	615	415	592
Costa Rica	118	51	115	49	5.2	5.3	5.0	...	...	110	101	83	258	68	141	69	102
Cuba	716	58	364	55	4.3	3.8	4.7	280	494	108	122	300	346	131	162	...	32
Dominica	...	...	...	...	...	...	...	203	408	–	–	419	597	–	73	16	191
Dominican Republic	842	51	908	49	17.9	18.0	17.8	...	...	39	36	158	173	70	88	19	65
El Salvador	904	56	975	56	28.5	26.5	30.2	...	11	64	90	343	413	66	93	15	31
Grenada	...	...	...	...	...	...	...	169	703	45	–	393	598	–	331	35	203
Guatemala	1 920	57	2 627	58	44.4	37.5	51.4	...	...	29	18	51	66	25	52	12	22
Haiti	2 145	55	2 360	54	55.0	52.0	57.8	...	...	7	7	20	47	3	5	...	7
Honduras	710	52	869	50	27.3	27.4	27.3	...	...	59	31	140	408	18	77	8	19
Jamaica	289	43	254	37	15.0	19.2	10.9	519	496	51	67	375	434	80	138	25	70
Mexico	6 452	61	6 246	61	10.4	8.2	12.6	36	182	124	116	134	255	57	149	38	79
Netherlands Antilles	...	...	...	...	...	...	...	571	...	299	275	1 006	1 062	247	332	218	253
Nicaragua	574	51	822	52	34.3	35.4	33.4	...	...	49	23	239	262	57	66	11	14
Panama	157	52	161	53	9.2	8.6	9.8	13	...	56	90	154	226	115	169	65	96
Saint Kitts and Nevis	...	...	...	...	...	...	...	...	...	–	–	...	648	91	206	...	277
Saint Lucia	...	...	...	...	...	...	...	...	...	–	–	704	759	80	190	39	131
Saint Vincent and the Grenadines	...	...	...	...	...	...	...	...	...	–	–	429	661	53	144	36	143
Trinidad and Tobago	35	69	19	72	2.1	1.2	3.0	...	...	143	138	277	494	194	316	40	142
United States	...	...	...	...	...	...	...	...	...	273	236	1 996	2 118	684	815	414	565
America, South																	
Argentina	1 185	54	935	52	3.8	3.8	3.8	...	...	142	143	427	671	183	219	67	111
Bolivia	937	69	745	73	16.9	9.5	24.0	23	...	42	57	523	669	56	112	24	26
Brazil	18 717	54	18 331	51	16.7	16.7	16.8	122	...	45	55	313	387	124	208	40	70
Chile	634	54	485	54	4.8	4.6	5.0	52	82	...	147	292	344	110	210	33	94
Colombia	2 080	53	2 046	51	8.7	8.8	8.6	...	59	53	63	124	177	85	117	41	84
Ecuador	815	60	719	60	9.9	8.0	11.8	...	...	70	64	305	327	63	88	28	48
Guyana	24	67	11	66	1.9	1.4	2.5	...	...	76	99	408	493	–	40	...	35
Paraguay	241	62	235	59	7.9	6.5	9.4	...	...	51	37	112	169	22	81	16	28
Peru	2 020	72	1 736	76	11.3	5.5	17.0	237	...	81	71	159	254	52	98	18	27
Suriname	27	67	19	66	7.0	4.9	9.0	...	...	127	105	532	683	113	141	43	108
Uruguay	110	47	65	45	2.7	3.1	2.3	...	...	240	240	559	604	126	232	75	157
Venezuela	1 417	56	1 244	54	8.9	8.2	9.7	65	178	195	205	391	442	113	161	54	90
Asia																	
Afghanistan	7 371	57	8 169	60	68.5	52.8	85.0	12	...	6	12	75	123	3	10	2	1
Armenia	58	85	10	66	0.4	0.3	0.5	...	4 268	...	24	...	...	...	...	97	157
Azerbaijan	111	86	18	66	0.4	0.3	0.5	...	5 494	...	59	...	...	...	...	55	89
Bahrain	63	54	56	55	14.8	10.9	20.6	...	459	40	83	360	552	259	427	123	212
Bangladesh	33 551	57	45 082	58	61.9	50.6	73.9	...	5	3	6	17	46	1	5	...	2
Bhutan	532	59	558	62	57.8	43.8	71.9	...	...	–	–	6	16	–	–	1	2

Table 2 (continued)

Country or territory	Estimated number of adult illiterates				Estimated adult illiteracy rate (%)			Culture and communication										
	1980		1995		1995			Number of volumes in public libraries (per 1,000 inhabitants)		Daily newspapers (number of copies per 1,000 inhabitants)		Radio receivers (per 1,000 inhabitants)		Television receivers (per 1,000 inhabitants)		Main telephone lines (per 1,000 inhabitants)	
	Total (000)	%F	Total (000)	%F	Total	Male	Female	1980	1992	1980	1992	1980	1992	1980	1992	1980	1992
Brunei Darussalam	27	65	22	67	11.8	7.4	16.6	503	1 059	–	74	212	271	135	238	60	176
Cambodia	...	...	...	...	...	...	...	...	...	–	–	92	105	5	8	...	1
China	218 848	68	166 173	72	18.5	10.1	27.3	...	263	34	43	55	183	4	31	2	10
Cyprus	...	...	...	...	...	...	...	371	...	127	107	258	292	135	149	106	470
Dem. People's Rep. of Korea	...	...	...	...	...	...	...	...	...	219	221	82	122	7	18	...	48
Georgia	149	87	19	71	0.4	0.3	0.6	...	5 939	...	...	...	...	...	...	63	105
Hong Kong	520	78	370	74	7.8	4.0	11.8	204	725	...	822	506	671	221	282	254	485
India	250 592	61	290 705	63	48.0	34.5	62.3	...	...	21	31	38	79	4	37	3	8
Indonesia	28 325	66	21 507	68	16.2	10.4	22.0	3	...	15	24	99	149	20	61	3	9
Iran, Islamic Rep. of	11 027	61	11 926	64	31.4	22.3	40.7	55	...	25	20	163	229	51	62	23	50
Iraq	4 188	62	4 848	65	42.0	29.3	55.0	...	...	26	35	161	219	50	74	19	35
Israel	...	...	...	...	...	...	...	...	...	258	246	245	480	232	276	222	352
Japan	...	...	...	...	...	...	...	587	1 309	567	577	678	910	539	616	342	464
Jordan	464	71	414	75	13.4	6.6	20.6	24	...	23	53	188	235	59	75	3	70
Kazakstan	310	87	45	68	0.4	0.3	0.5	...	...	...	...	...	...	...	...	44	87
Kuwait	264	49	200	59	21.4	17.8	25.1	208	140	222	248	284	372	257	315	114	245
Kyrgyzstan	70	87	11	66	0.4	0.3	0.5	...	...	...	...	...	...	...	...	40	75
Lao People's Dem. Rep.	1 083	62	1 170	66	43.4	30.6	55.6	...	...	4	3	109	125	–	6	2	2
Lebanon	222	67	151	67	7.6	5.3	9.7	...	...	109	185	749	878	281	341	...	93
Malaysia	2 400	67	2 057	67	16.5	10.9	21.9	176	433	59	117	411	430	87	150	29	112
Maldives	9	50	9	49	6.8	6.7	7.0	...	...	6	13	44	117	7	24	...	37
Mongolia	261	67	256	67	17.1	11.4	22.8	...	...	106	92	96	135	3	41	...	30
Myanmar	4 727	69	4 913	67	16.9	11.3	22.3	...	...	10	7	23	82	0	2	...	2
Nepal	6 784	56	9 149	59	72.5	59.1	86.0	...	...	8	7	20	34	–	2	...	3
Oman	...	...	...	...	...	...	...	...	1	–	41	272	546	32	626	13	79
Pakistan	34 575	56	48 693	58	62.2	50.0	75.6	1	...	12	6	64	87	11	18	4	10
Palestine																	
Gaza Strip	...	...	...	...	...	...	...	...	...	...	...	...	...	...	...	...	...
West Bank	...	...	...	...	...	...	...	...	...	...	...	...	...	...	...	...	...
Philippines	2 911	55	2 234	53	5.4	5.0	5.7	...	97	41	50	43	142	22	46	9	10
Qatar	47	36	82	27	20.6	20.8	20.1	...	327	131	135	393	389	331	397	134	206
Republic of Korea	1 566	79	697	82	2.0	0.7	3.3	37	153	210	412	525	1 013	165	213	71	357
Saudi Arabia	2 786	57	3 871	55	37.2	28.5	49.8	...	...	36	43	260	288	219	253	34	93
Singapore	301	75	196	77	8.9	4.1	13.7	...	...	286	336	373	648	311	380	235	415
Sri Lanka	1 410	68	1 241	67	9.8	6.6	12.8	...	28	30	27	98	199	2	49	4	8
Syrian Arab Republic	2 073	70	2 259	75	29.2	14.3	44.2	...	...	13	22	195	256	44	61	28	41
Tajikistan	58	84	11	63	0.3	0.3	0.4	...	...	...	21	...	...	...	...	30	48
Thailand	3 297	68	2 613	68	6.2	4.0	8.4	34	...	57	85	140	189	21	112	8	31
Turkey	9 384	73	7 231	76	17.7	8.3	27.6	114	155	56	71	113	161	79	175	26	160
Turkmenistan	42	85	8	63	0.3	0.2	0.4	...	...	...	...	...	...	...	...	38	64
United Arab Emirates	219	29	272	29	20.8	21.1	20.2	...	...	149	189	236	308	88	105	116	292
Uzbekistan	259	85	45	64	0.3	0.2	0.4	...	...	...	21	...	...	...	...	36	67
Viet Nam	5 133	72	2 916	73	6.3	3.5	8.8	...	...	10	8	93	103	...	42	...	2
Yemen	.	.	...	...	...	...	...	.	...	.	19	.	28	.	28	2	11
Former Dem. Yemen	...	...	.	.	.	.	.	...	.	8	.	63	.	19	.	...	.
Former Yemen Arab Rep.	...	...	.	.	.	.	.	...	.	13	.	17	.	1	.	...	.
Europe																	
Albania	...	...	...	...	...	...	...	2 139	...	54	49	150	173	36	86	10	13
Austria	...	...	...	...	...	...	...	699	1 179	351	398	507	618	391	478	290	440
Belarus	330	88	38	73	0.5	0.3	0.6	9 052	7 556	243	186	223	311	218	271	75	169
Belgium	...	...	...	...	...	...	...	2 450	...	232	310	731	768	387	452	248	425

Country or territory	Estimated number of adult illiterates 1980 Total (000)	%F	1995 Total (000)	%F	Estimated adult illiteracy rate (%) 1995 Total	Male	Female	Number of volumes in public libraries (per 1,000 inhabitants) 1980	1992	Daily newspapers (number of copies per 1,000 inhabitants) 1980	1992	Radio receivers (per 1,000 inhabitants) 1980	1992	Television receivers (per 1,000 inhabitants) 1980	1992	Main telephone lines (per 1,000 inhabitants) 1980	1992
Bosnia and Herzegovina	...	...	...	...	...	...	...	...	...	...	131	...	...	...	...	...	137
Bulgaria	...	...	...	...	...	...	...	5 521	6 400	253	164	395	446	243	258	102	275
Croatia	...	...	...	...	...	...	...	840	1 025	...	...	251	299	215	337	79	199
Czech Republic	...	...	...	...	...	...	...	...	3 648	...	583	...	602	...	476	115	176
Former Czechoslovakia	...	...	.	.	.	.	.	3 294	.	313	.	509	.	392	.	...	.
Denmark	...	...	...	...	...	...	...	5 761	6 299	366	332	927	1 034	498	537	434	581
Estonia	6	79	3	56	0.2	0.2	0.2	...	6 960	...	...	...	454	...	355	135	215
Finland	...	...	...	...	...	...	...	4 885	7 214	505	512	837	992	414	503	364	544
France	...	...	...	...	...	...	...	937	...	192	...	741	888	353	407	295	525
Germany	.	.	...	...	...	...	...	.	1 604	.	.	...	883	.	557	332	440
Former German Dem. Rep.	...	...	.	.	.	.	.	2 737	.	524	.	536	.	514	.	...	.
Germany, Federal Rep. of	...	...	.	.	.	.	.	1 011	.	335	.	894	.	439	.	.	.
Greece	666	79	283	74	3.3	1.7	4.7	...	723	120	135	343	415	171	198	235	437
Hungary	96	71	69	62	0.8	0.7	1.0	3 807	4 836	247	282	499	613	310	424	58	125
Iceland	...	...	...	...	...	...	...	...	7 112	548	519	711	788	285	331	372	537
Ireland	...	...	...	...	...	...	...	2 176	3 152	229	186	375	632	231	299	142	314
Italy	1 645	64	931	64	1.9	1.4	2.4	245	482	85	106	602	801	390	426	231	409
Latvia	18	83	5	64	0.2	0.2	0.3	...	9 780	...	98	...	607	...	455	161	247
Lithuania	81	79	16	67	0.5	0.4	0.7	...	...	...	225	...	384	...	379	115	222
Luxembourg	...	...	...	...	...	...	...	...	...	371	372	549	615	247	259	363	529
Malta	...	...	...	...	...	...	...	475	669	185	150	509	526	623	744	154	414
Monaco	...	...	...	...	...	...	...	...	...	381	258	967	981	630	715	521	1 040
Netherlands	...	...	...	...	...	...	...	2 172	2 754	326	303	650	907	399	488	346	487
Norway	...	...	...	...	...	...	...	3 435	4 648	463	607	661	797	350	425	293	529
Poland	188	66	84	57	0.3	0.3	0.3	2 658	3 550	236	159	298	436	246	297	55	103
Portugal	1 421	64	827	66	10.4	7.5	13.0	643	397	49	47	170	230	158	189	107	306
Republic of Moldova	126	...	34	...	1.1	...	...	...	...	...	47	...	...	...	...	56	117
Romania	766	78	388	75	2.1	1.1	3.1	2 695	...	181	324	177	201	184	198	73	109
Russian Federation	4 785	90	543	73	0.5	0.3	0.6	...	...	573	386	280	337	283	376	70	154
San Marino	...	...	...	...	...	...	...	...	...	48	...	476	565	300	337	...	675
Slovakia	...	...	...	...	...	...	...	...	3 731	...	317	...	567	...	472	94	155
Slovenia	...	...	...	...	...	...	...	...	2 736	108	160	273	373	251	295	...	247
Spain	1 709	72	957	70	2.9	1.8	3.9	312	693	93	104	258	309	253	398	193	353
Sweden	...	...	...	...	...	...	...	4 696	5 266	528	511	842	877	461	469	580	682
Switzerland	...	...	...	...	...	...	...	584	...	393	377	813	832	364	399	444	606
The FYR of Macedonia	...	...	...	...	...	...	...	...	1 303	...	...	...	176	146	161	...	144
Ukraine	2 219	...	483	...	1.2	...	...	7 420	7 766	...	118	579	804	255	335	76	145
United Kingdom	...	...	...	...	...	...	...	2 332	2 293	417	383	950	1 144	401	435	322	473
Yugoslavia	...	...	...	...	...	...	...	...	1 467	...	52	...	191	...	172	...	177
Former Yugoslavia	...	...	.	.	.	.	.	1 079	.	119	.	224	.	190	.	...	.

Oceania

Country or territory	1980 Total (000)	%F	1995 Total (000)	%F	Total	Male	Female	1980	1992	1980	1992	1980	1992	1980	1992	1980	1992
Australia	...	...	...	...	...	...	...	...	...	323	265	1 098	1 289	384	488	323	471
Fiji	66	62	43	63	8.4	6.2	10.7	...	...	102	36	473	603	–	16	38	66
Kiribati	...	...	...	...	...	...	...	...	...	–	–	193	203	–	–	...	18
New Zealand	...	...	...	...	...	...	...	1 957	...	340	305	885	935	332	445	361	449
Papua New Guinea	737	62	724	65	27.8	19.0	37.3	...	40	9	16	58	74	–	2	8	9
Samoa	...	...	...	...	...	...	...	...	...	–	–	201	461	16	38	...	40
Solomon Islands	...	...	...	...	...	...	...	...	...	–	–	88	120	–	6	...	15
Tonga	...	...	...	...	...	...	...	...	...	–	72	217	555	–	10	...	60
Tuvalu	...	...	...	...	...	...	...	...	...	–	–	206	307	–	–	...	14
Vanuatu	...	...	...	...	...	...	...	...	...	–	–	197	287	–	10	...	23

Table 3
Enrolment in pre-primary education and access to schooling

Country or territory	Pre-primary education					Access to schooling								
	Age-group	Gross enrolment ratio (%)				Apparent intake rate in first-level education (%)			School life expectancy (expected number of years of formal schooling)					
		Total	Total	Male	Female	Total	Male	Female	Total		Male		Female	
	1992	1980	1992			1992			1980	1992	1980	1992	1980	1992
Africa														
Algeria	5–5	...	3	3	3	98	102	95	7.9	10.2	9.2	11.0	6.4	9.2
Angola	♦5–5	60	53	71	36	75	...	...	7.4	...	8.1	...	6.6	...
Benin	♦3–5	2	3	3	2	77	101	52	...	...	...	...	...	...
Botswana	–	–	–	–	–	124	125	123	7.3	10.7	6.7	10.4	7.9	10.9
Burkina Faso	4–6	0	...	...	...	38	48	29	1.5	2.7	1.9	3.4	1.1	2.1
Burundi	4–6	0	...	...	...	61	67	56	2.0	4.5	2.5	5.1	1.5	4.0
Cameroon	4–5	7	13	13	13	85	91	80	6.8	...	7.7	...	5.8	...
Cape Verde	5–6	...	...	...	...	117	116	117	...	...	...	...	...	...
Central African Republic	4–5	7	7	9	5	71	85	58	...	...	...	...	...	...
Chad	4–5	...	...	...	...	64	80	47	...	...	...	...	...	...
Comoros	♦4–6	68	...	...	...	70	72	68	...	...	...	...	...	...
Congo	3–5	...	...	...	...	...	...	...	...	...	...	...	...	...
Côte d'Ivoire	5–6	1	1	1	1	63	71	54	...	...	...	...	...	...
Djibouti	5–5	...	1	1	2	35	...	...	...	...	...	...	...	...
Egypt	4–5	3	7	8	7	94	100	88	...	9.8	...	10.8	...	8.8
Equatorial Guinea	...	...	...	...	...	...	...	...	...	...	...	...	...	...
Eritrea	5–6	...	4	4	4	47	53	42	...	...	...	...	...	...
Ethiopia	4–6	1	1	1	1	♦42	50	34	...	...	...	...	...	...
Gabon	3–5	...	...	...	...	...	...	...	...	...	...	...	...	...
Gambia	♦5–6	...	24	...	...	77	90	64	4.1	5.0	5.4	6.1	2.8	4.0
Ghana	4–5	23	39	40	37	81	85	77	...	...	...	...	...	...
Guinea	–	–	–	–	–	53	70	36	...	2.7	...	3.8	...	1.6
Guinea–Bissau	4–6	2	...	...	...	...	...	...	4.3	...	6.0	...	2.6	...
Kenya	3–5	24	35	35	35	♦113	115	111	...	...	...	...	...	...
Lesotho	–	–	–	–	–	101	99	103	8.2	8.6	6.8	7.8	9.6	9.5
Liberia	♦4–6	67	...	...	...	...	...	...	...	...	...	...	...	...
Libyan Arab Jamahiriya	4–5	4	...	...	...	...	...	...	...	...	...	...	...	...
Madagascar	3–5	...	...	...	...	79	80	79	...	...	...	...	...	...
Malawi	–	–	–	–	–	102	106	99	...	5.6	...	6.3	...	5.0
Mali	5–7	...	2	2	2	32	37	27	...	1.8	...	2.3	...	1.2
Mauritania	...	...	...	...	...	88	97	80	...	...	...	...	...	...
Mauritius	3–4	27	...	...	...	♦96	97	95	...	...	...	...	...	...
Morocco	5–6	50	62	85	37	87	98	75	6.1	6.9	7.7	8.0	4.5	5.7
Mozambique	–	...	–	–	–	62	69	55	4.3	3.4	5.1	4.0	3.5	2.9
Namibia	6–6	...	13	13	13	143	143	143	...	12.6	...	12.0	...	13.0
Niger	5–6	1	2	2	2	26	...	...	1.7	2.1	...	2.8	...	1.4
Nigeria	3–5	...	...	...	...	♦101	112	90	...	...	...	...	...	...
Rwanda	4–6	...	...	...	...	102	103	101	...	5.7	...	5.9	...	5.5
Sao Tome and Principe	3–6	...	...	...	...	...	...	...	...	...	...	...	...	...
Senegal	♦4–6	2	2	2	2	55	61	49	...	4.6	...	5.6	...	3.6
Seychelles	...	...	...	...	...	...	...	...	...	...	...	...	...	...
Sierra Leone	3–4	...	...	...	...	...	...	...	...	...	...	...	...	...
Somalia	4–5	1	...	...	...	...	...	...	1.9	...	2.5	...	1.3	...
South Africa	5–5	...	22	22	22	131	133	128	...	12.0	...	11.7	...	12.2
Sudan	5–6	13	23	24	22	62	70	54	...	...	...	...	...	...
Swaziland	3–5	...	26	...	...	130	133	127	...	...	...	...	...	...
Togo	3–5	3	3	3	3	88	99	77	...	8.2	...	10.6	...	5.9
Tunisia	3–5	...	9	...	...	104	106	102	8.2	10.3	9.7	10.9	6.7	9.7
Uganda	...	...	...	...	...	♦106	114	98	...	...	...	...	...	...
United Rep. of Tanzania	4–6	...	...	...	...	78	80	76	...	...	...	...	...	...

Country or territory	Pre-primary education				Access to schooling								
	Age-group	Gross enrolment ratio (%)			Apparent intake rate in first-level education (%)			School life expectancy (expected number of years of formal schooling)					
		Total	Total	Male	Female	Total	Male	Female	Total		Male		Female	
	1992	1980	1992			1992			1980	1992	1980	1992	1980	1992
Zaire	3–5	...	1	1	1	70	78	61	...	5.6	...	6.7	...	4.4
Zambia	3–6	...	...	...	...	...	...	...	...	...	...	...	...	...
Zimbabwe	5–6	...	...	...	...	133	135	132	...	...	...	...	...	...
America, North														
Antigua and Barbuda	3–4	...	...	...	...	...	...	...	...	...	...	...	...	...
Bahamas	3–4	...	7	7	7	89	80	98	12.0	12.7	...	12.2	...	13.1
Barbados	3–4	41	...	...	...	89	88	91	12.3	12.9	12.1	12.8	12.3	12.9
Belize	3–4	20	28	27	28	...	...	...	...	10.3	...	10.4	...	10.3
British Virgin Islands	...	...	...	...	...	...	...	...	...	...	...	...	...	...
Canada	4–5	54	58	59	58	♦107	109	105	14.7	17.6	14.6	17.2	14.8	17.9
Costa Rica	5–5	39	67	67	67	113	113	113	9.7	9.5	9.7	9.6	9.7	9.4
Cuba	5–5	59	94	104	83	97	...	...	...	12.3	...	11.8	...	12.9
Dominica	...	...	...	...	...	...	...	...	...	...	...	...	...	...
Dominican Republic	3–6	4	20	19	20	♦185	193	177	...	10.3	...	10.1	...	10.4
El Salvador	4–6	11	22	21	22	129	131	128	...	8.6	...	8.7	...	8.5
Grenada	...	...	...	...	...	...	...	...	...	...	...	...	...	...
Guatemala	5–6	21	31	32	31	♦152	160	145	5.5	...	...	...	...	...
Haiti	3–5	...	41	42	40	71	73	70	...	...	...	...	...	...
Honduras	5–6	14	20	20	20	133	135	131	...	8.2	...	...	...	...
Jamaica	3–5	70	73	77	70	101	103	98	10.7	11.0	10.4	10.9	11.0	11.1
Mexico	4–5	25	63	62	64	112	...	...	...	10.7	...	...	...	...
Netherlands Antilles	...	...	...	...	...	...	...	...	...	...	...	...	...	...
Nicaragua	3–6	8	15	14	15	124	125	123	8.5	8.5	8.4	8.4	8.7	8.7
Panama	5–5	33	53	53	53	112	113	110	11.1	11.1	10.9	11.0	11.3	11.3
Saint Kitts and Nevis	...	...	...	...	...	...	...	...	...	...	...	...	...	...
Saint Lucia	...	...	...	...	...	...	...	...	...	...	...	...	...	...
Saint Vincent and the Grenadines	...	...	...	...	...	...	...	...	...	...	...	...	...	...
Trinidad and Tobago	3–4	8	9	9	9	80	80	79	10.9	10.6	10.9	10.6	10.9	10.6
United States	3–5	53	61	...	...	♦110	109	111	14.6	16.0	14.4	15.6	14.7	16.3
America, South														
Argentina	4–5	40	47	...	...	121	123	119	...	13.2	...	13.0	...	13.5
Bolivia	4–5	27	32	32	32	140	140	139	8.3	9.7	9.2	10.5	7.5	8.9
Brazil	4–6	14	36	...	...	137	...	...	9.3	10.9	9.3	...	9.3	...
Chile	5–5	71	86	85	86	♦100	101	99	...	11.8	...	11.8	...	11.8
Colombia	3–5	9	20	20	21	132	133	131	...	10.3	...	...	...	...
Ecuador	4–5	11	23	23	24	♦186	188	185	...	...	...	...	...	...
Guyana	4–5	67	79	79	79	...	...	...	...	...	...	...	...	...
Paraguay	6–6	12	31	30	32	113	115	112	7.8	8.5	...	8.6	...	8.3
Peru	3–5	16	34	...	...	♦175	...	...	10.6	12.5	11.2	...	10.0	...
Suriname	4–5	...	...	...	...	...	...	...	...	...	...	...	...	...
Uruguay	2–5	19	34	33	34	102	102	102	...	...	...	...	...	...
Venezuela	♦3–5	36	43	42	43	108	110	106	9.8	10.6	...	10.4	...	10.7
Asia														
Afghanistan	3–6	0	...	...	...	28	41	14	...	...	...	...	...	...
Armenia	...	...	...	...	...	...	...	...	...	...	...	...	...	...
Azerbaijan	3–6	...	24	26	22	102	102	102	...	...	...	...	...	...
Bahrain	3–5	15	33	33	32	108	105	111	10.1	12.9	10.9	12.5	9.4	13.2
Bangladesh	5–5	...	...	...	...	101	...	...	3.9	5.2	5.0	5.9	2.8	4.4
Bhutan	...	...	...	...	...	...	...	...	...	...	...	...	...	...

World education report

Table 3 *(continued)*

Country or territory	Pre-primary education					Access to schooling								
	Age-group	Gross enrolment ratio (%)				Apparent intake rate in first-level education (%)			School life expectancy (expected number of years of formal schooling)					
		Total	Total	Male	Female	Total	Male	Female	Total		Male		Female	
	1992	1980	1992			1992			1980	1992	1980	1992	1980	1992
Brunei Darussalam	3–5	42	50	52	49	100	...	...	10.6	11.2	10.6	11.2	10.6	11.2
Cambodia	5–5	...	...	...	...	...	...	...	...	...	...	...	...	...
China	3–6	13	26	27	26	104	...	...	...	...	...	...	...	...
Cyprus	2–5	...	59	59	60	...	...	...	...	...	...	...	...	...
Dem. People's Rep. of Korea	4–5	...	...	...	...	...	...	...	...	...	...	...	...	...
Georgia	...	...	...	...	...	...	...	...	...	...	...	...	...	...
Hong Kong	3–5	81	81	...	...	...	...	...	12.0	...	12.1	...	11.8	...
India	♦4–5	5	3	4	3	♦133	144	120	...	...	...	...	...	...
Indonesia	5–6	12	18	...	...	110	...	...	...	9.6	...	10.0	...	9.2
Iran, Islamic Rep. of	5–5	15	13	14	13	100	101	98	...	8.8	...	9.9	...	7.6
Iraq	4–5	9	8	8	7	83	87	80	10.2	8.3	11.7	9.4	8.5	7.1
Israel	2–5	71	81	...	...	♦99	98	100	...	...	...	...	...	...
Japan	3–5	41	48	48	49	102	102	103	12.8	13.5	13.2	...	12.3	...
Jordan	4–5	12	25	27	24	112	112	112	12.0	11.5	11.7	11.4	12.3	11.6
Kazakstan	...	...	...	...	...	98	98	98	...	...	...	...	...	...
Kuwait	4–5	37	44	44	44	64	64	64	11.1	...	11.4	...	10.9	...
Kyrgyzstan	...	...	...	...	...	...	...	...	...	...	...	...	...	...
Lao People's Dem. Rep.	3–5	2	6	6	7	120	135	106	...	6.7	...	7.9	...	5.5
Lebanon	3–5	59	68	69	68	...	...	...	...	...	...	...	...	...
Malaysia	4–5	23	36	35	36	97	97	97	...	...	...	...	...	...
Maldives	4–5	...	21	22	20	♦143	145	141	...	...	...	...	...	...
Mongolia	4–7	25	39	...	...	...	...	...	9.3	...	...	...	...	...
Myanmar	4–4	...	...	...	...	...	...	...	...	...	...	...	...	...
Nepal	3–5	...	...	...	...	125	138	111	...	...	...	...	...	...
Oman	4–5	1	3	4	3	77	77	76	3.7	7.9	5.0	8.4	2.3	7.4
Pakistan	3–4	...	...	...	...	♦74	91	56	...	...	...	...	...	...
Palestine														
Gaza Strip	...	...	...	...	...	...	...	...	...	...	...	...	...	...
West Bank	...	...	...	...	...	...	...	...	...	...	...	...	...	...
Philippines	5–6	4	12	...	...	♦136	...	...	10.3	10.8	10.1	10.7	10.5	10.9
Qatar	4–5	25	28	31	26	57	56	59	10.5	11.1	10.3	10.5	10.8	11.8
Republic of Korea	5–5	8	65	65	65	92	91	92	11.7	13.7	12.3	14.3	11.1	13.0
Saudi Arabia	4–5	5	8	9	8	76	74	78	5.6	8.1	6.7	8.6	4.5	7.7
Singapore	4–5	13	21	22	21	102	103	102	10.5	...	10.6	...	10.5	...
Sri Lanka	4–4	...	...	...	...	95	94	95	...	...	...	...	...	...
Syrian Arab Republic	3–5	4	6	7	6	100	104	96	9.2	9.5	10.8	10.2	7.5	8.7
Tajikistan	3–6	...	16	...	...	♦76	...	...	...	...	...	...	...	...
Thailand	♦3–5	10	50	49	50	♦107	...	...	...	...	...	...	...	...
Turkey	4–5	0	5	5	5	91	94	87	...	9.3	...	...	...	...
Turkmenistan	...	...	...	...	...	...	...	...	...	...	...	...	...	...
United Arab Emirates	4–5	37	61	62	60	107	107	107	7.5	11.2	7.7	10.7	7.3	11.7
Uzbekistan	...	...	...	...	...	103	...	...	...	...	...	...	...	...
Viet Nam	3–5	35	28	...	...	...	...	...	...	...	...	...	...	...
Yemen	...	.												
Former Dem. Yemen	3–6	2		.	.	.	.	.	...	.	...	.	...	.
Former Yemen Arab Rep.	...	...	.	.	.	.	.	.	...	.	...	.	...	.
Europe														
Albania	3–5	46	59	...	...	♦109	110	109	...	...	...	...	...	...
Austria	3–5	63	72	72	72	♦104	105	104	11.2	14.6	11.3	14.9	11.0	14.2
Belarus	♦3–5	58	79	...	...	94	95	94	...	...	...	...	...	...
Belgium	3–5	103	111	111	111	94	93	96	13.4	14.4	13.5	14.4	13.3	14.4

Country or territory	Pre-primary education					Access to schooling								
	Age-group	Gross enrolment ratio (%)				Apparent intake rate in first-level education (%)			School life expectancy (expected number of years of formal schooling)					
		Total	Total	Male	Female	Total	Male	Female	Total		Male		Female	
	1992	1980		1992			1992		1980	1992	1980	1992	1980	1992
Bosnia and Herzegovina	...	...	...	...	...	...	...	...	...	...	...	...	...	...
Bulgaria	♦3–5	104	79	80	79	91	91	92	11.0	11.7	10.9	11.4	11.1	11.9
Croatia	3–6	...	23	24	23	♦84	84	83	...	11.2	...	11.1	...	11.3
Czech Republic	3–5	...	88	...	...	104	104	104	...	...	...	...	...	...
Former Czechoslovakia	3–5	84	.	.	.	.	.	.	...	.	...	.	...	.
Denmark	6–6	88	98	98	98	101	101	101	13.5	15.1	13.6	14.9	13.5	15.4
Estonia	3–6	...	60	60	60	81	81	81	...	12.4	...	12.1	...	12.7
Finland	3–6	27	37	37	37	99	98	99	...	...	...	...	...	...
France	2–5	76	83	83	83	♦108	109	107	12.7	14.6	12.5	14.3	12.8	15.0
Germany	3–5	.	101	101	101	97	96	98	.	14.6	.	15.0	.	14.2
Former German Dem. Rep.	3–5	115	.	.	.	.	.	.	...	.	...	.	...	.
Germany, Federal Rep. of	3–5	92	.	.	.	.	.	.	...	.	...	.	...	.
Greece	4–5	54	55	55	56	♦95	94	95	12.1	13.2	12.4	13.2	11.7	13.2
Hungary	3–5	96	114	115	112	♦106	106	105	9.5	12.0	9.3	12.0	9.9	12.0
Iceland	5–6	50	46	46	46	...	...	...	...	...	...	...	...	...
Ireland	4–5	97	106	106	106	99	99	100	11.3	13.1	11.2	12.9	11.4	13.3
Italy	3–5	78	95	94	95	95	94	95	...	...	...	...	...	...
Latvia	3–6	...	40	42	39	♦77	80	75	...	...	...	...	...	...
Lithuania	3–6	...	34	34	35	♦98	99	96	...	...	...	...	...	...
Luxembourg	4–5	93	95	...	...	...	...	...	11.0	...	11.1	...	10.9	...
Malta	♦3–4	145	113	113	114	104	103	106	11.8	13.1	12.2	13.3	11.3	12.8
Monaco	3–5	...	...	...	...	...	...	...	...	...	...	...	...	...
Netherlands	4–5	107	98	98	98	...	...	...	13.3	15.5	13.7	15.7	12.8	15.2
Norway	4–6	44	106	...	...	97	97	97	12.9	15.5	12.8	15.3	13.0	15.6
Poland	3–6	55	41	...	...	♦99	100	99	11.8	12.1	11.6	12.0	12.0	12.3
Portugal	3–5	20	49	49	49	100	100	100	...	...	...	...	...	...
Republic of Moldova	3–5	...	61	62	60	♦100	101	99	...	...	...	...	...	...
Romania	3–5	83	76	74	78	94	94	94	...	10.8	...	10.9	...	10.7
Russian Federation	3–6	67	63	66	60	102	104	101	...	...	...	...	...	...
San Marino	3–5		...	...	...	...	...	...	...	...	...	...	...	...
Slovakia	3–5	81	78	...	...	101	102	101	...	...	...	...	...	...
Slovenia	3–6	...	57	58	56	♦99	98	98	...	...	...	...	...	...
Spain	2–5	44	65	64	66	104	103	105	12.5	14.7	12.6	14.4	12.4	15.0
Sweden	♦3–6	71	67	...	...	104	104	103	12.7	13.8	12.3	13.6	13.2	14.0
Switzerland	4–6	53	59	60	59	96	94	98	13.2	14.1	13.9	14.6	12.5	13.6
The FYR of Macedonia	3–6	...	21	21	21	♦91	91	90	...	...	...	...	...	...
Ukraine	♦3–5	60	75	...	...	97	99	95	...	...	...	...	...	...
United Kingdom	3–4	42	52	52	52	...	...	...	13.1	14.9	13.2	14.7	12.9	15.0
Yugoslavia	3–6	...	25	25	25	♦81	80	82	...	...	...	...	...	...
Former Yugoslavia	3–6	20	.	.	.	.	.	.	11.8	.	...	.	...	.
Oceania														
Australia	5–5	68	71	71	70	♦102	102	101	12.0	13.6	12.1	13.4	12.0	13.9
Fiji	3–5	9	15	15	16	♦116	118	114	...	...	...	...	...	...
Kiribati	4–5	...	...	...	...	...	...	...	...	...	...	...	...	...
New Zealand	♦2–4	73	81	82	80	♦100	102	99	13.4	15.4	13.6	15.2	13.2	15.5
Papua New Guinea	5–6	0	0	0	0	97	104	89	...	...	...	...	...	...
Samoa	...	...	...	...	...	...	...	...	10.5	...	10.5	...	10.4	...
Solomon Islands	...	...	...	...	...	110			...	...	...	...	...	...
Tonga	...	...	...	...	...	...	...	...	...	...	...	...	...	...
Tuvalu	...	...	...	...	...	...	...	...	...	...	...	...	...	...
Vanuatu	...	...	...	...	...	100	100	100	...	6.9	...	7.3	...	6.5

Table 4
First-level education: duration, population and enrolment ratios

Country or territory	Duration in years Compulsory education	Duration in years First-level education	School-age population (000) 1980	School-age population (000) 1992	Gross enrolment ratio (%) Total 1980	Total 1992	Male 1980	Male 1992	Female 1980	Female 1992	Net enrolment ratio (%) Total 1980	Total 1992	Male 1980	Male 1992	Female 1980	Female 1992
Africa																
Algeria	9	6	3 302	4 290	94	103	108	111	81	96	81	94	91	99	71	89
Angola	8	4	743	1 089	175	91	...	95	...	87	...	...	...	...	...	...
Benin	6	6	596	812	64	66	87	88	41	44	...	53	...	71	...	35
Botswana	–	7	189	260	91	116	83	113	100	120	75	97	69	93	82	100
Burkina Faso	6	6	1 099	1 474	18	38	23	47	14	30	15	31	19	38	11	24
Burundi	6	6	666	942	26	69	32	76	21	62	20	51	23	56	16	47
Cameroon	6	6	1 406	1 944	98	101	107	109	89	93	♦69	♦76	♦75	♦81	♦64	♦71
Cape Verde	6	6	50	55	114	122	119	125	110	119	90	100	93	100	88	99
Central African Republic	6	6	348	455	71	71	92	88	51	55	56	58	73	71	41	46
Chad	8	6	...	937	...	59	...	80	...	38	...	...	...	...	...	...
Comoros	9	6	68	103	88	75	100	81	75	69	♦65	51	...	55	...	46
Congo	10	6	...	...	...	...	...	...	...	...	...	...	...	...	...	...
Côte d'Ivoire	6	6	1 300	2 087	79	69	95	81	63	58	...	52	...	...	...	...
Djibouti	6	6	49	88	39	35	46	39	32	30	...	29	...	33	...	26
Egypt	8	♦5	6 375	7 964	73	97	84	105	61	89	...	89	...	95	...	82
Equatorial Guinea	8	6	33	...	135	...	...	...	...	...	...	...	...	...	...	...
Eritrea	7	4	...	445	...	47	...	52	...	41	...	26	...	27	...	24
Ethiopia	6	6	6 067	8 033	35	23	45	27	25	19	...	...	...	...	...	...
Gabon	10	6	...	...	...	...	...	...	...	...	...	...	...	...	...	...
Gambia	–	6	89	144	51	67	67	79	35	56	48	55	63	64	33	46
Ghana	9	6	1 804	2 635	80	76	89	83	71	70	...	...	...	...	...	...
Guinea	6	6	708	997	36	42	48	57	25	27	...	...	...	...	...	...
Guinea-Bissau	6	6	110	...	68	...	94	...	43	...	47	...	63	...	31	...
Kenya	–	♦8	3 409	6 017	115	92	120	93	110	91	91	...	92	...	89	...
Lesotho	7	7	239	354	102	102	85	94	120	111	66	68	54	61	78	75
Liberia	9	6	306	...	48	...	61	...	34	...	...	...	...	...	...	...
Libyan Arab Jamahiriya	9	♦9	...	1 189	...	106	...	107	...	104	...	97	...	98	...	96
Madagascar	5	5	1 268	1 971	136	76	139	77	133	74	...	...	...	...	...	...
Malawi	8	8	1 347	2 061	60	68	72	74	48	62	43	50	48	52	38	48
Mali	9	6	1 093	1 487	27	25	34	32	19	19	20	19	...	23	...	14
Mauritania	–	6	248	357	37	61	47	68	26	55	...	...	...	...	...	...
Mauritius	–	6	139	118	93	106	94	107	91	106	79	94	80	94	79	94
Morocco	6	♦6	2 617	3 746	83	73	102	85	63	60	62	63	75	73	47	53
Mozambique	7	♦5	1 321	1 992	99	60	114	69	84	52	36	42	39	47	33	37
Namibia	10	7	...	256	...	136	...	134	...	138	...	89	...	86	...	93
Niger	8	6	905	1 280	25	29	33	37	18	21	21	25	...	32	...	18
Nigeria	6	6	11 526	16 519	119	90	135	100	104	79	...	...	...	...	...	...
Rwanda	8	♦7	1 122	1 443	63	77	66	78	60	76	59	71	62	71	57	71
Sao Tome and Principe	4	4	...	...	...	...	...	...	...	...	...	...	...	...	...	...
Senegal	6	6	907	1 233	46	59	55	67	37	50	37	48	44	55	30	42
Seychelles	9	♦6	...	...	...	...	...	...	...	...	...	...	...	...	...	...
Sierra Leone	–	7	604	750	52	51	61	60	43	42	♦47	...	♦55	...	♦39	...
Somalia	8	8	1 438	...	19	...	24	...	14	...	14	...	18	...	10	...
South Africa	10	7	5 146	6 480	85	111	...	112	...	111	...	92	...	90	...	93
Sudan	–	6	2 932	4 163	50	52	59	59	41	45	...	...	...	...	...	...
Swaziland	–	7	109	154	103	117	104	120	102	114	80	93	...	93	...	93
Togo	6	6	441	652	113	102	137	122	89	81	76	69	91	80	60	58
Tunisia	11	6	1 022	1 227	103	116	118	122	88	110	83	96	93	100	72	93
Uganda	–	7	2 697	3 713	52	70	60	78	44	63	39	...	43	...	35	...
United Rep. of Tanzania	7	7	3 762	5 338	94	70	100	71	88	69	67	50	68	50	65	51

Country or territory	Duration in years		School-age population (000)		Gross enrolment ratio (%)						Net enrolment ratio (%)					
	Compulsory education	First-level education			Total		Male		Female		Total		Male		Female	
			1980	1992	1980	1992	1980	1992	1980	1992	1980	1992	1980	1992	1980	1992
Zaire	6	6	4 540	6 997	92	70	108	78	77	61	♦71	52	♦82	58	♦60	47
Zambia	7	7	1 159	1 593	90	92	97	...	83	...	77	...	81	...	73	...
Zimbabwe	8	7	1 491	1 941	115	119	120	120	110	117	100	...	100	...	100	...
America, North																
Antigua and Barbuda	11	6	...	...	...	...	...	...	...	...	...	...	...	...	...	...
Bahamas	10	6	33	33	98	101	96	100	100	103	...	94	...	93	...	96
Barbados	11	6	31	25	99	105	98	105	100	105	96	89	94	89	97	88
Belize	10	8	33	44	107	109	...	111	...	107	...	96	...	97	...	95
British Virgin Islands	10	7	...	...	...	...	...	...	...	...	...	...	...	...	...	...
Canada	10	6	2 181	2 333	105	105	106	106	105	104	96	98	96	98	96	97
Costa Rica	9	6	332	441	105	103	106	103	104	102	89	87	89	87	90	88
Cuba	6	6	1 388	920	106	102	109	103	103	102	95	97	95	97	95	98
Dominica	10	7														
Dominican Republic	8	♦8	946	1 375	121	97	120	95	123	99	73	81	73	79	73	83
El Salvador	9	9	1 114	1 313	75	78	75	78	75	79	...	70	...	70	...	71
Grenada	11	7	...	...	...	...	...	...	...	...	...	...	...	...	...	...
Guatemala	6	6	1 135	1 666	71	84	77	89	65	78	58	...	...	...	...	...
Haiti	6	6	841	993	76	56	82	58	70	54	38	26	38	25	37	26
Honduras	6	6	612	887	98	112	98	111	99	112	78	90	78	89	78	91
Jamaica	6	6	348	307	103	109	103	109	104	108	96	100	95	100	97	100
Mexico	6	6	12 058	12 772	122	113	122	114	121	111	...	100	...	...	...	...
Netherlands Antilles	–	6	...	...	...	...	...	...	...	...	...	...	...	...	...	...
Nicaragua	6	6	484	715	98	103	95	101	101	105	73	80	72	79	74	81
Panama	6	6	317	331	106	106	108	108	105	104	89	91	88	91	89	92
Saint Kitts and Nevis	12	7	...	...	...	...	...	...	...	...	...	...	...	...	...	...
Saint Lucia	10	7	...	...	...	...	...	...	...	...	...	...	...	...	...	...
Saint Vincent and the Grenadines	–	7	...	...	...	...	...	...	...	...	...	...	...	...	...	...
Trinidad and Tobago	6	7	168	208	100	95	100	95	100	95	92	88	92	88	93	88
United States	10	6	20 343	22 162	100	107	101	107	100	106	96	100	96	99	97	100
America, South																
Argentina	7	7	3 814	4 680	106	108	106	108	106	107	...	95	...	95	...	95
Bolivia	8	8	1 130	1 350	87	95	92	99	81	90	79	91	84	95	74	87
Brazil	8	8	22 858	27 041	99	111	101	...	97	...	81	90	...	...	...	...
Chile	8	8	2 010	2 064	109	99	110	99	108	98	...	86	...	87	...	84
Colombia	5	5	3 350	3 881	124	117	123	116	126	117	...	83	...	...	...	...
Ecuador	6	6	1 306	1 615	117	123	119	124	116	122	♦88	...	♦89	...	♦88	...
Guyana	8	6	126	...	103	...	104	...	102	...	94	...	95	...	94	...
Paraguay	6	6	501	686	104	109	107	111	100	108	87	97	88	98	86	96
Peru	6	6	2 836	3 283	115	119	117	...	112	...	91	88	93	...	89	...
Suriname	6	6	60	57	125	125	...	127	...	124	...	...	...	...	...	...
Uruguay	6	6	310	313	107	108	107	108	107	107	...	93	...	92	...	93
Venezuela	10	9	3 445	4 398	94	96	92	95	96	97	83	88	...	87	...	90
Asia																
Afghanistan	6	8	3 307	2 531	34	31	54	46	12	16	29	29	46	42	11	14
Armenia	...	3	...	216	...	90	...	87	...	93	...	...	...	...	...	...
Azerbaijan	11	4	...	637	...	87	...	87	...	86	...	...	...	...	...	...
Bahrain	–	6	46	63	104	110	111	109	97	111	80	100	84	99	76	100
Bangladesh	5	5	13 746	15 193	60	79	70	84	50	73	59	70	68	74	48	66
Bhutan	–	♦7	...	...	...	...	...	...	...	...	...	...	...	...	...	...

Table 4 *(continued)*

Country or territory	Duration in years — Compulsory education	First-level education	School-age population (000) 1980	1992	Gross enrolment ratio (%) Total 1980	1992	Male 1980	1992	Female 1980	1992	Net enrolment ratio (%) Total 1980	1992	Male 1980	1992	Female 1980	1992
Brunei Darussalam	9	6	28	38	109	105	111	108	106	102	82	86	83	87	82	86
Cambodia	6	6	...	...	...	...	...	...	...	...	...	...	...	...	...	...
China	9	5	129 902	101 330	113	120	121	124	104	117	...	96	...	98	...	95
Cyprus	9	6	...	...	104	102	104	101	104	102	100	98	100	98	100	99
Dem. People's Rep. of Korea	10	4	...	...	...	...	...	...	...	...	...	...	...	...	...	...
Georgia	...	...	...	...	...	...	...	...	...	...	...	...	...	...	...	...
Hong Kong	9	6	507	509	107	102	107	...	106	...	95	...	95	...	96	...
India	8	5	88 726	104 455	83	101	98	112	67	89	...	...	...	...	...	...
Indonesia	6	6	23 812	25 895	107	114	115	116	100	112	88	97	93	99	83	95
Iran, Islamic Rep. of	5	5	5 763	8 816	92	111	107	117	75	105	...	97	...	100	...	93
Iraq	6	6	2 308	3 157	113	91	119	98	107	83	99	79	100	83	94	74
Israel	11	8	636	801	95	95	94	95	96	96	...	...	...	...	...	...
Japan	9	6	11 699	9 115	101	100	101	100	101	101	100	100	100	100	100	100
Jordan	10	♦10	439	1 074	104	94	105	94	102	95	93	89	94	89	91	89
Kazakstan	11	4	...	1 431	...	86	...	86	...	86	...	...	...	...	...	...
Kuwait	8	4	146	205	102	60	105	60	100	60	85	...	89	...	80	...
Kyrgyzstan	...	...	...	...	...	...	...	...	...	...	...	...	...	...	...	...
Lao People's Dem. Rep.	8	5	422	613	113	104	123	119	104	89	...	64	...	71	...	57
Lebanon	–	5	356	292	112	118	116	120	108	116	...	...	...	...	...	...
Malaysia	9	6	2 168	2 838	93	93	93	93	92	94	...	...	...	...	...	...
Maldives	–	5	...	35	...	130	...	132	...	128	...	...	...	...	...	...
Mongolia	8	3	135	171	107	97	107	95	107	100	...	...	...	...	...	...
Myanmar	5	5	4 562	5 111	91	105	93	107	89	104	...	...	...	...	...	...
Nepal	5	♦5	1 266	2 783	84	109	117	130	49	87	...	...	...	...	...	...
Oman	–	6	175	336	52	86	69	90	36	83	44	73	56	74	32	71
Pakistan	–	5	12 185	17 737	39	44	51	57	27	30	...	...	...	...	...	...
Palestine																
Gaza Strip	...	6	...	...	...	...	...	...	...	...	...	...	...	...	...	...
West Bank	...	6	...	...	...	...	...	...	...	...	...	...	...	...	...	...
Philippines	6	6	7 601	9 546	112	112	114	...	110	...	94	99	95	...	92	...
Qatar	–	6	29	55	105	89	108	91	103	86	85	79	88	80	83	78
Republic of Korea	6	6	5 148	4 406	110	103	109	103	111	104	100	100	100	100	100	100
Saudi Arabia	–	6	1 511	2 686	61	75	74	78	49	73	49	61	60	65	37	57
Singapore	–	6	271	244	108	107	109	...	106	...	99	...	100	...	99	...
Sri Lanka	10	♦5	2 023	1 956	103	105	105	106	100	104	...	...	...	...	...	...
Syrian Arab Republic	6	6	1 562	2 412	100	107	111	112	88	101	89	96	99	100	80	92
Tajikistan	9	4	...	609	...	85	...	87	...	84	...	...	...	...	...	...
Thailand	6	6	7 477	6 915	99	99	100	...	97	...	...	...	...	...	...	...
Turkey	5	5	5 869	6 539	96	103	102	107	90	98	...	93	...	...	...	...
Turkmenistan	...	...	...	...	...	...	...	...	...	...	...	...	...	...	...	...
United Arab Emirates	6	6	100	216	89	110	90	111	88	109	74	100	72	100	75	99
Uzbekistan	...	4	...	2 329	...	80	...	80	...	79	...	...	...	...	...	...
Viet Nam	5	5	7 251	8 737	109	108	111	...	106	...	95	...	...	...	...	...
Yemen	...	...														
Former Dem. Yemen	8	8	411	.	65	.	93	.	36	.	.	.	.	.	.	.
Former Yemen Arab Rep.	6	6	1 199	.	38	.	65	.	10	.	.	.	.	.	.	.
Europe																
Albania	8	8	488	558	113	96	116	95	111	97	...	...	...	...	...	...
Austria	9	4	406	369	99	104	99	104	98	104	87	90	87	89	88	91
Belarus	11	♦4	720	660	104	96	...	96	...	96	...	...	...	...	...	...
Belgium	12	6	810	716	104	99	104	99	103	100	97	96	97	95	98	97

Country or territory	Duration in years		School-age population (000)		Gross enrolment ratio (%)						Net enrolment ratio (%)					
	Compulsory education	First-level education			Total		Male		Female		Total		Male		Female	
			1980	1992	1980	1992	1980	1992	1980	1992	1980	1992	1980	1992	1980	1992
Bosnia and Herzegovina	...	...	...	...	...	...	...	...	...	...	...	...	...	...	...	...
Bulgaria	8	8	1 016	984	98	89	98	90	98	88	96	80	96	80	96	79
Croatia	8	8	...	509	...	86	...	86	...	85	...	80	...	80	...	80
Czech Republic	9	4	...	535	...	99	...	99	...	99	...	...	...	...	...	...
Former Czechoslovakia	10	8	2 080	.	92	.	91	.	92	.	...	.	...	.	...	.
Denmark	9	6	455	333	96	98	96	97	95	98	96	98	96	97	95	98
Estonia	9	6	...	140	...	85	...	86	...	85	...	80	...	81	...	80
Finland	9	6	388	391	96	100	97	100	96	100	...	...	...	...	...	...
France	10	5	4 087	3 841	111	106	112	107	110	105	100	99	100	99	99	99
Germany	12	4	.	3 555	.	98	.	97	.	98	.	81	.	80	.	83
Former German Dem. Rep.	10	4	792	.	108	.	109	.	106	.	...	.	...	.	...	.
Germany, Federal Rep. of	12	4	2 809	.	99	.	99	.	99	.	82	.	81	.	83	.
Greece	9	6	875	834	103	98	103	97	103	98	96	94	96	93	97	94
Hungary	10	8	1 206	1 059	96	95	96	95	97	95	95	92	94	91	95	92
Iceland	8	6	25	25	101	100	101	102	101	98	...	...	...	...	...	...
Ireland	9	6	421	388	100	103	100	103	100	103	90	90	89	89	91	90
Italy	8	5	4 425	2 971	100	100	100	98	100	101	...	...	...	...	...	...
Latvia	9	4	...	157	...	85	...	86	...	84	...	81	...	82	...	80
Lithuania	9	4	...	230	...	92	...	95	...	90	...	...	...	...	...	...
Luxembourg	9	6	28	26	87	91	86	88	88	94	77	...	76	...	78	...
Malta	10	6	29	33	113	108	114	109	112	106	98	100	99	100	98	99
Monaco	10	5	...	...	...	...	...	...	...	...	...	...	...	...	...	...
Netherlands	11	6	1 331	1 075	100	97	99	96	101	99	93	94	91	92	94	96
Norway	9	6	392	308	100	100	100	100	100	100	98	99	98	99	99	99
Poland	8	8	4 185	5 337	100	98	100	99	99	97	98	96	98	96	98	96
Portugal	9	6	1 006	838	123	120	124	122	123	118	98	100	97	100	100	100
Republic of Moldova	11	4	...	340	...	78	...	78	...	78	...	...	...	...	...	...
Romania	8	♦4	3 187	1 395	102	86	102	87	101	86	...	77	...	77	...	76
Russian Federation	9	3	5 882	7 181	102	109	102	109	102	109	...	♦96	...	♦96	...	♦96
San Marino	8	5	...	...	...	...	...	...	...	...	...	...	...	...	...	...
Slovakia	9	4	...	348	...	101	...	101	...	101	...	...	...	...	...	...
Slovenia	8	4	...	109	...	96	...	96	...	96	...	...	...	...	...	...
Spain	10	5	3 311	2 431	109	105	110	105	109	105	100	100	100	99	100	100
Sweden	9	6	682	588	97	101	97	101	97	101	97	100	96	100	97	100
Switzerland	8-9	6	...	463	...	102	...	101 *	...	103	...	94	...	93	...	95
The FYR of Macedonia	8	8	...	295	...	89	...	89	...	88	...	84	...	85	...	84
Ukraine	11	♦6	3 512	4 538	102	90	...	91	...	90	...	...	...	...	...	...
United Kingdom	11	6	4 774	4 409	103	103	103	103	103	104	97	100	96	100	97	100
Yugoslavia	8	4	...	648	...	72	...	71	...	73	...	69	...	69	...	70
Former Yugoslavia	8	4	1 431	.	100	.	100	.	100	.	80	.	...	.	...	.
Oceania																
Australia	10-11	6	1 534	1 501	112	108	113	108	111	108	100	99	100	99	100	99
Fiji	–	6	97	114	119	128	119	128	119	127	92	99	92	99	92	100
Kiribati	9	7	...	...	...	...	...	...	...	...	...	...	...	...	...	...
New Zealand	11	6	343	311	111	102	111	103	111	101	100	99	100	99	100	98
Papua New Guinea	–	6	509	600	59	74	66	80	51	67	...	...	...	...	...	...
Samoa	–	7	36	36	88	107	87	106	90	107	83	...	81	...	85	...
Solomon Islands	–	6	38	59	76	90	85	97	65	82	...	...	...	...	...	...
Tonga	6	6	...	...	...	...	...	...	...	...	...	...	...	...	...	...
Tuvalu	9	7	...	...	...	...	...	...	...	...	...	...	...	...	...	...
Vanuatu	–	6	...	27	...	106	...	105	...	107	...	...	...	...	...	...

Table 5
First-level education: internal efficiency

Country or territory	Percentage of repeaters						Percentage of 1991 cohort reaching					
	Total		Male		Female		Grade 2			Grade 5		
	1980	1992	1980	1992	1980	1992	Total	Male	Female	Total	Male	Female
Africa												
Algeria	12	9	12	11	11	7	99	98	99	93	93	92
Angola	29	33	...	...	...	...	76	...	...	34	...	...
Benin	20	23	19	23	22	24	84	84	84	55	54	56
Botswana	3	3	...	4	...	3	92	92	93	84	82	86
Burkina Faso	17	17	17	17	18	17	100	100	100	70	65	78
Burundi	30	24	30	24	30	23	89	89	88	74	74	75
Cameroon	30	29	30	30	30	28	83	81	85	66	63	69
Cape Verde	29	19	29	20	29	18	98	...	...	60	...	...
Central African Republic	35	31	34	31	37	32	90	90	90	65	66	63
Chad	...	32	...	32	...	34	79	82	73	49	57	33
Comoros	25	39	...	39	...	39	90	...	...	78	...	...
Congo	26	36	26	37	25	35	100	100	100	72	72	70
Côte d'Ivoire	20	25	20	26	20	25	91	91	90	73	75	70
Djibouti	...	14	...	...	...	...	100	...	...	98	...	...
Egypt	8	8	7	8	9	6	100	100	100	98	98	97
Equatorial Guinea	...	...	...	...	...	...	...	...	...	...	...	...
Eritrea	...	20	...	18	...	23	88	89	86	83	85	80
Ethiopia	12	...	11	...	14	...	◆55	57	53	22	22	21
Gabon	35	33	35	33	34	34	...	...	...	...	...	...
Gambia	13	14	14	15	13	14	90	90	90	87	85	89
Ghana	2	3	2	3	2	3	90	90	90	80	81	79
Guinea	22	21	...	19	...	23	97	98	95	80	82	75
Guinea-Bissau	29	...	28	...	30	...	...	...	...	...	...	...
Kenya	13	...	13	...	13	...	89	89	88	77	74	78
Lesotho	21	21	22	24	20	19	83	81	85	60	54	66
Liberia	...	...	...	...	...	...	...	...	...	...	...	...
Libyan Arab Jamahiriya	9	...	10	...	8	...	...	...	...	...	...	...
Madagascar	...	33	...	34	...	32	66	66	67	28	26	30
Malawi	17	18	18	19	17	18	73	75	71	46	48	44
Mali	30	25	29	26	30	25	94	93	96	76	76	77
Mauritania	14	16	13	16	17	17	88	89	88	72	74	69
Mauritius	...	8	...	8	...	8	100	100	100	100	100	99
Morocco	30	12	30	14	28	11	93	94	93	80	80	80
Mozambique	29	25	27	25	31	26	81	86	75	35	39	31
Namibia	...	25	...	26	...	23	79	78	80	64	62	67
Niger	14	18	15	...	14	...	96	96	96	82	83	81
Nigeria	...	...	...	...	...	...	◆88	88	89	87	83	84
Rwanda	6	14	6	15	6	14	86	86	87	59	58	60
Sao Tome and Principe	30	30	...	...	...	...	...	...	...	...	...	...
Senegal	16	16	15	16	16	16	97	98	97	88	92	83
Seychelles	–	–	–	–	–	–	100	99	100	97	99	92
Sierra Leone	15	...	...	...	...	...	...	...	...	...	...	...
Somalia	...	...	...	...	...	...	...	...	...	...	...	...
South Africa	...	12	...	14	...	11	◆80	79	81	71	68	74
Sudan	–	–	–	–	–	–	100	99	100	94	90	95
Swaziland	11	15	12	17	9	13	92	91	92	77	74	80
Togo	36	37	34	37	38	38	89	91	86	70	76	57
Tunisia	21	19	22	20	19	17	99	99	98	90	91	91
Uganda	10	...	...	...	...	...	◆75	...	...	55	...	...
United Rep. of Tanzania	1	3	1	3	1	4	94	93	94	83	81	86

Country or territory	Percentage of repeaters						Percentage of 1991 cohort reaching					
	Total		Male		Female		Grade 2			Grade 5		
	1980	1992	1980	1992	1980	1992	Total	Male	Female	Total	Male	Female
Zaire	19	21	19	21	19	21	84	86	81	64	73	54
Zambia	2	...	2	...	2	...	...	...	...	...	...	...
Zimbabwe	–	–	–	–	–	–	88	86	90	76	72	81
America, North												
Antigua and Barbuda	...	3	...	3	...	3	...	...	...	...	...	...
Bahamas	–	–	–	–	–	–	...	...	...	...	...	...
Barbados	–	–	–	–	–	–	...	...	...	...	...	...
Belize	...	7	...	8	...	6	◆76	77	74	69	70	68
British Virgin Islands	...	...	...	...	...	...	...	...	...	...	...	...
Canada	...	...	...	...	...	...	◆97	96	100	96	90	100
Costa Rica	8	10	9	11	7	8	96	95	96	86	84	87
Cuba	6	3	...	...	...	...	100	...	...	95	...	...
Dominica	...	...	...	...	...	...	◆97	98	97	93	90	94
Dominican Republic	18	...	...	...	...	...	...	...	...	...	...	...
El Salvador	9	7	9	7	8	6	76	75	77	58	58	59
Grenada	...	...	...	...	...	...	...	...	...	...	...	...
Guatemala	15	16	...	17	...	16	...	...	...	47	47	46
Haiti	21	13	21	13	21	13	80	80	80	...	...	...
Honduras	16	12	17	13	15	11	...	...	...	...	...	...
Jamaica	4	4	4	4	4	3	100	100	100	96	93	99
Mexico	10	9	...	...	...	...	◆94	91	91	84	77	78
Netherlands Antilles	...	...	...	...	...	...	...	...	...	...	...	...
Nicaragua	17	17	18	18	16	16	78	76	80	55	51	57
Panama	13	10	15	12	11	8	◆92	92	93	82	80	84
Saint Kitts and Nevis	–	–	–	–	–	–	...	...	...	...	...	...
Saint Lucia	3	...	3	...	3	...	◆100	100	99	96	94	95
Saint Vincent and the Grenadines	...	15	...	17	...	13	...	...	...	...	...	...
Trinidad and Tobago	4	4	4	4	4	4	100	100	100	95	95	95
United States	...	...	...	...	...	...	...	...	...	...	...	...
America, South												
Argentina	...	...	...	...	...	...	◆84	85	83	60	63	58
Bolivia	...	3	...	3	...	3	◆84	85	83	60	63	58
Brazil	20	17	...	...	...	...	◆80	...	...	72	...	...
Chile	...	...	...	...	...	...	◆98	98	98	95	94	96
Colombia	13	11	14	12	12	11	72	...	...	59	...	...
Ecuador	11	...	12	...	10	...	...	...	...	...	...	...
Guyana	3	...	...	...	...	...	...	...	...	...	...	...
Paraguay	14	9	15	10	12	8	93	93	94	74	73	75
Peru	19	...	19	...	18	...	...	...	...	...	...	...
Suriname	22	...	...	...	...	...	...	...	...	...	...	...
Uruguay	15	10	17	12	13	8	100	100	100	95	94	97
Venezuela	11	11	...	13	...	9	92	91	93	78	75	82
Asia												
Afghanistan	15	9	15	9	16	9	◆88	88	89	43	39	52
Armenia	...	...	...	...	...	...	...	...	...	...	...	...
Azerbaijan	...	0	...	0	...	0	...	...	...	...	...	...
Bahrain	11	5	12	5	10	5	100	100	100	99	98	100
Bangladesh	...	7	...	...	...	...	66	...	...	47	...	...
Bhutan	13	19	13	19	12	18	...	...	...	...	...	...

Table 5 (continued)

Country or territory	Percentage of repeaters						Percentage of 1991 cohort reaching					
	Total		Male		Female		Grade 2			Grade 5		
	1980	1992	1980	1992	1980	1992	Total	Male	Female	Total	Male	Female
Brunei Darussalam	13	10	15	...	10	...	100	...	...	100	...	...
Cambodia	...	...	...	...	...	...	...	...	...	...	...	...
China	...	5	...	...	...	...	98	...	...	88	...	...
Cyprus	1	0	1	0	1	0	100	100	100	100	100	100
Dem. People's Rep. of Korea	...	...	...	...	...	...	...	...	...	...	...	...
Georgia	...	...	...	...	...	...	...	...	...	...	...	...
Hong Kong	4	...	4	...	3	...	...	...	...	...	...	...
India	...	...	...	...	...	...	...	...	...	...	...	...
Indonesia	8	9	...	...	...	...	98	...	...	86	...	...
Iran, Islamic Rep. of	...	7	...	8	...	6	96	96	96	89	90	88
Iraq	23	17	25	19	21	14	...	...	...	...	...	...
Israel	...	...	...	...	...	...	♦100	100	100	100	100	100
Japan	–	–	–	–	–	–	100	100	100	100	100	100
Jordan	3	4	3	5	3	4	99	99	99	98	98	99
Kazakstan	...	1	...	1	...	1	...	...	...	...	...	...
Kuwait	6	4	6	4	6	4	...	...	...	...	...	...
Kyrgyzstan	...	...	...	...	...	...	...	...	...	...	...	...
Lao People's Dem. Rep.	...	28	...	29	...	26	76	77	75	53	55	50
Lebanon	...	...	...	...	...	...	...	...	...	...	...	...
Malaysia	–	–	–	–	–	–	100	100	100	98	98	98
Maldives	...	...	...	...	...	...	...	...	...	...	...	...
Mongolia	2	...	...	...	...	...	...	...	...	...	...	...
Myanmar	...	...	...	...	...	...	...	...	...	...	...	...
Nepal	...	27	...	28	...	24	65	68	62	52	52	52
Oman	12	8	14	10	9	7	100	100	100	96	96	96
Pakistan	...	...	...	...	...	...	♦67	70	61	48	48	48
Palestine												
Gaza Strip	...	...	...	...	...	...	...	...	...	...	...	...
West Bank	...	3	...	3	...	4	♦100	100	99	100	100	99
Philippines	2	2	3	...	2	...	87	...	...	75	...	...
Qatar	13	6	12	8	13	4	100	99	100	98	96	100
Republic of Korea	–	–	–	–	–	–	100	100	100	100	100	100
Saudi Arabia	16	11	19	14	10	8	98	98	98	96	96	95
Singapore	7	...	8	...	6	...	♦100	100	100	100	100	100
Sri Lanka	10	7	...	8	...	6	98	98	98	92	92	93
Syrian Arab Republic	8	7	9	8	7	6	98	98	98	92	94	91
Tajikistan	...	1	...	...	...	...	...	...	...	...	...	...
Thailand	8	...	9	...	7	...	♦95	...	...	88	...	...
Turkey	...	6	...	6	...	6	98	98	99	92	92	93
Turkmenistan	...	...	...	...	...	...	...	...	...	...	...	...
United Arab Emirates	9	6	9	7	9	5	99	100	98	99	100	98
Uzbekistan	...	0	...	...	...	...	...	...	...	...	...	...
Viet Nam	...	...	...	...	...	...	...	...	...	...	...	...
Yemen	.	.	.	.	.	.	.	.	.	.	.	.
Former Dem. Yemen	...	.	...	.	...	.	.	.	.	.	.	.
Former Yemen Arab Rep.	25	.	29	.	3	.	.	.	.	.	.	.
Europe												
Albania	...	...	...	...	...	...	100	100	100	98	97	98
Austria	...	...	...	...	...	...	97	97	98	97	96	98
Belarus	0	1	...	1	...	1	99	...	...	99	...	...
Belgium	19	16	21	17	18	14	...	...	...	...	...	...

Country or territory	Percentage of repeaters						Percentage of 1991 cohort reaching					
	Total		Male		Female		Grade 2			Grade 5		
	1980	1992	1980	1992	1980	1992	Total	Male	Female	Total	Male	Female
Bosnia and Herzegovina	...	...	...	...	...	...	...	...	...	...	...	...
Bulgaria	2	6	2	7	1	4	94	94	94	88	88	88
Croatia	...	1	...	...	...	...	100	...	...	100	...	...
Czech Republic	...	1	...	2	...	1	97	96	97	95	94	96
Former Czechoslovakia	1	.	1	.	1	.	.	.	.	.	.	.
Denmark	–	–	–	–	–	–	100	100	100	100	100	100
Estonia	...	3	...	4	...	2	99	99	100	93	92	94
Finland	...	0	...	1	...	0	100	100	100	100	100	100
France	9	4	...	...	...	...	99	99	99	...	...	...
Germany	.	2	.	2	.	2	♦100	100	100	99	99	100
Former German Dem. Rep.	...	.	...	.	...	.	.	.	.	.	.	.
Germany, Federal Rep. of	2	.	3	.	2	.	.	.	.	.	.	.
Greece	1	...	1	...	1	...	99	99	99	99	99	99
Hungary	2	3	3	...	2	...	98	...	...	97	...	...
Iceland	...	...	...	...	...	...	...	...	...	...	...	...
Ireland	...	2	...	2	...	2	100	100	100	100	100	100
Italy	1	1	2	1	1	1	100	100	100	100	100	100
Latvia	...	...	...	...	...	...	...	...	...	...	...	...
Lithuania	...	3	...	...	...	...	97	...	...	94	...	...
Luxembourg	6	...	7	...	5	...	...	...	...	...	...	...
Malta	2	2	2	2	2	1	100	100	99	100	100	99
Monaco	...	6	...	6	...	6	...	...	...	...	...	...
Netherlands	3	...	3	...	2	...	...	...	...	...	...	...
Norway	–	–	–	–	–	–	100	100	100	100	100	100
Poland	2	1	...	...	...	...	99	...	...	98	...	...
Portugal	...	14	...	16	...	12	...	...	...	...	...	...
Republic of Moldova	...	...	...	...	...	...	...	...	...	...	...	...
Romania	...	4	...	5	...	3	97	97	97	93	93	93
Russian Federation	...	2	...	2	...	2	96	95	96	...	...	...
San Marino	1	0	...	1	...	–	100	...	...	100	...	...
Slovakia	...	2	...	2	...	2	98	98	98	97	97	98
Slovenia	...	1	...	...	...	...	100	...	...	100	...	...
Spain	6	...	7	...	6	...	♦100	100	100	96	96	97
Sweden	–	–	–	–	–	–	99	98	99	98	97	98
Switzerland	2	2	2	2	2	2	100	100	100	100	100	100
The FYR of Macedonia	...	2	...	...	...	...	99	...	...	95	...	...
Ukraine	0	1	...	1	...	1	...	...	...	...	...	...
United Kingdom	–	–	–	–	–	–	...	...	...	...	...	...
Yugoslavia	...	2	...	...	...	...	...	...	...	...	...	...
Former Yugoslavia	2	.	...	.	...	.	.	.	.	.	.	.
Oceania												
Australia	...	...	...	...	...	...	♦99	99	99	99	98	99
Fiji	5	...	6	...	4	...	♦92	94	90	87	88	84
Kiribati	5	0	5	0	4	0	94	90	97	83	78	89
New Zealand	4	4	4	4	3	4	97	98	98	94	95	95
Papua New Guinea	–	–	–	–	–	–	88	90	87	69	70	68
Samoa	...	...	...	...	...	...	...	...	...	...	...	...
Solomon Islands	5	6	5	...	5	...	♦90	91	89	84	86	83
Tonga	9	8	10	8	9	8	100	99	100	84	85	75
Tuvalu	...	–	...	–	...	–	...	...	...	...	...	...
Vanuatu	...	13	...	14	...	11	92	93	91	61	62	60

Table 6
Second-level education: duration, population and enrolment ratios

Country or territory	Duration in years of second-level general education		School-age population (000)		Gross enrolment ratio (%)						Net enrolment ratio (%)					
					Total		Male		Female		Total		Male		Female	
	1st stage	2nd stage	1980	1992	1980	1992	1980	1992	1980	1992	1980	1992	1980	1992	1980	1992
Africa																
Algeria	♦3	3	3 115	3 792	33	61	40	66	26	55	31	55	37	59	24	50
Angola	♦4	3	968	1 513	14	12	20	...	9	...	11	...	14	...	7	...
Benin	4	3	546	722	16	12	24	17	9	7	...	...	...	...	...	...
Botswana	2	3	112	156	19	52	17	49	20	55	14	42	12	38	17	45
Burkina Faso	4	3	1 029	1 372	3	8	4	11	2	6	2	7	3	10	2	5
Burundi	4	3	671	841	3	7	4	8	2	5	2	5	3	6	2	4
Cameroon	4	3	1 282	1 817	18	28	24	32	13	23	15	...	19	...	11	...
Cape Verde	3	2	42	39	8	20	9	21	7	20	...	...	...	...	...	...
Central African Republic	4	3	331	424	14	12	21	17	7	6	...	...	...	...	...	...
Chad	4	3	...	883	...	9	...	...	...	...	...	...	...	...	...	...
Comoros	4	3	61	93	23	19	30	21	15	17	...	...	...	...	...	...
Congo	4	3	...	...	...	...	...	...	...	...	...	...	...	...	...	...
Côte d'Ivoire	4	3	1 147	1 801	19	24	27	32	12	16	...	...	...	...	...	...
Djibouti	4	3	46	85	12	11	16	13	9	10	...	...	...	...	...	...
Egypt	3	3	5 804	8 112	50	76	61	81	39	69	...	65	...	70	...	60
Equatorial Guinea	4	2	...	...	...	...	...	...	...	...	...	...	...	...	...	...
Eritrea	2	4	...	444	...	15	...	17	...	13	...	11	...	12	...	10
Ethiopia	2	4	5 038	6 514	9	11	11	12	6	11	...	...	...	...	...	...
Gabon	4	3	...	...	...	...	...	...	...	...	...	...	...	...	...	...
Gambia	5	2	84	138	11	19	16	25	7	13	...	18	...	24	...	12
Ghana	4	3	1 696	2 376	41	36	51	44	31	28	...	...	...	...	...	...
Guinea	♦4	3	576	914	17	12	24	17	10	6	...	...	...	...	...	...
Guinea-Bissau	3	2	78	...	6	...	10	...	2	...	3	...	4	...	1	...
Kenya	♦.	4	2 186	2 443	20	27	23	30	16	24	...	...	...	...	...	...
Lesotho	3	2	142	207	18	26	14	21	21	31	13	16	9	11	17	22
Liberia	3	3	249	...	22	...	31	...	12	...	...	...	...	...	...	...
Libyan Arab Jamahiriya	♦.	3	...	320	...	97	...	...	...	...	...	...	...	...	...	...
Madagascar	4	3	...	2 165	...	15	...	15	...	15	...	...	...	...	...	...
Malawi	2	2	537	799	3	4	5	5	2	3	...	2	...	2	...	2
Mali	3	3	892	1 209	9	7	12	10	5	5	...	♦5	...	♦7	...	♦3
Mauritania	3	3	203	296	11	15	17	19	4	10	...	...	...	...	...	...
Mauritius	3	4	164	153	50	59	51	58	49	60	...	...	...	...	...	...
Morocco	♦3	3	3 088	3 536	26	35	32	40	20	29	20	29	25	33	16	24
Mozambique	♦2	5	1 968	2 210	5	7	8	9	3	6	4	7	5	8	2	5
Namibia	.	5	...	153	...	55	...	49	...	61	...	30	...	26	...	35
Niger	4	3	836	1 161	5	7	7	9	3	4	4	6	5	8	2	3
Nigeria	♦3	3	11 327	13 225	21	27	27	30	14	25	...	...	...	...	...	...
Rwanda	♦.	6	624	960	3	10	4	11	3	9	...	8	...	9	...	7
Sao Tome and Principe	4	3	...	...	...	...	...	...	...	...	...	...	...	...	...	...
Senegal	4	3	844	1 149	11	17	15	22	7	12	...	...	...	...	...	...
Seychelles	♦.	5	...	...	...	...	...	...	...	...	...	...	...	...	...	...
Sierra Leone	5	2	479	606	14	17	20	22	8	12	...	...	...	...	...	...
Somalia	.	4	574	...	8	...	11	...	4	...	4	...	6	...	2	...
South Africa	3	2	...	4 118	...	71	...	66	...	77	...	46	...	43	...	49
Sudan	3	3	2 406	3 369	16	21	20	24	12	19	...	...	...	...	...	...
Swaziland	3	2	62	98	38	53	39	54	37	52	...	...	...	...	...	...
Togo	4	3	412	599	32	23	47	34	16	12	...	...	...	...	...	...
Tunisia	3	4	1 074	1 270	27	46	34	51	20	42	23	43	28	46	18	40
Uganda	4	2	1 792	2 566	5	11	7	14	3	8	...	...	...	...	...	...
United Rep. of Tanzania	4	2	2 474	3 650	3	5	4	6	2	5	...	...	...	...	...	...

Country or territory	Duration in years of second-level general education		School-age population (000)		Gross enrolment ratio (%)						Net enrolment ratio (%)					
					Total		Male		Female		Total		Male		Female	
	1st stage	2nd stage	1980	1992	1980	1992	1980	1992	1980	1992	1980	1992	1980	1992	1980	1992
Zaire	2	4	3 587	5 414	24	23	35	31	13	14	...	16	...	21	...	12
Zambia	2	3	635	...	16	...	22	...	11	...	...	...	...	...	...	...
Zimbabwe	.	6	1 009	1 389	15	47	17	53	12	41	...	...	...	...	...	...
America, North																
Antigua and Barbuda	3	2	...	...	...	...	...	...	...	...	...	89	...	88	...	89
Bahamas	3	3	32	31	86	95	80	95	91	95	...	89	...	88	...	89
Barbados	3	3	32	27	89	88	90	93	89	83	86	81	86	87	85	75
Belize	.	4	15	20	38	47	34	46	42	48	...	36	...	35	...	37
British Virgin Islands	3	2	...	...	...	...	...	...	...	...	...	...	...	...	...	...
Canada	3	3	2 572	2 308	91	104	90	104	92	103	83	90	82	90	84	90
Costa Rica	3	2	286	321	48	43	44	42	51	45	39	37	36	35	43	38
Cuba	3	3	1 421	1 003	81	82	79	77	83	87	...	...	...	...	...	...
Dominica	.	5	...	...	...	...	...	...	...	...	...	...	...	...	...	...
Dominican Republic	♦.	4	875	635	43	37	...	30	...	43	...	24	...	20	...	29
El Salvador	.	3	299	397	24	26	26	25	23	28	...	...	...	...	...	...
Grenada	.	5	...	...	...	...	...	...	...	...	...	...	...	...	...	...
Guatemala	3	3	934	1 386	18	24	20	25	17	23	13	...	...	...	...	...
Haiti	3	3	737	871	14	22	14	22	13	21	...	...	...	...	...	...
Honduras	3	2	424	588	30	33	29	29	31	37	...	21	...	...	...	...
Jamaica	3	4	372	358	67	66	63	62	71	70	64	64	61	61	68	68
Mexico	3	3	9 800	12 159	48	56	51	56	46	56	...	♦46	...	...	...	...
Netherlands Antilles	.	5	...	...	...	...	...	...	...	...	...	...	...	...	...	...
Nicaragua	3	2	330	493	42	41	39	39	45	44	23	26	21	25	25	28
Panama	3	3	280	313	61	63	58	60	65	65	46	51	43	48	49	53
Saint Kitts and Nevis	4	2	...	...	...	...	...	...	...	...	...	...	...	...	...	...
Saint Lucia	3	2	...	...	...	...	...	...	...	...	...	...	...	...	...	...
Saint Vincent and the Grenadines	5	2	...	...	...	...	...	...	...	...	...	...	...	...	...	...
Trinidad and Tobago	3	2	125	128	74	78	74	77	74	80	64	65	64	64	64	67
United States	.	6	23 721	21 170	91	97	...	98	...	97	...	90	...	89	...	90
America, South																
Argentina	3	2	2 382	3 126	57	72	53	70	62	75	...	59	...	55	...	62
Bolivia	.	4	465	599	37	37	42	40	32	34	16	29	18	32	14	27
Brazil	.	3	8 399	9 402	34	43	31	...	36	...	14	19	13	...	16	...
Chile	2	2	1 030	975	52	69	49	67	56	72	...	52	...	50	...	55
Colombia	4	2	4 250	4 383	41	61	40	56	41	67	...	44	...	...	...	...
Ecuador	3	3	1 109	1 482	53	55	53	54	53	56	...	...	...	...	...	...
Guyana	4	3	143	...	55	...	54	...	56	...	...	...	...	...	...	...
Paraguay	3	3	449	562	26	34	...	34	...	35	...	29	...	28	...	29
Peru	2	3	2 091	2 648	59	65	62	...	55	...	46	46	48	...	43	...
Suriname	4	3	69	...	35	...	...	...	...	...	...	...	...	...	...	...
Uruguay	3	3	291	330	62	83	61	...	62	...	...	...	...	...	...	...
Venezuela	.	2	1 073	859	21	35	18	29	25	41	14	20	11	16	16	24
Asia																
Afghanistan	.	4	1 346	2 216	10	15	16	22	4	8	...	...	...	...	...	...
Armenia	.	7	...	447	...	85	...	80	...	90	...	...	...	...	...	...
Azerbaijan	5	2	...	967	...	92	...	92	...	93	...	...	...	...	...	...
Bahrain	3	3	41	52	64	99	70	97	58	101	55	85	58	84	51	87
Bangladesh	5	2	15 656	18 627	15	19	24	25	6	13	15	17	23	22	6	12
Bhutan	2	2	...	...	...	...	...	...	...	...	...	...	...	...	...	...

Table 6 (continued)

Country or territory	Duration in years of second-level general education		School-age population (000)		Gross enrolment ratio (%)						Net enrolment ratio (%)					
					Total		Male		Female		Total		Male		Female	
	1st stage	2nd stage	1980	1992	1980	1992	1980	1992	1980	1992	1980	1992	1980	1992	1980	1992
Brunei Darussalam	5	2	29	39	61	69	59	65	63	73	51	60	48	56	54	64
Cambodia	4	3	...	...	...	...	...	...	...	...	...	...	...	...	...	...
China	3	2	123 654	99 658	46	54	54	59	37	48	...	...	...	...	...	...
Cyprus	3	3	...	...	95	98	95	96	95	101	87	94	86	92	88	96
Dem. People's Rep. of Korea	.	6	...	...	...	...	...	...	...	...	...	...	...	...	...	...
Georgia	...	...	...	...	...	...	...	...	...	...	...	...	...	...	...	...
Hong Kong	5	2	731	...	64	...	63	...	65	...	61	...	59	...	62	...
India	3	4	109 687	129 605	30	49	39	60	20	37	...	...	...	...	...	...
Indonesia	3	3	19 725	25 236	29	43	35	48	23	39	...	37	...	41	...	34
Iran, Islamic Rep. of	3	4	6 709	9 859	42	57	51	65	33	48	...	...	...	...	...	...
Iraq	3	3	1 812	2 630	57	44	76	53	38	34	47	37	62	44	31	30
Israel	.	4	269	384	72	87	67	84	77	91	...	...	...	...	...	...
Japan	3	3	10 253	11 083	93	96	92	95	94	97	93	96	92	...	94	...
Jordan	♦.	2	350	214	76	53	79	52	73	54	68	36	70	35	60	37
Kazakstan	5	2	...	2 227	...	90	...	89	...	91	...	...	...	...	...	...
Kuwait	4	4	227	322	80	55	84	55	76	55	...	...	...	...	...	...
Kyrgyzstan	...	...	...	...	...	...	...	...	...	...	...	...	...	...	...	...
Lao People's Dem. Rep.	3	3	437	597	21	24	25	30	16	18	...	15	...	18	...	13
Lebanon	4	3	485	390	60	74	59	71	61	76	...	...	...	...	...	...
Malaysia	3	4	2 273	2 609	48	60	50	58	46	62	...	...	...	...	...	...
Maldives	5	2	...	37	...	44	...	44	...	44	...	...	...	...	...	...
Mongolia	5	2	271	353	91	86	85	...	97	...	...	...	...	...	...	...
Myanmar	4	2	4 784	5 658	22	23	...	23	...	23	...	...	...	...	...	...
Nepal	♦2	3	2 416	2 447	21	35	33	46	9	23	...	...	...	...	...	...
Oman	3	3	136	254	12	55	19	59	6	52	11	...	16	...	5	...
Pakistan	3	4	15 206	19 172	14	21	20	28	8	13	...	...	...	...	...	...
Palestine																
Gaza Strip	3	3	...	...	...	...	...	...	...	...	...	...	...	...	...	...
West Bank	3	3	...	...	...	...	...	...	...	...	...	...	...	...	...	...
Philippines	.	4	4 561	5 723	64	77	60	...	69	...	45	59	42	...	48	...
Qatar	3	3	24	42	66	84	64	82	68	86	51	70	50	68	52	72
Republic of Korea	3	3	5 485	4 922	78	91	82	91	74	90	69	85	72	85	65	85
Saudi Arabia	3	3	1 185	2 210	29	49	36	54	23	43	21	34	26	38	16	30
Singapore	♦4	3	313	291	58	68	56	...	59	...	...	...	...	...	...	...
Sri Lanka	♦6	2	2 322	2 952	55	74	52	71	57	78	...	...	...	...	...	...
Syrian Arab Republic	3	3	1 302	1 893	46	48	57	54	35	43	39	44	48	49	30	39
Tajikistan	5	2	...	852	...	103	...	101	...	104	...	...	...	...	...	...
Thailand	3	3	6 668	7 269	29	39	30	...	28	...	...	...	...	...	...	...
Turkey	3	3	6 402	7 044	35	61	44	74	24	48	...	54	...	...	...	...
Turkmenistan	...	...	...	...	...	...	...	...	...	...	...	...	...	...	...	...
United Arab Emirates	3	3	62	156	52	83	55	78	49	89	...	74	...	70	...	79
Uzbekistan	5	2	...	3 347	...	94	...	96	...	92	...	...	...	...	...	...
Viet Nam	4	3	9 533	11 013	42	32	44	...	40	...	...	...	...	...	...	...
Yemen	...	...	...	...	...	...	...	...	...	...	.	...	.	...	.	...
Former Dem. Yemen	.	4	173	.	18	.	25	.	11	.	...	...	...	...	...	...
Former Yemen Arab Rep.	3	3	976	.	4	.	7	.	1	.	...	...	...	...	...	...
Europe																
Albania	.	4	245	263	67	78	70	84	63	72	...	...	...	...	...	...
Austria	4	4	1 012	719	93	107	98	110	87	104	...	91	...	92	...	91
Belarus	♦5	2	774	1 061	98	91	...	88	...	95	...	...	...	...	...	...
Belgium	3	3	901	740	93	103	92	103	94	104	83	88	82	87	85	90

Country or territory	Duration in years of second-level general education		School-age population (000)		Gross enrolment ratio (%)						Net enrolment ratio (%)					
					Total		Male		Female		Total		Male		Female	
	1st stage	2nd stage	1980	1992	1980	1992	1980	1992	1980	1992	1980	1992	1980	1992	1980	1992
Bosnia and Herzegovina	...	...	...	...	...	...	...	...	...	...	...	...	...	...	...	...
Bulgaria	♦.	4	373	535	84	70	85	68	84	72	73	61	73	59	72	62
Croatia	.	4		248	...	77	...	73	...	81	...	66	...	63	...	70
Czech Republic	4	4	...	1 339	...	88	...	86	...	90	...	...	...	...	...	...
Former Czechoslovakia	.	4	873	.	89	.	90	.	88	.	...	.	...	.	...	.
Denmark	3	3	476	401	105	114	105	112	104	115	88	87	87	86	89	88
Estonia	3	3	...	132	...	92	...	90	...	95	...	74	...	71	...	77
Finland	3	3	451	367	100	116	94	106	105	127	...	93	...	92	...	94
France	4	3	5 937	5 483	85	102	81	100	89	104	79	86	75	85	82	89
Germany	6	3	.	7 589	.	101	.	102	.	100	.	85	.	85	.	86
Former German Dem. Rep.	.	6	2 370	.	80	.	81	.	79	.	...	.	...	.	...	.
Germany, Federal Rep. of	6	3	9 074	.	94	.	96	.	92	.	...	.	...	.	...	.
Greece	3	3	915	861	85	99	88	100	81	98	77	88	78	87	75	89
Hungary	.	4	517	657	68	81	71	79	65	82	38	75	31	72	45	77
Iceland	3	4	31	29	86	103	89	105	84	101	...	...	...	...	...	...
Ireland	3	2	335	344	90	105	85	101	95	110	78	82	75	80	80	84
Italy	3	5	7 393	6 034	72	81	73	81	70	81	...	...	...	...	...	...
Latvia	5	3	...	281	...	87	...	84	...	90	...	77	...	...	...	...
Lithuania	5	3	...	425	...	78	...	76	...	79	...	...	...	...	...	...
Luxembourg	3	4	38	30	73	74	74	...	71	...	67	...	68	...	66	...
Malta	5	2	34	39	75	88	80	91	70	84	71	83	73	83	69	82
Monaco	...	...	...	...	...	...	...	...	...	...	...	...	...	...	...	...
Netherlands	3	3	1 504	1 115	93	123	95	126	90	120	81	86	80	84	82	87
Norway	3	3	384	338	94	113	92	114	96	111	84	90	82	90	86	90
Poland	.	4	2 171	2 446	77	83	75	81	80	85	70	77	68	74	74	81
Portugal	3	3	1 071	966	37	81	34	...	40	...	...	...	...	...	...	...
Republic of Moldova	5	2	...	535	...	70	...	69	...	72	...	...	...	...	...	...
Romania	♦4	4	1 222	2 975	71	82	73	83	69	82	...	72	...	71	...	73
Russian Federation	5	2	13 554	15 420	96	89	95	86	97	93	...	...	...	...	...	...
San Marino	...	...	...	...	...	...	...	...	...	...	...	...	...	...	...	...
Slovakia	4	4	...	746	...	88	...	86	...	90	...	...	...	...	...	...
Slovenia	4	4	...	238	...	89	...	88	...	91	...	...	...	...	...	...
Spain	3	4	4 578	4 315	87	110	85	105	89	115	74	90	74	88	74	92
Sweden	3	3	694	625	87	96	82	96	93	97	82	90	79	90	85	91
Switzerland	3	4	...	557	...	91	...	94	...	89	...	79	...	82	...	77
The FYR of Macedonia	.	4		137	...	54	...	53	...	55	...	...	...	...	...	...
Ukraine	3	2	3 514	3 681	95	89	...	84	...	94	...	...	...	...	...	...
United Kingdom	3	4	6 399	4 946	83	90	82	88	85	92	79	82	78	81	81	84
Yugoslavia	4	4	...	1 289	...	65	...	64	...	65	...	...	...	...	...	...
Former Yugoslavia	4	4	2 906	.	83	.	87	.	80	.	77	.	...	.	...	.
Oceania																
Australia	3	3	1 546	1 534	71	84	70	83	72	86	70	80	69	79	71	82
Fiji	.	6	91	104	55	64	53	64	57	65	...	...	...	...	...	...
Kiribati	3	3	* ...	...	...	...	...	...	...	...	...	...	...	...	...	...
New Zealand	4	3	428	370	83	95	82	95	84	95	82	88	81	87	83	89
Papua New Guinea	4	2	403	539	12	13	15	15	8	10	...	...	...	...	...	...
Samoa	4	3	34	...	64	...	61	...	67	...	...	...	...	...	...	...
Solomon Islands	3	2	25	42	16	16	22	19	9	12	...	...	...	...	...	...
Tonga	.	7	...	...	...	...	...	...	...	...	...	...	...	...	...	...
Tuvalu	.	6	...	...	...	...	...	...	...	...	...	...	...	...	...	...
Vanuatu	4	3		24	...	20	...	23	...	18	...	...	...	...	...	...

Table 7
Teaching staff in pre-primary, first- and second-level education

Country or territory	Pupil-teacher ratio						Percentage of female teachers					
	Pre-primary		First level		Second level		Pre-primary		First level		Second level	
	1980	1992	1980	1992	1980	1992	1980	1992	1980	1992	1980	1992
Africa												
Algeria	–	20	35	27	26	17	–	80	37	40	...	43
Angola	...	...	39	32	...	...	...	...	...	...	...	...
Benin	22	23	48	40	45	29	52	55	23	25	...	...
Botswana	–	–	32	29	22	20	–	–	72	77	35	41
Burkina Faso	...	22	54	60	26	39	...	90	20	24	...	...
Burundi	46	...	39	63	20	25	100	...	47	47	18	22
Cameroon	27	26	52	51	28	29	99	100	20	30	18	20
Cape Verde	...	...	38	33	23	30	...	...	...	60	...	45
Central African Republic	3	1	60	90	82	38	100	100	25	26	12	...
Chad	...	...	...	64	...	35	...	...	...	6	...	5
Comoros	30	...	46	39	31	24	33	...	7	...	20	...
Congo	9	10	58	63	50	31	100	100	26	33	8	...
Côte d'Ivoire	35	...	39	37	24	22	100	...	15	18	...	...
Djibouti	...	...	40	43	21	23	...	...	...	36	...	...
Egypt	44	26	34	22	25	19	98	96	49	54	35	42
Equatorial Guinea	...	...	57	...	...	...	...	...	...	...	...	...
Eritrea	...	32	...	41	...	30	...	100	...	...	...	...
Ethiopia	47	40	64	27	43	32	...	97	·22	26	10	10
Gabon	...	26	45	44	19	25	...	97	27	...	28	21
Gambia	...	32	23	30	17	29	...	...	33	31	27	17
Ghana	...	17	27	29	22	18	...	...	42	36	21	24
Guinea	–	–	36	49	26	29	–	–	14	23	...	15
Guinea-Bissau	10	...	23	...	11	...	98	...	24	...	20	...
Kenya	42	36	36	31	25	17	...	97	31	44	...	34
Lesotho	–	–	48	51	21	21	–	–	75	79	48	50
Liberia	...	...	33	...	13	...	...	...	21	...	19	...
Libyan Arab Jamahiriya	17	...	18	12	12	12	100	...	47	67	24	40
Madagascar	...	...	44	40	...	20	...	...	...	56	...	...
Malawi	–	–	67	68	20	27	–	–	32	34	...	23
Mali	...	32	42	47	17	16	...	...	20	24	...	17
Mauritania	...	...	41	51	31	20	...	...	9	18	8	10
Mauritius	26	...	20	21	26	21	100	...	43	46	40	42
Morocco	20	21	36	28	21	15	8	22	32	38	26	30
Mozambique	...	–	81	53	42	40	...	–	22	23	27	18
Namibia	...	25	...	32	...	...	...	100	...	65	...	...
Niger	30	34	41	38	31	35	100	100	30	34	22	18
Nigeria	...	...	37	39	32	27	...	...	33	45	8	27
Rwanda	...	...	59	58	12	14	...	...	38	47	19	14
Sao Tome and Principe	...	30	32	35	17	23	...	93	...	52	...	24
Senegal	23	24	46	59	23	23	100	74	24	27	24	16
Seychelles	31	20	21	18	15	13	100	100	82	88	34	55
Sierra Leone	...	...	34	34	21	18	...	...	22	...	21	17
Somalia	15	...	33	...	25	...	94	...	29	...	10	...
South Africa	...	25	27	27	...	26	...	98	...	58	...	64
Sudan	47	41	34	34	21	23	44	46	31	52	26	33
Swaziland	...	24	34	33	18	18	...	...	79	77	48	...
Togo	36	27	55	53	40	43	100	100	21	16	13	11
Tunisia	...	27	39	26	21	18	...	99	29	47	28	33
Uganda	...	...	34	32	23	15	...	...	30	30	20	16
United Rep. of Tanzania	...	...	43	36	21	20	...	...	37	41	28	23

Country or territory	Pupil-teacher ratio						Percentage of female teachers					
	Pre-primary		First level		Second level		Pre-primary		First level		Second level	
	1980	1992	1980	1992	1980	1992	1980	1992	1980	1992	1980	1992
Zaire	...	43	...	42	...	22	...	53	...	19	...	15
Zambia	...	...	49	...	22	...	...	...	40	...	...	...
Zimbabwe	...	...	45	38	24	28	...	...	38	41	...	33
America, North												
Antigua and Barbuda	...	...	...	...	...	15	...	...	...	...	...	87
Bahamas	...	7	24	21	22	16	...	100	85	91	...	69
Barbados	24	...	24	17	20	20	...	...	...	72	...	55
Belize	15	19	24	27	16	15	...	99	...	71	47	47
British Virgin Islands	20	...	18	...	14	...	80	...	84	...	58	...
Canada	...	31	17	17	18	16	...	69	58	69	44	53
Costa Rica	32	24	33	32	22	22	98	97	79	80	57	...
Cuba	25	23	17	12	13	9	99	100	75	73	50	59
Dominica	...	23	26	29	...	...	...	99	...	80	...	...
Dominican Republic	...	...	50	34	...	21	...	...	...	71	...	59
El Salvador	47	41	48	38	13	...	100	95	65	69	24	...
Grenada	22	...	23	23	32	27	99	...	68	70	52	52
Guatemala	17	25	37	32	15	16	93	...	62	...	33	...
Haiti	...	...	44	29	24	20	...	...	49	43	...	...
Honduras	46	29	37	37	38	28	100	100	74	73	55	...
Jamaica	...	32	37	33	22	22	...	...	88	89	46	68
Mexico	33	25	39	30	18	17	100	100	...	...	...	...
Netherlands Antilles	25	...	21	...	16	...	...	...	...	...	...	...
Nicaragua	33	32	35	37	...	30	99	99	78	84	...	55
Panama	28	...	27	...	22	...	100	...	80	...	55	...
Saint Kitts and Nevis	...	19	...	21	...	15	...	100	...	79	...	56
Saint Lucia	...	17	31	27	19	18	...	...	80	82	52	61
Saint Vincent and the Grenadines	...	14	18	20	24	25	...	99	62	67	52	51
Trinidad and Tobago	6	4	24	26	20	20	96	96	66	72	52	54
United States	...	...	22	...	14	...	...	...	...	...	...	...
America, South												
Argentina	21	19	20	16	7	8	100	...	92	...	75	...
Bolivia	...	42	20	25	...	18	...	96	48	57	...	48
Brazil	23	22	26	23	9	13	98	...	85	...	54	...
Chile	50	24	33	25	...	17	...	98	...	73	...	57
Colombia	26	24	31	28	21	21	...	96	79	80	41	...
Ecuador	27	22	36	31	19	13	95	94	65	65	38	46
Guyana	14	20	33	...	18	...	98	100	70	...	45	...
Paraguay	...	18	27	24	...	11	...	90	...	55	...	67
Peru	32	25	37	28	25	19	97	...	60	...	46	...
Suriname	...	...	27	23	18	...	...	...	...	85	...	...
Uruguay	31	28	22	21	...	...	...	...	...	...	...	...
Venezuela	28	24	26	23	...	8	98	99	75	74	...	54
Asia												
Afghanistan	12	...	32	...	20	...	100	...	21	...	21	...
Armenia	...	...	...	...	...	...	...	...	...	...	...	...
Azerbaijan	...	8	...	15	...	...	...	100	...	70	...	...
Bahrain	42	27	21	18	20	15	100	100	49	63	...	...
Bangladesh	...	...	54	63	24	28	...	...	8	19	7	10
Bhutan	...	...	36	31	...	13	...	...	...	...	...	...

World education report

Table 7 (continued)

Country or territory	Pupil-teacher ratio						Percentage of female teachers					
	Pre-primary		First level		Second level		Pre-primary		First level		Second level	
	1980	1992	1980	1992	1980	1992	1980	1992	1980	1992	1980	1992
Brunei Darussalam	21	21	18	16	14	13	77	90	45	58	37	50
Cambodia	...	...	...	...	...	...	...	...	...	...	...	...
China	28	30	27	22	18	15	82	95	37	44	25	33
Cyprus	25	20	22	19	17	13	100	99	45	63	47	53
Dem. People's Rep. of Korea	...	...	...	...	...	...	...	...	...	...	...	...
Georgia	...	...	...	...	...	...	...	...	...	...	...	...
Hong Kong	38	26	30	27	30	...	98	...	73	...	50	...
India	...	...	45	48	23	33	...	...	27	30	28	35
Indonesia	27	18	32	23	15	14	...	...	33	51	...	35
Iran, Islamic Rep. of	25	25	27	32	15	28	100	100	57	55	32	44
Iraq	24	19	28	22	33	20	100	100	48	68	42	55
Israel	...	...	14	14	6	7	...	...	...	83	57	69
Japan	22	19	25	20	17	17	88	94	57	60	26	30
Jordan	27	23	32	22	21	20	99	100	59	60	44	53
Kazakstan	...	...	...	...	...	...	...	...	...	...	...	...
Kuwait	18	18	19	16	12	11	100	100	56	69	50	53
Kyrgyzstan	...	...	...	...	...	...	...	...	...	...	...	...
Lao People's Dem. Rep.	21	16	30	29	21	12	100	100	30	42	26	39
Lebanon	19	...	18	21	12	...	...	...	...	...	...	...
Malaysia	...	34	27	20	23	19	...	96	44	58	46	54
Maldives	...	...	...	...	...	...	...	...	...	...	...	...
Mongolia	28	26	32	28	24	19	100	...	...	58	...	...
Myanmar	...	...	52	36	35	19	...	...	...	65	...	69
Nepal	...	...	38	39	31	34	...	...	10	15	7	10
Oman	36	20	23	27	9	17	91	100	34	48	27	46
Pakistan	...	...	37	41	18	19	...	...	32	31	30	32
Palestine												
Gaza Strip	...	...	...	...	...	...	...	...	...	...	...	...
West Bank	...	...	...	...	...	...	...	...	...	...	...	...
Philippines	43	41	31	34	34	33	49	...	83	...	...	...
Qatar	22	17	15	10	10	7	100	98	57	73	53	61
Republic of Korea	20	21	48	33	41	24	85	95	37	53	28	39
Saudi Arabia	25	16	18	14	14	12	97	100	39	48	33	41
Singapore	21	23	31	26	21	22	100	100	66	71	56	63
Sri Lanka	...	...	32	29	...	20	...	...	...	80	...	59
Syrian Arab Republic	31	23	28	24	20	18	97	95	54	64	22	45
Tajikistan	...	12	...	21	...	...	...	...	...	48	...	...
Thailand	...	...	23	17	18	18	...	...	33	...	57	...
Turkey	9	16	27	28	22	27	99	97	41	43	36	40
Turkmenistan	...	...	...	...	...	...	...	...	...	...	...	...
United Arab Emirates	15	20	16	17	11	13	100	99	52	68	48	57
Uzbekistan	...	...	...	20	...	...	...	...	...	80	...	53
Viet Nam	28	22	39	36	26	21	100	...	65	...	58	...
Yemen	.	...	.	...	.	...	.	...	.	...	.	...
Former Dem. Yemen	18	.	27	.	22	.	99	.	34	.	23	.
Former Yemen Arab Rep.	...	.	37	.	17	.	...	.	9	.	6	.
Europe												
Albania	22	18	21	17	31	18	100	100	50	60	46	58
Austria	23	20	15	11	12	8	99	100	75	83	54	60
Belarus	9	7	18	16	...	...	...	...	...	...	...	...
Belgium	22	...	18	14	10	6	100	...	59	69	49	52

Country or territory	Pupil-teacher ratio						Percentage of female teachers					
	Pre-primary		First level		Second level		Pre-primary		First level		Second level	
	1980	1992	1980	1992	1980	1992	1980	1992	1980	1992	1980	1992
Bosnia and Herzegovina	...	...	...	...	...	...	...	...	...	...	...	...
Bulgaria	15	10	19	14	13	13	100	100	72	78	64	75
Croatia	...	12	19	18	...	13	...	...	73	75	...	69
Czech Republic	...	12	...	21	...	12	...	100	...	93	...	66
Former Czechoslovakia	15	.	21	.	13	.	100	.	79	.	46	.
Denmark	...	12	...	11	...	...	...	...	...	58	...	...
Estonia	...	7	...	18	...	11	...	100	...	96	...	74
Finland	...	...	14	18	17	...	...	...	...	...	...	...
France	30	24	21	19	13	13	97	78	71	78	68	60
Germany	.	20	.	16	.	13	.	97	.	84	.	49
Former German Dem. Rep.	12	.	16	.	13	.	100	.	86	.	55	.
Germany, Federal Rep. of	...	.	...	.	...	.	...	.	...	.	...	.
Greece	22	16	24	19	20	14	100	100	48	52	55	57
Hungary	16	12	15	11	13	12	100	100	80	83	61	67
Iceland	...	...	...	...	...	...	...	...	...	...	...	...
Ireland	28	27	28	25	...	16	75	77	75	77	...	52
Italy	17	15	16	12	11	9	...	99	87	91	64	70
Latvia	...	7	...	10	...	10	...	...	...	90	...	76
Lithuania	...	7	...	17	...	...	...	100	...	...	...	...
Luxembourg	18	19	14	13	...	...	99	...	50	51	...	...
Malta	18	17	21	21	13	13	87	100	64	82	41	41
Monaco	...	11	...	16	...	10	...	71	...	64	...	58
Netherlands	18	16	23	16	15	14	100	100	46	55	26	30
Norway	5	4	17	15	...	...	...	96	63	69	...	...
Poland	23	13	21	17	16	20	99	...	80	...	69	...
Portugal	20	19	18	14	12	10	99	98	...	81	59	67
Republic of Moldova	...	...	...	32	...	13	...	...	...	79	...	71
Romania	24	21	21	21	10	14	100	100	70	83	53	65
Russian Federation	11	9	28	20	15	12	...	...	98	98	76	79
San Marino	10	8	10	5	11	...	100	100	88	88	62	...
Slovakia	14	11	...	22	...	14	...	...	...	92	...	73
Slovenia	...	11	...	18	...	16	...	98	...	92	...	75
Spain	33	22	28	21	21	17	97	96	67	74	43	53
Sweden	...	4	...	10	...	9	...	97	...	79	...	54
Switzerland	...	19	...	...	...	...	...	...	...	...	...	...
The FYR of Macedonia	...	10	23	20	...	16	...	97	...	52	...	62
Ukraine	9	8	18	17	...	...	...	...	...	...	...	...
United Kingdom	...	25	20	20	15	13	...	95	77	78	49	54
Yugoslavia	...	10	...	22	...	15	...	94	...	75	...	58
Former Yugoslavia	10	.	24	.	17	.	94	.	70	.	49	.
Oceania												
Australia	...	...	20	17	13	11	...	...	68	72	45	50
Fiji	23	19	28	31	21	20	100	...	57	56	43	47
Kiribati	...	...	30	29	14	16	...	...	48	59	43	43
New Zealand	19	24	20	16	21	15	...	98	63	80	50	54
Papua New Guinea	...	...	31	31	24	24	...	...	27	34	34	35
Samoa	...	...	29	...	25	...	...	...	71	...	55	...
Solomon Islands	...	...	25	21	18	17	...	...	26	...	31	...
Tonga	...	...	25	22	23	18	...	...	59	66	49	31
Tuvalu	...	...	...	...	...	...	...	...	...	...	...	...
Vanuatu	24	...	24	19	15	19	100	...	39	38	39	36

Table 8
Third-level education: enrolment and breakdown by ISCED level

Country or territory	Number of students per 100,000 inhabitants						Percentage of students by ISCED level 1992			Percentage of female students in each ISCED level 1992		
	Total		Male		Female							
	1980	1992	1980	1992	1980	1992	Level 5	Level 6	Level 7	Level 5	Level 6	Level 7
Africa												
Algeria	530	1 188	789	1 523	275	844	16	79	5	34	44	...
Angola	39	66	67	...	12	...	–	100	–	–	...	–
Benin	160	235	263	413	59	60	...	...	...	...	...	...
Botswana	119	294	163	306	79	280	56	42	3	...	...	...
Burkina Faso	24	60	37	94	10	28	6	94	./.	43	22	./.
Burundi	45	73	71	110	22	38	–	100	./.	–	26	./.
Cameroon	135	288	...	...	...	...	...	...	...	...	...	...
Cape Verde	–	–	–	–	–	–	–	–	–	–	–	–
Central African Rep.	74	150	142	252	12	55	23	76	1	34	11	17
Chad	...	...	...	...	...	...	...	...	...	...	...	...
Comoros	–	47	–	80	–	14	100	–	–	15	–	–
Congo	435	524	759	873	126	190	13	78	9	23	18	15
Côte d'Ivoire	240	...	386	...	86	...	...	...	...	...	...	...
Djibouti	–	–	–	–	–	–	100	–	–	30	–	–
Egypt	1 636	1 560	2 205	2 047	1 048	1 056	–	83	17	–	39	31
Equatorial Guinea	...	164	...	292	...	41	33	67	–	11	14	–
Eritrea	...	...	...	...	...	...	...	...	...	...	...	...
Ethiopia	40	70	70	113	11	25	48	50	3	25	14	7
Gabon	216	373	342	525	94	225	...	...	...	...	...	...
Gambia	–	–	–	–	–	–	–	–	–	–	–	–
Ghana	144	126	231	200	59	54	10	83	7	28	22	15
Guinea	410	123	663	218	157	28	...	...	...	...	...	...
Guinea-Bissau	–	–	–	–	–	–	–	–	–	–	–	–
Kenya	78	186	126	271	30	102	...	...	...	...	31	22
Lesotho	152	196	113	183	188	209	71	27	1	59	54	62
Liberia	208	...	298	...	117	...	...	...	...	...	...	...
Libyan Arab Jamahiriya	663	1 548	936	1 605	356	1 486	...	...	...	...	...	...
Madagascar	250	318	...	359	...	278	62	36	2	30	44	39
Malawi	56	78	80	120	34	37	31	68	1	28	21	18
Mali	64	73	116	128	14	19	26	74	./.	19	12	./.
Mauritania	...	356	...	613	...	104	1	99	–	7	15	–
Mauritius	107	378	151	443	65	313	74	22	5	44	38	28
Morocco	580	986	886	1 257	273	715	1	89	10	34	37	25
Mozambique	8	31	12	47	5	16	–	100	–	–	26	–
Namibia	...	300	...	217	...	382	54	41	5	63	65	66
Niger	26	60	42	104	10	18	16	84	–	15	15	–
Nigeria	208	360	...	531	...	192	...	...	...	...	...	...
Rwanda	24	50	44	82	5	19	86	14	–	19	17	–
Sao Tome and Principe	–	–	–	–	–	–	–	–	–	–	–	–
Senegal	246	306	402	495	90	117	...	...	...	...	25	19
Seychelles	–	–	–	–	–	–	–	–	–	–	–	–
Sierra Leone	67	119	...	...	...	...	...	...	...	...	...	...
Somalia	45	...	...	...	...	...	...	...	...	...	...	...
South Africa	...	1 264	...	1 361	...	1 168	...	...	...	...	...	...
Sudan	154	264	224	284	84	245	9	90	1	30	41	58
Swaziland	335	384	412	464	260	311	42	58	./.	39	45	./.
Togo	182	226	314	396	53	60	53	47	–	12	15	–
Tunisia	499	1 044	692	1 215	300	869	7	85	8	48	42	31
Uganda	45	112	70	161	20	63	61	36	3	29	28	23
United Rep. of Tanzania	22	21	36	...	8	...	...	...	...	...	...	...

Country or territory	Number of students per 100,000 inhabitants						Percentage of students by ISCED level			Percentage of female students in each ISCED level		
	Total		Male		Female		1992			1992		
	1980	1992	1980	1992	1980	1992	Level 5	Level 6	Level 7	Level 5	Level 6	Level 7
Zaire	105	...	...	...	...	...	...	...	...	...	...	...
Zambia	127	188	205	...	52	...	61	38	1	34	19	16
Zimbabwe	197	588	232	860	162	320	76	24	./.	33	27	./.
America, North												
Antigua and Barbuda	–	–	–	–	–	–	–	–	–	–	–	–
Bahamas	1 948	...	...	...	...	...	...	...	...	...	...	...
Barbados	1 620	1 647	1 579	1 389	1 656	1 885	63	34	3	53	60	53
Belize	–	–	–	–	–	–	–	–	–	–	–	–
British Virgin Islands	–	–	–	–	–	–	–	–	–	–	–	–
Canada	5 213	6 903	5 150	6 372	5 276	7 424	46	48	6	52	57	45
Costa Rica	2 433	2 767	...	...	...	...	11	88	1	...	...	...
Cuba	1 563	1 840	1 595	1 548	1 530	2 134	–	100	–	–	58	–
Dominica	...	...	...	...	...	...	100	–	–	55	–	–
Dominican Republic	...	...	...	...	...	...	...	...	...	...	...	...
El Salvador	372	1 512	521	1 753	227	1 281	7	92	1	52	32	15
Grenada	...	...	...	...	...	...	...	...	...	...	...	...
Guatemala	736	...	...	...	...	...	...	...	...	...	...	...
Haiti	87	...	124	...	52	...	...	...	...	...	...	...
Honduras	724	852	897	976	548	726	1	99	0	62	43	4
Jamaica	656	976	...	1 291	...	663	57	40	3	...	...	...
Mexico	1 387	1 477	1 859	1 622	912	1 333	–	96	4	–	46	37
Netherlands Antilles	–	–	–	–	–	–	–	–	–	–	–	–
Nicaragua	1 106	809	1 188	799	1 025	819	4	95	1	57	49	29
Panama	2 071	2 398	1 836	...	2 313	...	...	...	...	...	...	...
Saint Kitts and Nevis	...	...	...	...	...	...	100	–	–	55	–	–
Saint Lucia	...	...	...	...	...	...	...	...	...	...	...	...
Saint Vincent and the Grenadines	...	...	...	...	...	...	100	–	–	68	–	–
Trinidad and Tobago	522	593	601	748	444	440	9	74	17	68	48	40
United States	5 311	5 486	5 298	5 120	5 324	5 834	38	49	13	...	...	...
America, South												
Argentina	1 748	3 268	1 757	...	1 740	...	...	...	...	...	...	...
Bolivia	1 557	2 214	...	...	...	...	27	73	./.	...	...	...
Brazil	1 162	1 079	1 187	938	1 137	1 220	–	100	–	–	54	–
Chile	1 306	2 145	1 503	...	1 114	...	31	66	3	...	...	...
Colombia	1 024	1 554	1 142	1 530	908	1 578	23	74	2	54	51	41
Ecuador	3 389	2 012	4 221	...	2 547	...	...	...	...	...	...	...
Guyana	325	588	369	678	281	499	69	30	2	38	53	49
Paraguay	858	907	...	980	...	832	17	83	0	77	48	78
Peru	1 769	4 188	2 273	...	1 256	...	32	68	./.	...	...	...
Suriname	670	1 079	...	1 029	...	1 127	54	46	–	...	...	–
Uruguay	1 339	2 396	1 258	...	1 416	...	11	89	./.	...	...	...
Venezuela	2 035	2 853	...	...	...	...	...	...	...	...	...	...
Asia												
Afghanistan	142	162	235	217	44	102	62	38	./.	23	42	./.
Armenia	3 577	3 711	...	...	...	...	...	...	...	...	...	...
Azerbaijan	3 021	2 323	...	2 277	...	2 453	–	100	./.	–	38	./.
Bahrain	550	1 493	555	1 113	542	2 011	...	...	...	...	...	...
Bangladesh	272	402	455	655	78	132	–	92	8	–	16	12
Bhutan	26	...	41	...	11	...	...	...	...	...	...	...

Table 8 (continued)

Country or territory	Number of students per 100,000 inhabitants						Percentage of students by ISCED level 1992			Percentage of female students in each ISCED level 1992		
	Total		Male		Female							
	1980	1992	1980	1992	1980	1992	Level 5	Level 6	Level 7	Level 5	Level 6	Level 7
Brunei Darussalam	74	...	69	...	80	...	...	...	...	...	...	...
Cambodia	208	158	...	...	...	...	...	...	...	...	...	...
China	116	192	173	248	56	132	38	59	4	...	...	...
Cyprus	308	872	361	886	256	859	91	8	1	46	88	24
Dem. People's Rep. of Korea	...	...	...	...	...	...	...	...	...	...	...	...
Georgia	2 757	2 710	...	...	...	...	...	...	...	...	...	...
Hong Kong	1 201	1 540	1 636	1 749	727	1 320	32	57	11	44	43	30
India	515	...	732	...	281	...	1	88	11	25	32	34
Indonesia	367	1 045	508	1 341	227	751	...	...	...	...	...	...
Iran, Islamic Rep. of	317	1 232	439	1 685	192	764	12	71	17	16	31	25
Iraq	820	...	1 101	...	530	...	...	...	...	...	...	...
Israel	2 503	3 208	2 437	3 286	2 570	3 131	41	41	18	47	54	53
Japan	2 065	2 340	2 820	2 836	1 333	1 861	19	77	3	86	30	17
Jordan	1 250	1 893	1 313	1 881	1 183	1 906	36	58	6	62	44	26
Kazakstan	3 524	3 433	...	...	...	...	...	...	...	...	52	./.
Kuwait	991	1 370	739	1 215	1 330	1 569	29	70	1	43	68	45
Kyrgyzstan	2 897	1 837	...	...	...	...	...	...	...	...	...	...
Lao People's Dem. Rep.	44	112	60	167	28	60	33	67	–	6	37	–
Lebanon	2 962	3 275	3 854	4 114	2 101	2 482	...	...	...	...	...	...
Malaysia	419	679	512	716	325	640	52	44	4	42	48	43
Maldives	–	–	–	–	–	–	–	–	–	–	–	–
Mongolia	2 234	1 267	1 656	...	2 816	...	...	...	...	...	...	...
Myanmar	478	...	...	...	...	...	...	...	...	...	...	...
Nepal	259	558	408	837	101	270	63	30	7	27	19	17
Oman	2	400	...	389	...	413	51	48	1	45	53	63
Pakistan	189	258	264	359	107	149	...	...	...	...	...	...
Palestine												
Gaza Strip	...	720	...	...	...	...	21	79	0	44	35	27
West Bank	...	...	...	...	...	...	13	87	0	60	54	35
Philippines	2 641	2 696	2 455	2 257	2 828	3 140	17	79	4	69	56	66
Qatar	990	1 408	594	598	1 682	3 072	6	91	4	48	73	78
Republic of Korea	1 698	4 253	2 531	5 624	848	2 866	25	69	6	36	31	25
Saudi Arabia	646	1 145	863	1 092	392	1 215	11	86	3	57	45	34
Singapore	963	...	1 150	...	768	...	...	...	...	...	...	...
Sri Lanka	288	504	320	607	255	402	23	66	11	14	37	39
Syrian Arab Republic	1 611	1 700	2 231	1 976	964	1 419	8	89	3	39	38	39
Tajikistan	2 450	2 298	...	...	...	...	...	...	...	...	...	...
Thailand	1 284	2 029	...	1 921	...	2 138	20	77	3	50	53	45
Turkey	554	1 567	808	2 002	292	1 111	15	79	6	31	35	36
Turkmenistan	2 437	2 078	...	...	...	...	...	...	...	...	...	...
United Arab Emirates	282	601	210	281	442	1 185	8	91	1	12	75	21
Uzbekistan	3 237	3 054	...	...	...	...	...	...	...	...	...	...
Viet Nam	214	149	336	...	98	...	...	...	...	...	...	...
Yemen	.	438	.	740	.	147	...	...	...	...	...	...
Former Dem. Yemen	177	.	173	.	181	.	.	.	.	.	.	.
Former Yemen Arab Rep.	71	.	134	.	15	.	.	.	.	.	.	.
Europe												
Albania	545	679	533	638	559	722	–	100	–	–	52	–
Austria	1 812	2 836	2 223	3 129	1 444	2 560	7	87	7	67	44	35
Belarus	3 530	3 317	3 413	3 630	3 317	3 060	–	99	1	–	51	...
Belgium	2 111	2 776	2 451	2 939	1 787	2 621	45	49	6	56	43	32

Country or territory	Number of students per 100,000 inhabitants						Percentage of students by ISCED level 1992			Percentage of female students in each ISCED level 1992		
	Total		Male		Female		Level 5	Level 6	Level 7	Level 5	Level 6	Level 7
	1980	1992	1980	1992	1980	1992						
Bosnia and Herzegovina	...	...	...	...	...	...	...	...	...	...	...	...
Bulgaria	1 144	2 085	1 006	1 978	1 281	2 189	15	83	2	70	55	39
Croatia	...	1 720	...	1 846	...	1 603	...	...	...	...	...	...
Czech Republic	...	1 132	...	1 298	...	974	...	...	...	...	...	...
Former Czechoslovakia	1 287	.	1 542	.	1 045	.	.	.	.	.	.	.
Denmark	2 074	3 045	2 148	2 940	2 001	3 147	15	85	./.	57	52	./.
Estonia	3 339	2 603	...	2 748	...	2 475	17	77	6	50	52	42
Finland	2 577	3 739	2 761	3 615	2 404	3 856	24	68	8	67	49	43
France	1 998	3 409	...	3 202	...	3 605	23	67	10	54	56	42
Germany	.	2 319	.	2 854	.	1 813	...	...	...	...	...	...
Former German Dem. Rep.	2 395	.	2 147	.	2 613	.	.	.	.	.	.	.
Germany, Federal Rep. of	1 987	.	2 447	.	1 556	.	.	.	.	.	.	.
Greece	1 256	1 907	1 498	1 930	1 023	1 884	40	60	./.	45	53	./.
Hungary	945	1 145	980	1 178	912	1 113	42	58	./.	52	50	./.
Iceland	1 592	2 393	1 263	1 976	1 927	2 812	...	...	...	...	...	...
Ireland	1 610	3 087	1 901	2 979	1 316	3 195	34	59	7	45	52	44
Italy	1 981	2 829	2 336	2 878	1 644	2 782	1	96	3	68	51	44
Latvia	3 528	2 786	...	2 799	...	2 775	...	...	...	...	...	...
Lithuania	4 061	2 802	...	2 474	...	3 097	...	...	...	...	...	...
Luxembourg	205	...	271	...	142	...	...	...	...	...	...	...
Malta	292	1 300	454	1 365	139	1 236	25	70	5	52	48	38
Monaco	–	–	–	–	–	–	–	–	–	–	–	–
Netherlands	2 546	3 339	3 091	3 646	2 008	3 038	./.	97	3	./.	47	36
Norway	1 936	3 890	2 039	3 656	1 836	4 120	31	68	./.	52	54	./.
Poland	1 656	1 527	1 504	1 366	1 800	1 680	16	77	8	78	52	57
Portugal	944	1 936	1 008	1 585	883	2 264	–	98	2	–	56	49
Republic of Moldova	2 747	2 665	...	...	...	...	...	...	...	...	...	...
Romania	868	1 019	1 010	1 102	730	939	...	...	...	...	...	...
Russian Federation	4 116	3 174	3 918	3 024	4 286	3 307	44	55	1	...	...	...
San Marino	–	–	–	–	–	–	–	–	–	–	–	–
Slovakia	...	1 247	...	1 324	...	1 173	4	94	2	57	49	37
Slovenia	...	2 033	...	1 916	...	2 143	30	66	5	49	57	46
Spain	1 859	3 306	2 132	3 283	1 595	3 328	1	96	3	49	51	45
Sweden	2 423	2 622	2 669	2 458	2 182	2 783	49	44	7	60	49	35
Switzerland	1 347	2 095	1 931	2 714	794	1 490	40	49	11	31	41	32
The FYR of Macedonia	...	1 260	...	1 208	...	1 313	10	90	./.	62	51	./.
Ukraine	3 370	3 152	...	3 384	...	2 954	–	98	2	–	50	...
United Kingdom	1 468	2 405	1 911	2 525	1 049	2 291	31	55	14	52	49	42
Yugoslavia	...	1 296	...	1 243	...	1 348	19	81	./.	51	54	./.
Former Yugoslavia	1 847	.	2 048	.	1 652	.	.	.	.	.	.	.
Oceania												
Australia	2 222	3 219	2 434	3 003	2 011	3 435	11	71	17	66	52	49
Fiji	275	1 076	329	...	219	...	60	39	1	...	...	...
Kiribati	...	...	...	...	...	...	...	...	...	...	...	...
New Zealand	2 462	4 251	2 941	3 983	1 988	4 512	37	53	10	53	55	47
Papua New Guinea	163	...	243	...	76	...	...	...	...	...	...	...
Samoa	404	...	729	...	58	...	...	...	...	...	...	...
Solomon Islands	–	–	–	–	–	–	–	–	–	–	–	–
Tonga	...	...	...	...	...	...	...	...	...	...	...	...
Tuvalu	–	–	–	–	–	–	–	–	–	–	–	–
Vanuatu	–	–	–	–	–	–	–	–	–	–	–	–

World education report

Table 9
Third-level education: students and graduates by broad field of study, 1992

Country or territory	Percentage of students (and graduates) by field of study					Percentage of female students in each field of study						Gender segregation index (%)
	Education	Humanities	Law and social sciences	Natural sciences, engin. & agric.	Medical sciences	All fields	Education	Humanities	Law and social sciences	Natural sciences, engin. & agric.	Medical sciences	
Africa												
Algeria	5 (9)	11 (11)	22 (24)	50 (45)	12 (11)	40	48	60	41	32	46	8
Angola	29 (13)	– (–)	29 (30)	30 (39)	12 (17)	...	...	–	...	...	...	...
Benin	9 (...)	18 (...)	54 (...)	16 (...)	3 (...)	13	11	20	12	10	17	3
Botswana	8 (20)	11 (28)	34 (49)	28 (3)	10 (–)	...	...	...	...	...	...	...
Burkina Faso	4 (...)	17 (...)	51 (...)	20 (...)	8 (...)	23	15	39	25	9	18	7
Burundi	11 (10)	15 (15)	32 (30)	32 (37)	8 (7)	26	29	30	35	18	27	7
Cameroon	8 (...)	./. (...)	62 (...)	28 (...)	2 (...)	...	...	...	13	14	13	...
Cape Verde	– (–)	– (–)	– (–)	– (–)	– (–)	–	–	–	–	–	–	–
Central African Republic	3 (...)	7 (...)	53 (...)	9 (...)	26 (...)	15	5	11	10	5	31	9
Chad	... (...)	... (...)	... (...)	... (...)	... (...)	...	...	...	...	...	...	...
Comoros	– (–)	54 (...)	16 (...)	29 (...)	– (–)	15	–	15	23	10	–	3
Congo	10 (...)	6 (...)	68 (...)	12 (...)	3 (...)	19	17	25	20	10	24	3
Côte d'Ivoire	... (...)	... (...)	... (...)	... (...)	... (...)	...	...	...	...	...	...	...
Djibouti	40 (...)	– (–)	60 (...)	– (–)	– (–)	30	38	–	25	–	–	6
Egypt	18 (19)	16 (17)	37 (35)	18 (17)	9 (9)	37	50	48	31	25	43	9
Equatorial Guinea	12 (...)	2 (...)	31 (...)	4 (...)	– (–)	13	51	10	10	–	–	...
Eritrea	... (...)	... (...)	... (...)	... (...)	... (...)	...	...	...	...	...	...	...
Ethiopia	9 (24)	4 (3)	37 (31)	43 (36)	7 (7)	19	19	30	29	10	14	8
Gabon	... (...)	... (...)	... (...)	... (...)	... (...)	...	...	...	...	...	...	...
Gambia	– (–)	– (–)	– (–)	– (–)	– (–)	–	–	–	–	–	–	–
Ghana	5 (3)	34 (38)	19 (23)	32 (29)	9 (7)	22	21	30	27	11	22	7
Guinea	♦33 (...)	./. (...)	11 (...)	46 (...)	10 (...)	7	♦7	./.	5	5	13	2
Guinea-Bissau	– (–)	– (–)	– (–)	– (–)	– (–)	–	–	–	–	–	–	–
Kenya	36 (34)	20 (19)	17 (17)	22 (24)	4 (6)	28	39	25	27	13	28	8
Lesotho	42 (35)	4 (3)	37 (44)	16 (19)	– (–)	58	67	53	60	29	–	9
Liberia	... (...)	... (...)	... (...)	... (...)	... (...)	...	...	...	...	...	...	...
Libyan Arab Jamahiriya	... (...)	... (...)	... (...)	... (...)	... (...)	...	...	...	...	...	...	...
Madagascar	2 (3)	14 (14)	49 (44)	23 (28)	13 (11)	35	36	66	25	31	46	12
Malawi	12 (10)	4 (1)	39 (36)	36 (40)	9 (13)	23	22	40	18	15	79	11
Mali	11 (...)	♦15 (...)	20 (...)	43 (...)	12 (...)	...	...	...	...	...	...	...
Mauritania	2 (8)	22 (39)	68 (39)	9 (14)	– (–)	15	4	18	14	14	–	2
Mauritius	40 (47)	20 (22)	19 (15)	16 (13)	5 (3)	42	49	57	36	21	21	11
Morocco	2 (7)	36 (40)	25 (22)	34 (27)	3 (3)	36	17	45	35	29	36	6
Mozambique	24 (26)	– (–)	27 (4)	39 (76)	10 (19)	26	28	–	28	18	49	6
Namibia	58 (67)	5 (4)	18 (13)	3 (2)	14 (12)	64	67	42	52	32	91	11
Niger	9 (...)	16 (...)	38 (...)	21 (...)	10 (...)	15	28	14	13	5	26	4
Nigeria	15 (23)	13 (12)	24 (26)	36 (24)	7 (5)	...	...	...	...	...	...	...
Rwanda	8 (8)	18 (23)	36 (39)	21 (25)	5 (5)	19	30	12	30	9	23	...
Sao Tome and Principe	– (–)	– (–)	– (–)	– (–)	– (–)	–	–	–	–	–	–	–
Senegal	3 (...)	35 (...)	31 (...)	20 (...)	11 (...)	24	20	29	23	11	38	6
Seychelles	– (–)	– (–)	– (–)	– (–)	– (–)	–	–	–	–	–	–	–
Sierra Leone	57 (...)	16 (...)	10 (...)	15 (...)	2 (...)	...	...	24	14	15	25	...
Somalia	... (...)	... (...)	... (...)	... (...)	... (...)	...	...	...	...	...	...	...
South Africa	... (...)	... (...)	... (...)	... (...)	... (...)	...	...	...	...	...	...	...
Sudan	6 (5)	18 (18)	28 (39)	16 (15)	5 (11)	48	34	45	40	28	42	...
Swaziland	25 (11)	8 (18)	24 (44)	43 (28)	– (–)	42	56	68	43	29	–	11
Togo	0 (1)	25 (27)	46 (48)	16 (13)	9 (7)	13	11	20	13	4	17	4
Tunisia	5 (14)	28 (16)	30 (32)	27 (20)	10 (13)	41	42	51	40	28	52	8
Uganda	38 (38)	6 (5)	36 (43)	15 (11)	4 (2)	29	27	29	36	13	26	6
United Rep. of Tanzania	... (...)	... (...)	... (...)	... (...)	... (...)	...	...	...	...	...	...	...

Country or territory	Percentage of students (and graduates) by field of study												Percentage of female students in each field of study													Gender segregation index (%)
	Education		Humanities		Law and social sciences		Natural sciences, engin. & agric.		Medical sciences				All fields	Education	Humanities	Law and social sciences	Natural sciences, engin. & agric.	Medical sciences								
Zaire	...	(...)	...	(...)	...	(...)	...	(...)	...	(...)			...	...	...	...	...	...								...
Zambia	44	(56)	♦9	(4)	14	(14)	25	(18)	4	(4)			28	37	♦29	43	6	24								12
Zimbabwe	43	(49)	5	(2)	26	(21)	25	(25)	2	(1)			32	40	34	34	16	27								8
America, North																											
Antigua and Barbuda	−	(−)	−	(−)	−	(−)	−	(−)	−	(−)			−	−	−	−	−	−								−
Bahamas	...	(...)	...	(...)	...	(...)	...	(...)	...	(...)			...	...	...	...	...	...								...
Barbados	2	(...)	40	(...)	43	(...)	8	(...)	6	(...)			55	70	64	48	44	60								9
Belize	−	(−)	−	(−)	−	(−)	−	(−)	−	(−)			−	−	−	−	−	−								−
British Virgin Islands	−	(−)	−	(−)	−	(−)	−	(−)	−	(−)			−	−	−	−	−	−								−
Canada	5	(4)	8	(7)	21	(18)	16	(19)	5	(5)			54	76	61	59	20	74								...
Costa Rica	12	(19)	4	(4)	39	(46)	18	(13)	4	(16)			...	...	...	...	...	...								...
Cuba	39	(50)	2	(1)	7	(11)	23	(18)	20	(15)			58	71	62	65	38	68								15
Dominica	−	(−)	8	(16)	37	(29)	42	(55)	−	(−)			55	−	77	73	27	−								−
Dominican Republic	...	(...)	...	(...)	...	(...)	...	(...)	...	(...)			...	...	...	...	...	...								...
El Salvador	18	(34)	2	(0)	46	(29)	19	(23)	15	(9)			33	47	49	38	15	20								11
Grenada	...	(...)	...	(...)	...	(...)	...	(...)	...	(...)			...	...	...	...	...	...								...
Guatemala	...	(...)	...	(...)	...	(...)	...	(...)	...	(...)			...	...	...	...	...	...								...
Haiti	...	(...)	...	(...)	...	(...)	...	(...)	...	(...)			...	...	...	...	...	...								...
Honduras	17	(5)	2	(1)	41	(35)	25	(21)	14	(38)			43	65	87	41	23	56								13
Jamaica	26	(12)	11	(21)	32	(43)	22	(14)	7	(10)			...	...	...	...	...	...								...
Mexico	10	(15)	1	(1)	45	(45)	34	(28)	9	(10)			45	67	55	53	26	55								13
Netherlands Antilles	−	(−)	−	(−)	−	(−)	−	(−)	−	(−)			−	−	−	−	−	−								−
Nicaragua	13	(11)	1	(1)	31	(38)	40	(28)	14	(22)			49	59	73	52	38	62								9
Panama	3	(18)	8	(11)	30	(32)	21	(25)	5	(14)			...	...	...	...	...	...								...
Saint Kitts and Nevis	15	(16)	5	(5)	12	(16)	57	(57)	11	(5)			55	83	50	55	38	100								19
Saint Lucia	...	(...)	...	(...)	...	(...)	...	(...)	...	(...)			...	...	...	...	...	...								...
Saint Vincent and the Grenadines	17	(...)	27	(...)	11	(...)	26	(...)	18	(...)			68	74	54	71	55	97								14
Trinidad and Tobago	5	(13)	15	(15)	25	(31)	45	(37)	10	(4)			49	68	73	58	34	43								14
United States	7	(11)	13	(18)	30	(38)	17	(19)	10	(9)			...	...	...	...	...	...								...
America, South																											
Argentina	...	(...)	...	(...)	...	(...)	...	(...)	...	(...)			...	...	...	...	...	...								...
Bolivia	1	(1)	2	(3)	41	(45)	32	(29)	20	(21)			...	...	...	...	...	...								...
Brazil	13	(19)	9	(10)	43	(41)	22	(16)	9	(10)			54	81	73	50	31	64								12
Chile	11	(26)	4	(5)	37	(22)	41	(31)	6	(13)			...	...	...	...	...	...								...
Colombia	18	(22)	4	(4)	39	(39)	31	(26)	9	(9)			51	68	59	55	32	63								12
Ecuador	25	(21)	1	(1)	41	(36)	21	(16)	11	(25)			...	...	...	...	...	...								...
Guyana	16	(26)	4	(3)	27	(19)	45	(48)	5	(4)			43	78	70	61	16	49								24
Paraguay	19	(33)	2	(4)	40	(35)	25	(19)	6	(6)			53	77	41	48	42	64								11
Peru	11	(13)	2	(1)	42	(43)	29	(25)	11	(11)			...	...	...	...	...	...								...
Suriname	45	(89)	1	(1)	32	(8)	6	(1)	8	(1)			...	...	...	...	...	...								...
Uruguay	10	(21)	9	(1)	40	(34)	22	(17)	17	(23)			...	...	...	...	...	...								...
Venezuela	...	(...)	...	(...)	...	(...)	...	(...)	...	(...)			...	...	...	...	...	...								...
Asia																											
Afghanistan	28	(30)	44	(32)	14	(19)	12	(14)	3	(5)			31	54	9	43	39	44								19
Armenia	...	(...)	...	(...)	...	(...)	...	(...)	...	(...)			...	...	...	...	...	...								...
Azerbaijan	35	(35)	3	(3)	9	(9)	51	(43)	./.	(7)			38	66	45	19	23	./.								19
Bahrain	14	(5)	13	(./.)	21	(37)	39	(42)	14	(16)			57	79	66	70	34	72								18
Bangladesh	1	(...)	30	(...)	42	(...)	25	(...)	2	(...)			16	35	16	15	15	27								1
Bhutan	...	(...)	...	(...)	...	(...)	...	(...)	...	(...)			...	...	...	...	...	...								...

Table 9 (continued)

Country or territory	Education		Humani-ties		Law and social sciences		Natural sciences, engin. & agric.		Medical sciences		All fields	Edu-cation	Humani-ties	Law and social sciences	Natural sciences, engin. & agric.	Medical sciences	Gender segre-gation index (%)
	Percentage of students (and graduates) by field of study										*Percentage of female students in each field of study*						
Brunei Darussalam	...	(...)	...	(...)	...	(...)	...	(...)	...	(...)	...	...	...	...	...	...	...
Cambodia	...	(...)	...	(...)	...	(...)	...	(...)	...	(...)	...	...	...	...	...	...	...
China	24	(29)	6	(6)	13	(13)	47	(44)	10	(8)	...	...	...	...	...	...	...
Cyprus	11	(24)	3	(3)	53	(50)	26	(19)	5	(4)	49	90	72	51	22	74	15
Dem. People's Rep. of Korea	...	(...)	...	(...)	...	(...)	...	(...)	...	(...)	...	...	...	...	...	...	...
Georgia	...	(...)	...	(...)	...	(...)	...	(...)	...	(...)	...	...	...	...	...	...	...
Hong Kong	7	(12)	8	(9)	26	(34)	35	(40)	5	(5)	42	64	74	58	18	46	...
India	2	(9)	♦40	(47)	27	(24)	26	(17)	3	(2)	32	53	♦44	19	27	32	10
Indonesia	18	(25)	3	(3)	55	(49)	22	(22)	2	(2)	...	...	...	...	...	...	...
Iran, Islamic Rep. of	13	(11)	11	(8)	15	(10)	37	(28)	22	(23)	28	35	40	23	15	45	11
Iraq	...	(...)	...	(...)	...	(...)	...	(...)	...	(...)	...	...	...	...	...	...	...
Israel	♦41	♦(25)	./.	(./.)	25	(35)	27	(30)	6	(10)	51	♦61	./.	50	32	69	10
Japan	8	(9)	19	(21)	39	(38)	22	(22)	6	(5)	40	73	74	33	10	46	18
Jordan	12	(14)	19	(26)	28	(24)	29	(23)	11	(11)	49	73	64	41	36	53	12
Kazakstan	14	(18)	22	(2)	13	(1)	26	(58)	8	(./.)	52	60	68	61	38	69	...
Kuwait	13	(14)	13	(12)	28	(30)	29	(32)	13	(8)	61	88	72	64	50	48	12
Kyrgyzstan	...	(...)	...	(...)	...	(...)	...	(...)	...	(...)	...	...	...	...	...	...	...
Lao People's Dem. Rep.	23	(28)	11	(11)	8	(7)	45	(38)	13	(17)	27	38	40	35	11	50	15
Lebanon	...	(...)	...	(...)	...	(...)	...	(...)	...	(...)	...	...	...	...	...	...	...
Malaysia	25	(11)	9	(10)	30	(44)	27	(32)	3	(3)	45	57	53	52	32	52	12
Maldives	–	(–)	–	(–)	–	(–)	–	(–)	–	(–)	–	–	–	–	–	–	–
Mongolia	...	(...)	...	(...)	...	(...)	...	(...)	...	(...)	...	...	...	...	...	...	...
Myanmar	...	(...)	...	(...)	...	(...)	...	(...)	...	(...)	...	...	...	...	...	...	...
Nepal	8	(...)	♦42	(...)	34	(...)	14	(...)	2	(...)	24	23	♦33	16	12	52	9
Oman	59	(84)	3	(2)	5	(4)	21	(10)	11	(–)	49	53	53	39	31	59	8
Pakistan	...	(...)	...	(...)	...	(...)	...	(...)	...	(...)	...	...	...	...	...	...	...
Palestine																	
Gaza Strip	10	(42)	15	(35)	5	(15)	3	(8)	–	(–)	44	22	32	16	27	–	–
West Bank	19	(3)	35	(58)	16	(2)	27	(11)	3	(2)	39	47	45	27	30	69	9
Philippines	18	(18)	9	(8)	26	(32)	26	(23)	19	(17)	59	77	60	67	27	76	18
Qatar	23	(36)	31	(14)	20	(31)	24	(17)	1	(1)	71	83	84	69	48	100	13
Republic of Korea	7	(9)	17	(18)	27	(29)	40	(35)	6	(8)	32	65	53	31	14	48	14
Saudi Arabia	40	(38)	31	(26)	8	(9)	16	(23)	4	(4)	46	65	38	32	25	37	15
Singapore	...	(...)	...	(...)	...	(...)	...	(...)	...	(...)	...	...	...	...	...	...	...
Sri Lanka	7	(5)	10	(42)	41	(21)	34	(25)	9	(7)	32	59	28	33	23	39	6
Syrian Arab Republic	2	(4)	21	(15)	35	(25)	29	(36)	11	(19)	38	55	61	32	30	34	11
Tajikistan	...	(...)	...	(...)	...	(...)	...	(...)	...	(...)	...	...	...	...	...	...	...
Thailand	12	(15)	14	(17)	50	(38)	19	(24)	5	(6)	53	60	68	56	23	77	11
Turkey	9	(11)	5	(7)	54	(34)	23	(34)	8	(12)	35	43	46	34	28	47	5
Turkmenistan	...	(...)	...	(...)	...	(...)	...	(...)	...	(...)	...	...	...	...	...	...	...
United Arab Emirates	33	(36)	6	(9)	24	(39)	13	(16)	1	(–)	76	89	75	63	53	69	...
Uzbekistan	...	(...)	...	(...)	...	(...)	...	(...)	...	(...)	...	...	...	...	...	...	...
Viet Nam	...	(...)	...	(...)	...	(...)	...	(...)	...	(...)	...	...	...	...	...	...	...
Yemen	43	(60)	10	(4)	34	(26)	8	(7)	5	(3)	17	19	32	9	14	39	6
Former Dem. Yemen	.	(.)	.	(.)	.	(.)	.	(.)	.	(.)	.	.	.	.	.	.	.
Former Yemen Arab Rep.	.	(.)	.	(.)	.	(.)	.	(.)	.	(.)	.	.	.	.	.	.	.
Europe																	
Albania	30	(29)	6	(5)	13	(13)	30	(32)	10	(11)	52	68	53	61	40	51	...
Austria	6	(16)	17	(13)	39	(32)	29	(27)	8	(11)	45	73	61	46	25	57	12
Belarus	21	(20)	18	(16)	9	(10)	40	(41)	8	(8)	50	77	58	70	30	60	19
Belgium	10	(13)	7	(6)	44	(45)	24	(22)	13	(13)	48	72	60	51	22	64	13

Country or territory	Percentage of students (and graduates) by field of study					Percentage of female students in each field of study						Gender segregation index (%)
	Education	Humanities	Law and social sciences	Natural sciences, engin. & agric.	Medical sciences	All fields	Education	Humanities	Law and social sciences	Natural sciences, engin. & agric.	Medical sciences	
Bosnia and Herzegovina	... (...)	... (...)	... (...)	... (...)	... (...)	...	...	...	...	...	...	...
Bulgaria	15 (22)	7 (6)	26 (17)	37 (36)	10 (13)	57	77	75	61	46	65	13
Croatia	8 (14)	9 (6)	28 (26)	44 (38)	8 (14)	48	79	68	62	28	64	19
Czech Republic	19 (21)	7 (4)	20 (20)	42 (46)	10 (8)	44	69	48	52	26	59	16
Former Czechoslovakia	. (.)	. (.)	. (.)	. (.)	. (.)	.	.	.	.	.	.	.
Denmark	12 (18)	19 (9)	28 (23)	27 (28)	11 (16)	53	76	69	44	28	82	19
Estonia	13 (13)	13 (9)	28 (30)	36 (40)	6 (6)	51	84	67	57	26	74	19
Finland	11 (13)	14 (6)	19 (14)	38 (35)	18 (32)	53	76	70	57	23	84	23
France	3 (4)	♦24 (23)	21 (24)	19 (20)	11 (8)	54	72	♦70	54	34	60	...
Germany	♦26 ♦(18)	./. (./.)	29 (29)	39 (43)	6 (11)	40	♦63	./.	41	25	45	12
Former German Dem. Rep.	. (.)	. (.)	. (.)	. (.)	. (.)	.	.	.	.	.	.	.
Germany, Federal Rep. of	. (.)	. (.)	. (.)	. (.)	. (.)	.	.	.	.	.	.	.
Greece	9 (11)	13 (14)	28 (25)	37 (31)	13 (19)	50	65	76	56	28	63	16
Hungary	36 (40)	5 (4)	17 (16)	29 (27)	9 (8)	51	72	50	55	24	56	18
Iceland	16 (...)	21 (...)	30 (...)	16 (...)	18 (...)	59	78	65	52	25	74	14
Ireland	3 (6)	19 (18)	27 (32)	31 (39)	4 (4)	48	74	64	55	31	57	...
Italy	2 (3)	15 (15)	43 (34)	28 (23)	11 (25)	51	87	79	51	33	49	10
Latvia	14 ♦(20)	11 (./.)	24 (12)	46 (51)	6 (5)	...	...	...	...	...	...	...
Lithuania	... (...)	... (...)	... (...)	... (...)	... (...)	...	...	...	...	...	...	...
Luxembourg	... (...)	... (...)	... (...)	... (...)	... (...)	...	...	...	...	...	...	...
Malta	18 (21)	26 (23)	24 (32)	13 (14)	18 (9)	48	60	52	44	20	56	10
Monaco	− (−)	− (−)	− (−)	− (−)	− (−)	−	−	−	−	−	−	−
Netherlands	11 (12)	12 (10)	39 (34)	24 (25)	9 (15)	46	64	62	47	18	70	13
Norway	13 (36)	11 (5)	34 (18)	20 (18)	10 (15)	53	75	65	51	28	82	...
Poland	19 (28)	10 (7)	28 (21)	28 (19)	12 (23)	56	79	65	60	31	69	16
Portugal	13 (18)	11 (17)	39 (28)	31 (29)	6 (6)	39	69	57	31	32	60	12
Republic of Moldova	... (...)	... (...)	... (...)	... (...)	... (...)	...	...	...	...	...	...	...
Romania	2 (3)	8 (4)	21 (12)	57 (70)	10 (10)	47	33	60	59	39	60	11
Russian Federation	10 (13)	7 (7)	20 (18)	51 (47)	9 (13)	55	88	76	74	34	80	22
San Marino	− (−)	− (−)	− (−)	− (−)	− (−)	−	−	−	−	−	−	−
Slovakia	18 (17)	8 (3)	18 (19)	47 (55)	8 (6)	49	73	55	60	31	66	17
Slovenia	13 (10)	8 (5)	36 (38)	34 (33)	6 (9)	54	80	68	64	27	73	18
Spain	7 (13)	11 (12)	46 (37)	26 (19)	8 (12)	51	73	64	55	29	65	12
Sweden	15 (19)	15 (3)	26 (17)	29 (33)	14 (25)	54	79	64	55	24	74	18
Switzerland	5 (3)	14 (16)	41 (37)	32 (29)	8 (14)	36	70	57	38	14	52	14
The FYR of Macedonia	7 (12)	9 (10)	26 (27)	47 (41)	9 (10)	52	74	74	60	37	67	15
Ukraine	19 (20)	14 (15)	7 (10)	52 (48)	7 (7)	...	...	...	...	...	...	...
United Kingdom	6 (6)	12 (18)	27 (32)	28 (39)	12 (4)	49	71	61	50	24	76	...
Yugoslavia	7 (14)	12 (9)	22 (23)	49 (39)	9 (13)	53	68	76	66	38	65	15
Former Yugoslavia	. (.)	. (.)	. (.)	. (.)	. (.)	.	.	.	.	.	.	.
Oceania												
Australia	15 (22)	♦23 ♦(22)	24 (22)	26 (22)	12 (12)	53	73	♦68	42	30	74	18
Fiji	16 (20)	− (4)	37 (45)	25 (23)	17 (8)	35	...	...	...	...	...	...
Kiribati	... (...)	... (...)	... (...)	... (...)	... (...)	...	...	...	...	...	...	...
New Zealand	12 (8)	19 (10)	36 (38)	20 (17)	7 (6)	54	80	65	50	27	76	14
Papua New Guinea	... (...)	... (...)	... (...)	... (...)	... (...)	...	...	...	...	...	...	...
Samoa	... (...)	... (...)	... (...)	... (...)	... (...)	...	...	...	...	...	...	...
Solomon Islands	− (−)	− (−)	− (−)	− (−)	− (−)	−	−	−	−	−	−	−
Tonga	... (...)	... (...)	... (...)	... (...)	... (...)	...	...	...	...	...	...	...
Tuvalu	− (−)	− (−)	− (−)	− (−)	− (−)	−	−	−	−	−	−	−
Vanuatu	− (−)	− (−)	− (−)	− (−)	− (−)	−	−	−	−	−	−	−

Table 10
Private enrolment and public expenditure on education

| Country or territory | Private enrolment as percentage of total enrolment | | | | | | Public expenditure on education | | | | | | |
| | Pre-primary | | First level | | Second level | | As percentage of GNP | | As percentage of government expenditure | | Average annual growth rate (%) | Current expenditure as percentage of total | |
	1980	1992	1980	1992	1980	1992	1980	1992	1980	1992	1980–92	1980	1992
Africa													
Algeria	–	–	–	–	–	–	7.8	8.1	24.3	27.0	5.2	66.9	78.3
Angola	...	...	–	–	–	–	...	...	...	10.7	...	...	89.9
Benin	...	8	3	4	1	...	4.2	...	...	...	...	...	...
Botswana	–	–	5	4	41	72	7.0	8.3	16.1	18.7	12.1	75.2	77.1
Burkina Faso	90	...	8	7	51	35	2.6	2.7	19.8	17.5	4.2	93.0	99.7
Burundi	31	...	4	1	10	11	3.0	3.7	17.5	11.9	5.5	86.9	96.0
Cameroon	49	36	36	25	47	39	3.2	♦3.1	20.3	♦16.9	2.4	81.3	88.9
Cape Verde	...	...	–	...	–	–	...	4.2	...	19.9	...	...	98.6
Central African Republic	...	...	...	...	1	4	3.8	2.8	20.9	...	– 2.4	97.2	97.6
Chad	...	...	5	14	...	9	...	2.3	...	...	...	...	99.1
Comoros	–	–	–	1	–	12	...	♦4.1	...	♦22.0	...	...	...
Congo	–	9	–	–	–	1	7.0	8.6	23.6	...	3.2	93.8	99.0
Côte d'Ivoire	76	67	14	10	29	27	7.2	...	22.6	...	...	83.5	...
Djibouti	100	100	9	9	5	18	...	3.8	11.5	11.1	...	76.5	100.0
Egypt	94	83	5	7	11	4	5.7	5.0	9.4	11.0	2.9	78.6	80.2
Equatorial Guinea	...	...	...	...	...	...	...	1.8	...	...	...	...	...
Eritrea	...	97	...	17	...	...	...	...	...	...	...	...	...
Ethiopia	100	40	13	12	7	9	3.3	5.1	10.4	12.9	4.4	79.5	80.1
Gabon	...	52	39	31	45	19	2.7	...	...	...	...	72.3	...
Gambia	...	...	16	15	42	...	3.3	2.7	8.7	12.9	– 0.3	88.1	95.8
Ghana	11	...	...	7	2	...	3.1	3.1	17.1	24.3	6.9	...	86.7
Guinea	–	–	–	4	–	2	...	2.4	...	...	...	...	...
Guinea-Bissau	–	–	–	–	–	–	...	...	...	...	...	...	...
Kenya	...	...	...	...	33	11	6.8	♦5.4	18.1	♦16.1	3.9	92.1	93.2
Lesotho	–	–	98	100	...	...	5.1	6.0	14.8	17.6	2.6	79.9	78.1
Liberia	42	...	...	...	...	...	5.7	...	24.3	...	...	85.9	...
Libyan Arab Jamahiriya	–	–	–	–	–	–	3.4	...	...	...	...	63.0	...
Madagascar	...	...	13	22	42	41	4.4	...	...	...	...	85.5	...
Malawi	–	–	7	10	12	18	3.4	3.3	8.4	10.3	3.9	75.6	71.0
Mali	...	...	4	4	9	7	3.8	2.8	30.8	...	– 0.2	98.8	...
Mauritania	...	56	...	1	–	2	5.0	...	...	...	...	...	...
Mauritius	100	...	26	24	88	80	5.3	3.7	11.6	11.8	2.1	89.9	93.0
Morocco	100	100	3	4	5	3	6.1	5.8	18.5	26.7	1.8	80.8	88.1
Mozambique	–	–	–	–	–	–	4.4	6.2	12.1	12.0	– 1.5	86.2	63.7
Namibia	...	14	...	4	...	4	1.6	...	...	...	...	89.3	...
Niger	54	22	3	3	...	10	3.1	...	22.9	...	...	...	...
Nigeria	...	...	...	...	...	...	6.4	...	...	...	...	80.0	...
Rwanda	...	...	0	1	24	31	2.7	3.8	21.6	25.4	2.5	84.7	94.1
Sao Tome and Principe	–	–	–	–	–	–	8.0	...	...	...	...	...	...
Senegal	80	59	11	10	30	24	4.4	4.2	23.2	27.4	1.6	...	...
Seychelles	–	2	–	2	–	1	5.8	8.5	14.4	12.9	4.1	95.7	85.6
Sierra Leone	...	...	...	...	...	...	3.8	1.4	11.8	...	– 10.9	95.3	95.5
Somalia	–	...	–	...	–	...	...	...	...	...	...	...	...
South Africa	...	4	...	1	...	2	...	7.0	...	22.1	...	...	92.1
Sudan	69	...	3	2	5	21	4.8	...	9.1	...	...	92.2	...
Swaziland	...	...	80	81	...	46	6.1	6.0	...	22.5	– 4.7	76.4	86.7
Togo	54	51	23	25	11	16	5.6	6.7	19.4	21.6	1.8	96.4	97.4
Tunisia	...	...	1	1	7	11	5.4	6.1	16.4	13.5	5.0	87.6	87.8
Uganda	...	...	...	...	23	...	1.2	2.0	11.3	15.0	...	88.3	94.3
United Rep. of Tanzania	...	...	0	0	43	55	4.4	5.0	11.2	11.4	2.3	82.7	87.9

Country or territory	Private enrolment as percentage of total enrolment						Public expenditure on education							
	Pre-primary		First level		Second level		As percentage of GNP		As percentage of government expenditure		Average annual growth rate (%)		Current expenditure as percentage of total	
	1980	1992	1980	1992	1980	1992	1980	1992	1980	1992	1980–92		1980	1992
Zaire	...	86	...	6	...	26	2.6	...	24.2	...	...		98.3	...
Zambia	...	...	1	...	3	...	4.5	2.6	7.6	8.7	– 6.6		95.1	87.0
Zimbabwe	...	...	83	88	49	69	6.6	9.1	13.7	19.4	6.4		97.4	...
America, North														
Antigua and Barbuda	...	...	...	...	...	...	3.0	...	7.6	...	...		98.9	...
Bahamas	...	69	21	...	21	25	4.4	3.6	...	...	4.5		...	...
Barbados	20	...	9	10	16	...	6.5	7.0	20.5	16.9	3.2		82.8	89.3
Belize	...	...	...	...	...	47	...	5.7	...	15.5	...		...	79.9
British Virgin Islands	100	...	9	...	–	...	...	...	...	...	...		...	...
Canada	3	4	3	4	7	6	6.9	7.6	16.3	14.3	2.8		...	...
Costa Rica	13	10	3	5	9	10	7.8	4.4	22.2	21.4	– 0.8		91.3	96.4
Cuba	–	–	–	–	–	–	7.2	6.6	...	12.3	...		89.5	93.1
Dominica	...	100	4	4	...	5	...	5.8	...	10.6	...		...	91.0
Dominican Republic	87	55	18	22	24	32	2.2	1.6	16.0	8.9	– 1.6		...	...
El Salvador	20	33	7	14	50	62	3.9	1.6	17.1	...	– 6.6		94.1	99.8
Grenada	4	...	92	8	...	...	...	...	...	...	...		...	...
Guatemala	21	32	14	17	38	...	1.8	1.5	11.9	11.6	– 0.9		89.4	95.7
Haiti	100	86	57	61	82	82	1.5	1.8	14.9	20.0	3.9		80.1	99.9
Honduras	16	21	5	5	46	...	3.2	4.1	14.2	15.9	4.6		91.0	97.7
Jamaica	85	86	4	8	4	...	7.0	4.7	13.1	11.8	– 2.5		99.6	87.9
Mexico	11	9	5	6	19	12	4.7	4.9	...	...	0.4		...	...
Netherlands Antilles	80	...	80	...	...	...	3.5	...	13.6	...	...		97.7	78.3
Nicaragua	43	28	12	14	18	19	3.4	...	10.4	...	...		87.5	...
Panama	34	27	6	8	11	13	4.8	5.5	19.0	18.9	2.1		93.7	93.2
Saint Kitts and Nevis	68	71	...	16	...	3	5.2	♦3.3	9.4	...	– 1.2		99.5	95.2
Saint Lucia	...	100	2	1	11	8	7.7	...	...	...	...		83.9	...
Saint Vincent and the Grenadines	100	100	4	3	37	46	...	6.7	...	13.8	...		...	75.3
Trinidad and Tobago	...	...	73	...	...	...	4.0	4.0	11.5	11.6	– 2.2		76.4	92.2
United States	36	34	11	10	8	8	...	5.3	...	12.3	...		...	90.5
America, South														
Argentina	32	...	18	20	39	...	2.7	3.1	15.1	15.7	3.6		84.5	...
Bolivia	8	10	8	10	17	26	4.4	...	25.3	...	...		96.0	...
Brazil	46	26	13	12	...	...	3.6	4.6	...	...	4.0		...	...
Chile	20	49	20	40	24	43	4.6	2.9	11.9	12.9	– 1.6		94.9	96.3
Colombia	64	58	14	17	45	40	1.9	3.1	14.3	10.9	4.5		93.3	95.2
Ecuador	42	40	16	16	34	...	5.6	2.7	...	19.2	– 4.3		94.0	84.6
Guyana	–	–	–	–	–	–	9.7	7.8	14.0	8.9	– 7.2		73.6	80.2
Paraguay	63	50	15	14	27	22	1.5	♦2.6	16.4	♦11.9	2.5		...	98.2
Peru	27	20	13	12	15	16	3.1	...	15.2	...	...		94.4	...
Suriname	54	...	55	52	...	...	6.7	7.3	22.5	...	0.3		100.0	99.6
Uruguay	25	29	16	16	17	16	2.3	2.8	10.0	15.4	3.6		94.7	91.1
Venezuela	17	17	13	15	26	35	4.4	5.3	14.7	23.5	0.2		95.1	...
Asia														
Afghanistan	–	–	–	–	–	–	2.0	...	12.7	...	...		90.0	93.2
Armenia	–	...	–	...	–	...	...	7.3	...	20.5	...		...	...
Azerbaijan	–	...	–	...	–	...	...	7.7	...	24.7	...		...	...
Bahrain	100	100	9	16	7	12	2.9	...	10.3	...	...		86.5	...
Bangladesh	...	...	15	14	95	90	1.5	2.3	7.8	7.8	8.3		66.8	79.7
Bhutan	...	...	...	...	...	...	...	...	...	...	...		...	...

Table 10 (continued)

Country or territory	Private enrolment as percentage of total enrolment						Public expenditure on education						
	Pre-primary		First level		Second level		As percentage of GNP		As percentage of government expenditure		Average annual growth rate (%)	Current expenditure as percentage of total	
	1980	1992	1980	1992	1980	1992	1980	1992	1980	1992	1980–92	1980	1992
Brunei Darussalam	51	57	29	26	18	12	1.2	...	11.8	...	...	88.8	90.4
Cambodia	...	...	...	...	...	...	...	...	...	...	...	...	...
China	–	–	–	–	–	–	2.5	2.0	9.3	12.2	7.6	90.7	90.9
Cyprus	49	68	3	5	10	13	3.5	4.0	12.9	12.5	6.0	94.0	92.6
Dem. People's Rep. of Korea	–	–	–	–	–	–	...	...	...	...	...	...	...
Georgia	–	...	–	...	–	...	...	...	...	...	...	...	...
Hong Kong	100	...	94	...	96	...	...	...	14.6	18.1	...	88.1	86.5
India	...	...	...	...	...	...	2.8	3.7	10.0	11.9	8.5	98.8	98.5
Indonesia	99	100	21	17	49	44	1.7	2.2	8.9	9.4	8.3	...	65.4
Iran, Islamic Rep. of	–	–	–	1	–	1	7.5	4.6	15.7	28.2	– 1.7	88.4	82.2
Iraq	–	–	–	–	–	–	3.0	...	...	...	...	...	88.5
Israel	17	...	...	...	...	...	7.9	5.8	7.3	10.5	– 1.7	92.3	91.6
Japan	73	80	1	1	13	16	5.8	4.7	19.6	16.6	2.0	...	...
Jordan	99	96	6	24	19	7	...	6.5	11.3	13.3	...	79.2	93.8
Kazakstan	–	...	–	...	–	...	...	7.7	...	19.1	...	...	...
Kuwait	41	17	16	30	16	22	2.4	6.1	8.1	11.4	...	93.1	...
Kyrgyzstan	–	...	–	...	–	...	...	6.9	...	24.1	...	...	...
Lao People's Dem. Rep.	–	8	–	2	–	1	...	2.3	...	...	...	...	75.8
Lebanon	81	83	61	68	47	58	...	♦1.9	13.2	♦12.5	...	...	*98.8
Malaysia	53	43	...	...	...	5	6.0	♦5.5	14.7	♦16.9	...	83.0	...
Maldives	...	97	...	53	...	38	...	6.6	...	...	...	...	54.7
Mongolia	–	–	–	–	–	–	...	8.5	...	...	...	...	...
Myanmar	...	...	–	–	–	–	1.7	2.4	...	...	2.3	...	...
Nepal	...	...	...	6	...	24	1.8	2.9	10.5	13.2	8.2	...	...
Oman	100	100	0	2	–	1	2.1	3.8	...	16.2	12.4	81.3	89.8
Pakistan	...	...	...	...	...	...	2.0	2.7	5.0	...	11.7	73.1	86.7
Palestine													
Gaza Strip	...	87	...	1	...	1	...	...	...	...	...	...	...
West Bank	...	100	...	7	...	6	...	...	...	...	...	...	...
Philippines	66	53	5	7	48	35	1.7	2.9	9.1	10.5	6.6	96.0	88.8
Qatar	100	100	16	30	8	21	2.6	3.4	7.2	...	...	75.5	93.6
Republic of Korea	97	74	1	2	46	39	3.7	4.2	...	14.8	13.2	84.3	79.8
Saudi Arabia	87	78	3	5	2	4	4.1	6.4	8.7	17.0	2.1	63.5	95.5
Singapore	63	72	26	24	28	27	2.8	...	7.3	...	...	85.6	...
Sri Lanka	...	...	1	2	2	2	♦2.7	3.3	♦7.7	8.8	6.2	85.3	76.3
Syrian Arab Republic	100	92	5	4	7	6	4.6	4.2	8.1	14.2	– 1.9	...	...
Tajikistan	–	...	–	...	–	...	...	...	...	...	...	...	...
Thailand	55	23	8	10	13	10	3.4	4.0	20.6	19.6	7.7	70.6	82.0
Turkey	5	4	0	1	2	3	2.8	...	10.5	...	...	83.7	...
Turkmenistan	–	...	–	...	–	...	...	7.9	...	19.7	...	...	...
United Arab Emirates	69	66	17	36	10	24	1.3	2.0	...	15.2	...	79.0	93.3
Uzbekistan	–	...	–	...	–	...	...	...	...	...	...	...	...
Viet Nam	–	–	–	–	–	–	...	...	...	...	...	...	...
Yemen	.	...	.	...	.	...	.	...	.	...	.	.	...
Former Dem. Yemen	–	.	–	.	–	.	.	.	16.9	.	.	85.3	.
Former Yemen Arab Rep.	...	.	5	.	9	.	.	.	15.8	.	.	...	.
Europe													
Albania	–	–	–	–	–	–	...	...	10.3	...	...	...	...
Austria	28	26	3	4	6	8	5.6	5.8	8.0	7.7	1.9	85.3	88.2
Belarus	–	–	–	–	–	–	5.4	6.6	...	19.3	...	83.9	81.8
Belgium	58	57	53	56	64	66	6.1	5.2	16.3	...	0.0	98.9	99.2

Country or territory	Private enrolment as percentage of total enrolment						Public expenditure on education						
	Pre-primary		First level		Second level		As percentage of GNP		As percentage of government expenditure		Average annual growth rate (%)	Current expenditure as percentage of total	
	1980	1992	1980	1992	1980	1992	1980	1992	1980	1992	1980–92	1980	1992
Bosnia and Herzegovina	–	...	–	...	–	...	...	...	...	...	...	...	...
Bulgaria	–	0	–	0	–	0	4.5	5.9	...	...	2.9	95.9	95.6
Croatia	–	0	–	–	–	–	...	...	...	...	...	...	...
Czech Republic	–	0	–	0	–	6	...	4.6	...	...	...	...	91.1
Former Czechoslovakia	–	.	–	.	–	.	4.0	.	...	.	.	94.1	.
Denmark	8	10	9	10	11	16	6.9	7.4	9.5	11.8	1.9	88.7	93.1
Estonia	–	–	–	–	–	–	...	5.8	...	31.4	...	...	91.7
Finland	...	2	...	1	...	5	5.3	7.3	11.2	11.6	4.1	...	...
France	13	12	15	15	21	21	5.0	5.7	...	...	2.5	92.5	92.3
Germany	.	53	.	1	.	6	.	...	...	...	.	...	...
Former German Dem. Rep.	–	.	.	.	–	.	...	.	...	.	.	...	.
Germany, Federal Rep. of	...	.	...	.	6	.	4.7	.	9.5	.	.	86.4	.
Greece	9	5	6	7	4	4	2.4	3.1	8.4	...	4.5	94.3	94.1
Hungary	–	2	–	2	–	–	4.7	7.0	5.2	7.7	2.8	83.1	92.4
Iceland	...	...	...	...	...	...	4.6	5.8	14.0	...	5.5	...	73.9
Ireland	100	100	100	100	...	...	6.3	6.2	11.2	10.9	2.2	86.6	95.3
Italy	38	29	7	7	6	7	4.4	5.4	11.1	...	3.4	86.5	...
Latvia	–	–	–	0	–	0	...	6.7	...	16.8	...	...	97.4
Lithuania	–	0	–	0	–	0	...	5.5	...	22.1	...	...	95.5
Luxembourg	1	...	1	1	8	...	5.7	4.1	14.9	...	– 0.3	95.0	82.1
Malta	51	37	27	32	35	29	3.0	4.6	7.8	10.9	6.3	99.3	97.1
Monaco	37	30	34	35	...	30	...	...	...	5.6	...	...	91.4
Netherlands	70	68	68	69	72	76	7.6	5.9	...	...	– 0.1	...	...
Norway	41	37	1	1	3	5	7.1	8.4	13.5	13.6	3.9	...	...
Poland	0	1	–	0	–	3	...	5.6	...	14.0	...	...	93.6
Portugal	31	58	7	8	9	8	3.8	5.0	10.7	...	5.0	85.4	93.7
Republic of Moldova	–	...	–	–	–	–	...	6.5	...	26.4	...	...	91.8
Romania	–	0	–	–	–	–	3.3	3.6	6.7	14.2	– 1.3	88.8	96.5
Russian Federation	–	0	–	0	–	0	3.4	4.0	...	...	...	...	...
San Marino	–	–	–	–	–	–	...	...	7.5	...	...	86.4	94.5
Slovakia	–	–	–	3	–	4	...	6.6	...	...	...	...	88.6
Slovenia	–	–	–	–	–	–	...	5.7	...	23.2	...	...	94.2
Spain	45	36	36	35	37	31	2.6	4.6	...	9.3	1.1	86.3	90.4
Sweden	...	8	1	2	...	2	9.0	8.3	14.1	12.6	0.5	86.4	90.9
Switzerland	7	6	2	2	7	6	5.0	5.2	18.8	18.8	2.2	89.5	88.7
The FYR of Macedonia	–	–	–	–	–	–	...	5.3	...	...	...	...	97.7
Ukraine	–	–	–	–	–	–	5.6	7.8	24.5	...	...	86.3	85.6
United Kingdom	8	6	4	5	8	9	5.6	5.2	13.9	...	1.7	94.1	95.0
Yugoslavia	–	–	–	–	–	–	...	...	...	...	...	...	94.1
Former Yugoslavia	–	.	–	.	–	.	4.7	.	...	.	.	85.1	.
Oceania													
Australia	22	26	20	22	26	32	5.5	5.5	14.8	14.1	2.1	90.9	93.0
Fiji	100	100	94	96	89	87	5.1	◆5.6	11.3	◆18.6	0.2	96.4	96.9
Kiribati	...	...	2	–	59	78	7.7	7.4	13.0	14.8	0.1	100.0	100.0
New Zealand	–	–	8	3	13	5	5.8	7.1	23.1	...	3.7	89.9	96.2
Papua New Guinea	...	100	2	2	...	3	4.7	...	14.2	...	...	96.7	...
Samoa	...	...	13	...	...	...	...	4.2	...	10.7	...	...	94.3
Solomon Islands	...	9	13	10	89	...	5.6	4.2	11.2	7.9	4.3	76.2	100.0
Tonga	...	...	6	8	...	80	3.3	4.8	11.6	17.3	– 0.9	89.8	...
Tuvalu	...	...	...	...	...	...	...	...	...	16.2	...	...	100.0
Vanuatu	66	100	27	22	...	6	...	4.5	...	18.8	...	...	100.0

Table 11
Public current expenditure on education

Country or territory	Teachers' emoluments as percentage of total current expenditure 1992	Percentage distribution of current expenditure by level						Current expenditure per pupil as a percentage of GNP per capita					
		1980			1992			1980			1992		
		Pre-prim. + 1st level	2nd level	3rd level	Pre-prim. + 1st level	2nd level	3rd level	Pre-prim. + 1st level	2nd level	3rd level	Pre-prim. + 1st level	2nd level	3rd level
Africa													
Algeria	...	28.5	25.2	17.3	...	...	...	9	24	170	...	...	...
Angola	♦86.3	...	...	...	♦96.3	./.	3.7	...	...	...	...	...	...
Benin	...	...	...	...	...	...	...	...	...	...	...	...	...
Botswana	43.3	52.1	29.2	13.2	31.1	48.8	12.2	15	69	707	9	52	265
Burkina Faso	54.0	32.3	19.8	33.7	41.7	25.8	32.1	26	119	3 395	21	67	1 345
Burundi	56.1	38.8	35.3	23.8	44.5	28.2	24.6	24	222	1 480	14	105	1 199
Cameroon	...	♦76.0	./.	24.0	♦86.6	./.	13.4	♦8	./.	360	♦11	./.	120
Cape Verde	...	...	...	...	54.7	17.5	2.7	...	...	...	10	26	.
Central African Republic	68.1	54.9	13.9	16.3	52.7	14.6	21.5	21	27	671	10	20	395
Chad	58.6	...	...	...	47.1	20.9	8.2	...	...	...	10	36	196
Comoros	♦75.8	...	...	...	39.5	33.6	16.3	...	...	...	10	53	1 770
Congo	♦85.2	35.8	29.1	24.3	...	...	...	10	17	370	...	...	...
Côte d'Ivoire	...	46.8	37.2	14.9	...	...	...	22	83	376	...	...	...
Djibouti	♦76.8	58.4	18.2	19.1	53.4	21.1	13.9	...	...	...	...	...	...
Egypt	♦81.8	♦69.1	./.	30.9	♦63.5	./.	36.5	♦13	./.	62	♦11	./.	93
Equatorial Guinea	...	...	...	...	...	...	...	...	...	...	...	...	...
Eritrea	...	...	...	...	...	...	...	...	...	...	...	...	...
Ethiopia	...	42.0	29.8	19.0	53.2	26.6	12.4	18	65	1 251	58	76	731
Gabon	...	...	...	...	...	...	...	...	...	...	7	35	.
Gambia	38.5	49.2	23.5	10.8	42.7	21.4	9.1	20	45	...	10	25	.
Ghana	♦62.7	...	...	...	29.2	34.3	11.0	3	10	...	5	16	234
Guinea	58.7	24.7	28.9	31.9	35.1	29.7	17.5	...	...	...	12	41	342
Guinea-Bissau	...	76.3	16.2	–	...	...	...	76	16	–	...	...	...
Kenya	...	64.4	14.9	13.8	59.3	17.6	17.2	15	34	982	12	34	396
Lesotho	...	38.6	33.4	21.8	51.0	30.4	15.9	9	72	629	13	50	382
Liberia	...	17.6	26.6	19.0	...	...	...	6	36	361	...	...	...
Libyan Arab Jamahiriya	...	...	...	...	...	...	...	...	...	...	...	...	...
Madagascar	...	41.4	25.5	27.5	...	...	...	8	21	411	6	20	...
Malawi	52.8	38.9	15.7	30.2	55.4	10.7	19.3	8	133	1 371	11	101	890
Mali	...	42.0	22.3	16.3	...	...	...	39	81	998	...	...	...
Mauritania	52.1	35.4	50.3	13.5	37.0	39.2	20.0	30	177	524	12	72	196
Mauritius	62.5	44.1	36.5	7.7	41.2	39.6	7.2	14	20	339	10	18	115
Morocco	♦88.1	35.4	46.3	18.3	33.0	50.7	16.3	12	55	155	12	54	84
Mozambique	♦74.5	...	...	...	49.8	15.7	9.9	...	...	...	22	55	1 838
Namibia	...	...	...	...	...	...	...	...	...	...	...	...	...
Niger	...	36.8	46.2	17.0	...	...	...	25	170	1 509	29	93	...
Nigeria	...	17.2	39.8	25.0	...	...	...	5	52	534	...	...	...
Rwanda	80.7	67.1	19.9	9.6	67.7	14.1	16.2	11	112	902	16	53	1 167
Sao Tome and Principe	...	...	...	...	...	...	...	...	...	...	...	...	...
Senegal	♦70.4	42.8	27.8	25.0	43.9	25.7	24.0	24	70	443	18	42	382
Seychelles	♦58.0	...	...	...	28.2	40.7	9.5	...	...	...	9	53	.
Sierra Leone	...	...	...	...	...	...	...	...	...	...	...	...	...
Somalia	...	...	...	...	...	...	...	...	...	...	...	...	...
South Africa	78.6	...	...	...	♦83.2	./.	13.8	...	...	...	♦20	./.	74
Sudan	...	48.0	31.0	20.7	...	...	...	24	66	590	...	...	...
Swaziland	61.6	45.8	34.3	10.7	32.9	29.0	20.5	11	38	149	7	26	244
Togo	57.6	30.2	31.0	29.8	31.8	28.1	12.4	8	33	892	12	51	351
Tunisia	...	41.2	36.6	20.5	42.7	36.2	18.8	11	38	194	12	25	94
Uganda	...	16.2	58.0	18.0	...	...	...	4	205	917	...	...	...
United Rep. of Tanzania	...	54.4	21.1	11.1	41.6	32.1	17.1	11	204	1 914	11	189	2 787

Country or territory	Teachers' emoluments as percentage of total current expenditure 1992	Percentage distribution of current expenditure by level 1980 Pre-prim. + 1st level	1980 2nd level	1980 3rd level	1992 Pre-prim. + 1st level	1992 2nd level	1992 3rd level	Current expenditure per pupil as a percentage of GNP per capita 1980 Pre-prim. + 1st level	1980 2nd level	1980 3rd level	1992 Pre-prim. + 1st level	1992 2nd level	1992 3rd level
Zaire	...	41.5	26.7	31.8	...	...	...	7	20	771	...	...	...
Zambia	...	45.3	25.5	18.0	31.7	34.5	17.3	11	61	585	4	37	230
Zimbabwe	...	66.5	21.4	7.5	54.7	29.5	11.6	25	131	413	22	38	241
America, North													
Antigua and Barbuda	...	33.3	24.1	13.8	...	...	...	6	7	.	...	...	...
Bahamas	...	...	...	...	...	...	...	...	...	...	...	...	...
Barbados	♦71.2	32.0	32.0	18.1	37.5	37.6	19.2	12	15	60	20	26	74
Belize	...	...	...	...	...	...	...	...	...	...	...	...	...
British Virgin Islands	...	45.1	42.7	4.3	...	...	...	...	...	...	...	...	...
Canada	50.6	♦65.3	./.	27.4	♦60.8	./.	27.9	♦22	./.	36	♦26	./.	27
Costa Rica	♦94.5	28.0	21.5	26.1	38.2	21.6	36.1	12	26	76	10	21	61
Cuba	♦57.4	29.4	40.8	6.9	25.7	39.0	14.4	12	22	29	16	25	39
Dominica	59.1	...	...	...	59.5	27.1	2.5	...	...	...	15	18	47
Dominican Republic	...	36.8	22.9	23.9	...	...	...	3	6	37	...	...	...
El Salvador	...	♦68.1	./.	14.2	...	...	...	♦12	./.	140	...	...	...
Grenada	...	...	...	...	...	...	...	...	...	...	...	...	...
Guatemala	42.4	37.4	12.4	18.4	32.7	12.0	16.6	5	8	41	3	5	38
Haiti	♦95.3	59.3	20.4	9.6	53.1	19.0	9.1	6	13	130	8	12	144
Honduras	♦78.6	61.9	17.9	19.3	49.1	17.2	18.2	10	15	77	10	18	88
Jamaica	56.9	34.7	36.9	19.2	32.2	30.8	21.4	11	22	205	6	12	123
Mexico	...	...	...	...	...	...	...	...	...	...	...	...	...
Netherlands Antilles	...	...	...	...	44.6	44.7	4.8	...	...	...	...	...	...
Nicaragua	...	45.1	25.1	10.5	...	...	...	7	15	25	...	...	...
Panama	♦60.1	46.3	22.0	13.4	31.5	20.4	26.1	11	11	29	11	13	52
Saint Kitts and Nevis	75.5	50.0	40.6	2.9	34.7	45.4	12.2	16	21	111	5	14	67
Saint Lucia	...	45.6	23.7	14.7	48.5	23.0	13.2	12	42	387	9	17	233
Saint Vincent and the Grenadines	82.9	...	...	...	...	...	...	...	...	...	...	...	...
Trinidad and Tobago	75.4	46.9	34.9	10.2	42.5	36.8	11.9	9	13	59	10	17	74
United States	...	...	...	...	38.9	37.0	24.1	...	...	...	13	36	21
America, South													
Argentina	...	40.1	25.6	22.7	50.5	26.1	17.6	6	12	29	9	12	17
Bolivia	...	58.9	11.4	17.1	...	...	...	14	14	46	8	10	...
Brazil	...	44.8	7.1	18.9	48.8	6.9	25.6	8	11	59	11	13	109
Chile	...	44.7	18.0	33.2	56.0	14.9	20.6	9	16	112	9	8	24
Colombia	...	44.5	27.0	24.1	43.6	37.3	19.1	5	7	41	9	15	38
Ecuador	♦81.6	20.6	18.5	15.6	32.1	33.7	22.7	5	13	24	4	10	25
Guyana	...	40.1	28.5	12.6	...	...	...	15	22	275	...	...	...
Paraguay	...	...	...	...	42.2	25.0	19.3	...	...	...	5	12	44
Peru	...	47.9	19.9	...	...	...	...	7	8	...	...	...	...
Suriname	33.4	64.0	8.4	7.4	60.5	14.5	8.8	16	8	74	21	13	66
Uruguay	♦79.5	48.4	33.2	16.1	35.7	29.9	24.6	8	12	26	7	9	26
Venezuela	...	...	...	...	...	...	...	...	...	...	...	...	...
Asia													
Afghanistan	...	43.5	22.3	18.4	♦87.6	./.	12.4	11	46	248	...	...	...
Armenia	...	...	...	...	...	...	...	...	...	...	...	...	...
Azerbaijan	...	...	...	...	♦79.2	./.	10.4	...	...	...	...	...	...
Bahrain	...	...	...	...	...	...	...	...	...	...	9	23	...
Bangladesh	♦59.0	45.3	39.2	12.9	44.2	43.3	7.9	5	13	48	6	23	29
Bhutan	...	...	...	...	...	...	...	...	...	...	...	...	...

World education report

Table 11 (continued)

Country or territory	Teachers' emoluments as percentage of total current expenditure 1992	Percentage distribution of current expenditure by level						Current expenditure per pupil as a percentage of GNP per capita					
		1980			1992			1980			1992		
		Pre-prim. + 1st level	2nd level	3rd level	Pre-prim. + 1st level	2nd level	3rd level	Pre-prim. + 1st level	2nd level	3rd level	Pre-prim. + 1st level	2nd level	3rd level
Brunei Darussalam	33.7	31.4	46.0	16.7	24.1	26.1	9.5	2	6	245	...	...	...
Cambodia	...	...	...	...	...	...	...	...	...	...	...	...	...
China	69.7	27.6	34.3	20.0	34.5	34.7	19.1	3	10	276	4	11	140
Cyprus	80.8	37.9	50.5	4.1	38.6	49.6	6.0	13	22	44	12	26	25
Dem. People's Rep. of Korea	...	...	...	...	...	...	...	...	...	...	...	...	...
Georgia	...	...	...	...	...	...	...	...	...	...	...	...	...
Hong Kong	...	33.7	35.7	24.6	26.9	39.3	30.0	...	...	...	...	...	...
India	...	36.9	24.2	13.5	38.0	27.0	14.7	9	14	72	12	16	70
Indonesia	...	...	...	...	...	...	...	...	...	...	...	...	...
Iran, Islamic Rep. of	...	43.7	38.1	7.1	32.7	42.6	15.0	16	28	115	8	16	46
Iraq	...	47.5	17.3	24.1	...	...	...	7	7	88	...	...	...
Israel	...	40.4	29.2	24.8	41.5	31.5	17.3	13	42	72	10	25	33
Japan	...	39.6	34.6	11.1	...	...	...	13	17	21	...	...	...
Jordan	♦85.1	♦75.1	./.	22.8	♦64.4	./.	33.0	♦15	./.	95	♦16	./.	118
Kazakstan	...	...	...	...	...	...	...	...	...	...	...	...	...
Kuwait	...	35.8	41.9	16.5	...	...	...	6	7	38	...	...	...
Kyrgyzstan	...	...	...	...	...	...	...	...	...	...	...	...	...
Lao People's Dem. Rep.	65.0	...	...	...	42.2	43.5	3.9	...	...	...	5	25	62
Lebanon	...	...	...	...	...	...	...	...	...	...	...	...	...
Malaysia	87.4	35.0	34.0	12.4	38.6	37.4	16.1	11	22	149	11	21	117
Maldives	...	...	...	...	...	...	...	...	...	...	...	...	...
Mongolia	...	...	...	...	♦78.3	./.	21.7	...	...	...	♦27	./.	145
Myanmar	...	...	...	...	...	...	...	...	...	...	...	...	...
Nepal	...	♦58.8	./.	35.0	44.5	17.7	28.1	♦10	./.	247	11	15	161
Oman	♦84.7	...	...	...	50.4	42.6	5.7	...	...	...	11	20	43
Pakistan	...	39.4	31.0	18.8	...	...	...	9	18	134	...	...	...
Palestine													
Gaza Strip	...	...	...	...	...	...	...	...	...	...	...	...	...
West Bank	...	...	...	...	...	...	...	...	...	...	...	...	...
Philippines	♦96.1	♦77.1	./.	22.1	...	...	...	♦5	./.	14	...	...	...
Qatar	♦80.3	...	...	...	...	...	...	...	...	...	...	...	...
Republic of Korea	59.7	49.9	33.2	8.7	43.5	39.4	6.9	11	9	16	13	13	5
Saudi Arabia	...	...	...	...	♦80.3	./.	19.7	...	...	...	♦27	./.	111
Singapore	...	35.8	41.1	17.1	...	...	...	7	13	43	...	...	...
Sri Lanka	...	♦91.1	./.	8.9	♦81.6	./.	13.7	♦9	./.	72	♦7	./.	54
Syrian Arab Republic	...	38.8	28.5	32.7	46.4	27.7	23.4	8	15	75	9	14	51
Tajikistan	...	...	...	...	...	...	...	...	...	...	...	...	...
Thailand	64.3	55.3	28.3	13.3	54.5	21.2	16.3	10	19	20	12	14	26
Turkey	...	43.7	22.9	28.3	...	...	...	8	11	119	18	14	...
Turkmenistan	...	...	...	...	...	...	...	...	...	...	...	...	...
United Arab Emirates	♦71.7	...	...	...	...	...	...	...	...	...	...	...	...
Uzbekistan	...	...	...	...	...	...	...	...	...	...	...	...	...
Viet Nam	...	...	...	...	...	...	...	...	...	...	...	...	...
Yemen	...	.	.	.	...	...	...	.	.	.	...	...	...
Former Dem. Yemen	.	♦64.8	./.	11.6	.	.	.	...	...	...	.	.	.
Former Yemen Arab Rep.	.	...	...	...	.	.	.	...	...	...	.	.	.
Europe													
Albania	...	...	...	...	...	...	...	...	...	...	...	...	...
Austria	50.6	24.0	53.2	14.5	24.4	46.8	18.7	15	20	38	17	24	34
Belarus	...	♦74.3	./.	13.9	♦82.1	./.	12.2	♦18	./.	34	♦23	./.	36
Belgium	78.4	25.3	47.3	17.3	23.6	41.7	16.4	12	34	49	11	28	29

Country or territory	Teachers' emoluments as percentage of total current expenditure 1992	Percentage distribution of current expenditure by level						Current expenditure per pupil as a percentage of GNP per capita					
		1980			1992			1980			1992		
		Pre-prim. + 1st level	2nd level	3rd level	Pre-prim. + 1st level	2nd level	3rd level	Pre-prim. + 1st level	2nd level	3rd level	Pre-prim. + 1st level	2nd level	3rd level
Bosnia and Herzegovina	...	...	...	...	...	...	...	...	...	...	...	...	...
Bulgaria	♦66.1	♦65.0	./.	13.6	♦75.9	./.	13.7	♦14	./.	51	♦28	./.	41
Croatia	...	...	...	...	...	...	...	...	...	...	...	...	...
Czech Republic	♦41.1	...	...	...	50.0	29.2	13.0	...	...	...	15	23	48
Former Czechoslovakia	.	53.3	14.2	16.1	.	.	.	12	11	47	.	.	.
Denmark	♦57.8	♦72.1	./.	17.6	♦67.4	./.	18.4	♦23	./.	52	♦29	./.	44
Estonia	...	...	...	...	♦74.5	./.	15.9	...	...	...	♦21	./.	53
Finland	47.9	31.8	40.7	18.9	27.3	36.8	27.6	18	22	37	21	30	55
France	♦72.3	30.4	40.3	12.5	26.4	40.4	14.1	11	20	29	12	22	22
Germany	...				...	...	...				...	...	...
Former German Dem. Rep.	.	♦62.0	./.	20.5	.	.	.	...	...	...	.	.	.
Germany, Federal Rep. of	.	19.6	53.6	15.1	.	.	.	11	16	31	.	.	.
Greece	85.2	39.1	40.4	20.4	34.1	45.1	19.5	8	11	36	11	16	30
Hungary	♦42.9	52.4	21.6	19.3	54.9	24.5	15.3	14	26	85	23	29	89
Iceland	53.5	...	...	...	59.5	25.6	14.9	...	...	...	22	10	31
Ireland	75.3	34.8	39.2	17.6	37.2	39.4	20.9	12	24	60	15	23	40
Italy	...	35.1	41.0	9.1	...	...	...	12	17	18	13	21	...
Latvia	...	...	...	...	...	...	...	...	...	...	...	...	...
Lithuania	♦40.8	...	...	...	♦69.3	./.	14.9	...	...	...	♦25	./.	44
Luxembourg	72.9	49.3	29.1	1.5	44.4	41.9	3.3	32	22	43	19	25	63
Malta	38.7	31.4	44.3	9.3	22.5	40.4	17.9	7	17	94	7	17	57
Monaco	♦83.8	...	...	...	22.3	61.7	−	...	...	...	...	...	...
Netherlands	64.7	24.7	33.8	27.5	22.6	37.0	31.9	14	23	73	14	23	54
Norway	♦58.7	♦72.2	./.	13.6	♦62.6	./.	16.9	♦21	./.	42	♦23	./.	33
Poland	...	36.9	21.0	23.6	48.9	19.5	16.9	8	15	47	16	19	58
Portugal	♦85.7	52.8	25.4	10.5	39.6	37.5	15.5	14	23	41	18	26	42
Republic of Moldova	...	...	...	...	20.5	53.1	11.1	...	...	...	10	31	53
Romania	♦56.6	...	...	...	52.1	22.1	9.6	...	...	...	17	5	34
Russian Federation	...	...	...	...	...	...	...	...	...	...	...	...	...
San Marino	...	60.4	31.6	2.1	50.7	30.9	11.2	...	...	...	...	...	...
Slovakia	♦55.3	...	...	...	38.6	18.5	15.0	...	...	...	22	9	70
Slovenia	61.9	...	...	...	33.7	44.1	19.3	...	...	...	22	21	51
Spain	♦69.0	♦81.7	./.	14.0	28.7	46.8	16.0	♦8	./.	17	13	16	20
Sweden	39.0	♦58.2	./.	9.3	♦59.4	./.	15.9	♦25	./.	35	♦26	./.	49
Switzerland	60.5	♦76.5	./.	18.6	♦75.2	./.	19.4	♦18	./.	62	♦22	./.	44
The FYR of Macedonia	♦82.7	...	...	...	56.5	23.5	17.1	...	...	...	...	...	...
Ukraine	...	♦72.6	./.	14.0	♦70.3	./.	12.6	♦20	./.	39	♦28	./.	50
United Kingdom	49.9	26.6	40.1	22.4	29.8	42.3	20.7	14	22	80	16	27	43
Yugoslavia	♦60.2	...	...	...	44.3	25.6	18.8	...	...	...	...	...	...
Former Yugoslavia	.	♦73.0	./.	18.5	.	.	.	♦16	./.	40	.	.	.
Oceania													
Australia	♦74.1	♦68.7	./.	22.6	♦62.6	./.	29.5	♦17	./.	51	♦18	./.	48
Fiji	♦73.5	53.0	45.1	1.9	50.5	37.0	9.0	16	33	38	11	24	84
Kiribati	♦57.7	37.6	44.8	−	50.5	28.7	7.9	12	108	−	12	39	39
New Zealand	34.4	36.9	29.7	28.3	26.1	20.9	36.7	13	14	60	14	14	59
Papua New Guinea	...	...	...	...	...	...	...	...	...	...	...	...	...
Samoa	...	...	...	...	...	...	...	...	...	...	8	8	...
Solomon Islands	71.9	44.1	42.2	13.3	56.5	29.8	13.7	15	105	.	13	65	.
Tonga	♦70.7	55.0	25.4	14.7	38.8	24.2	7.3	8	5	95	10	8	47
Tuvalu	58.1	...	...	...	35.9	59.0	−	...	...	...	...	...	...
Vanuatu	♦90.4	...	...	...	58.1	29.1	3.2	...	...	...	12	48	.

IV. National reports and UNESCO reports, publications and periodicals concerning education, 1993–1995

This Appendix is in four parts: 1. National reports on education presented by Member States and Observers at the 44th session of the International Conference on Education (Geneva, October 1994); 2. Reports of UNESCO meetings concerning education; 3. UNESCO publications on education; and 4. UNESCO periodicals relating to education. The period covered by this listing is June 1993 to mid-1995.

National reports are listed by country in alphabetical order. Country names are given as they appear on their national reports. UNESCO reports, publications and periodicals are listed alphabetically by title.

For each title, the English version of the publication is given. When a title is not published in English, it is presented in its original language of publication. Besides English, some titles are published in other languages. An indication of the different language versions is given in parentheses: for example (F, S) indicates that the title is also published in French and in Spanish. The abbreviations for the different languages are as follows: Ar: Arabic; Ch: Chinese; E: English; F: French; G: German; Port.: Portuguese; S: Spanish; Ukr: Ukrainian.

For periodicals which present each issue with a special theme, this is indicated.

National reports presented at the 44th session of the International Conference on Education (Geneva, October 1994)

ANGOLA. *Développement de l'éducation: Rapport national de la République d'Angola.* Luanda, Ministère de l'Éducation, 1994. 23 pp., annexes.

ARGENTINA. *Educational Development in Argentina, 1993–1994.* Buenos Aires, Ministry of Culture and Education, 1994. 34 pp., annexes. (S)

ARMENIA. *Educational Policy Report: Educational Policy Making during a Situation of National Emergency.* Yerevan, Armenian National Commission for UNESCO, 1994. 44 pp., appendices.

AUSTRIA. *Austria: Development of Education, 1992–1994.* Vienna, Federal Ministry of Education and the Arts in Co-operation with the Federal Ministry of Science and Research, 1994. 146 pp.

AZERBAIJAN. *System of Education in Azerbaijan Republic: Problems of Development.* Baku, Ministry of Education, 1994. 7 pp.

BAHRAIN. *Development of Education in Bahrain, 1992/93–1993/94.* Manama, Ministry of Education, 1994. Bilingual: English (88 pp., appendices)/Arabic (95 pp., appendices).

BELARUS. *Education Development: National Report of the Republic of Belarus.* Minsk, Ministry of Education of the Republic of Belarus, National Education Institute, 1994. Bilingual: English (62 pp.)/Russian (69 pp.).

BELGIUM. *Educational Developments in Belgium, 1992–1994: The Flemish Community.* Brussels, Ministerie van de Vlaamse Gemeenschap, Departement Onderwijs, Centrum voor Informatie en Documentatie, 1994. 32 pp. + xvi pp.

Le système éducatif de la Communauté française de Belgique. Brussels, Ministère de l'Éducation, de la Recherche et de la Formation, 1994. 138 pp.

BENIN. *Développement de l'éducation: Rapport national de la République du Bénin.* Porto-Novo, Ministère de l'Éducation Nationale, Commission Nationale pour l'UNESCO, Institut National pour la Formation et la Recherche en Éducation, 1994. 10 pp.

BOLIVIA. *Informe nacional sobre el desarrollo de la educación.* La Paz, Ministerio de Desarrollo Humano, Secretaría Nacional de Educación, Dirección General de Planeamiento Educativo, 1993. 69 pp., annexes.

BRAZIL. *The Development of Education: National Report, 1992–1994.* Brasilia, Ministry of Education and Sports, 1994. 64 pp. (F, Port.)

BULGARIA. *National Report on the Development of Education in the Republic of Bulgaria in 1992–1994.* Sofia, Ministry of Science and Education, 1994. 29 pp.

CAMEROON. *Développement de l'éducation: Rapport national du Cameroun.* Yaoundé, Ministère de l'Éducation Nationale, 1994. 34 pp.

CANADA. *The Global Classroom: Appraisal and Perspectives on Education for International Understanding/Salle de classe ouverte sur le monde: bilan et perspectives de l'éducation pour la compréhension internationale.* Toronto, Council of Ministers of Education/Conseil des Ministres de l'Éducation, 1994. Bilingual: English (75 pp.)/French (79 pp.).

CENTRAL AFRICAN REPUBLIC. *Rapport national sur*

le développement de l'éducation en République centrafricaine. Bangui, Ministère des Enseignements, de la Coordination des Recherches et de la Technologie, Commission Nationale Centrafricaine pour l'UNESCO, 1994. 43 pp.

CHAD. *Rapport national du Tchad*. Ndjamena, Ministère de l'Éducation Nationale, de la Culture, de la Jeunesse et des Sports, Commission Nationale Tchadienne pour l'UNESCO, 1994. 30 pp.

CHINA. *The Development and Reform of Education in China, 1993–1994*. Beijing, State Education Commission, 1994. 53 pp.

CROATIA. *Information on the Educational System in the Republic of Croatia*. Zagreb, Ministry of Culture and Education, 1994. 25 pp.

CUBA. *Cuba: Organization of Education, 1992–1994*. Havana, Ministry of Education, 1994. 33 pp. (S)

CYPRUS. *Development of Education, 1992–1994: National Report of Cyprus*. Nicosia, Ministry of Education and Culture, 1994. 59 pp., appendices.

CZECH REPUBLIC. *National Report on the Development of Education, 1992–1994*. Prague, Ministry of Education, Youth and Sports, 1994. 96 pp.

DEMOCRATIC PEOPLE'S REPUBLIC OF KOREA. *L'enseignement en République populaire démocratique de Corée (1993/94): Rapport présenté par la Délégation de la République populaire démocratique de Corée*. Pyongyang, Commission Nationale pour l'UNESCO, 1994. 12 pp.

DENMARK. *Development of Education, 1992–1994: National Report of Denmark*. Copenhagen, Danish National Commission for UNESCO, Ministry of Education, 1994. 14 pp.

EGYPT. *Development of Education in the Arab Republic of Egypt, 92/1993–93/1994*. Cairo, National Centre for Educational Research and Development, 1994. 85 pp.

ESTONIA. *The Development of Education: National Report from Estonia*. Tallinn, Ministry of Culture and Education, 1994. 49 pp., annexes.

ETHIOPIA. *Educational Development, 1993–1994*. Addis Ababa, Ministry of Education, 1994. 11 pp.

FINLAND. *Developments in Education, 1992–1994*. Helsinki, Ministry of Education, 1994. 98 pp.

FRANCE. *Rapport de la France*. Paris, Ministère de l'Éducation Nationale, 1994. 37 pp.

   Rapport de la France. Paris, Ministère de l'Enseignement Supérieur et de la Recherche, 1994. 14 pp.

GAMBIA. *The Development of Education: National Report from The Gambia*. Banjul, Ministry of Education, 1994. 30 pp., annexes.

GERMANY. *Bericht über die Entwicklung des Bildungswesens, 1992–1994: Bestandsaufnahme und Perspektiven Internationaler Erziehung/Report on the Development of Education, 1992–1994: Appraisal and Perspectives of Education for International Understanding*. Bonn, Sekretariat der Ständigen Konferenz der Kultusminister der Länder in der Bundesrepublik Deutschland/Secretariat of the Standing Conference of the Ministers of Education and Cultural Affairs of the Länder in the Federal Republic of Germany, 1994. Bilingual: German (109 pp., annexes)/English (114 pp., annexes).

GHANA. *The Development of Education: National Report from Ghana, 1992–1994*. Accra, Ministry of Education, 1994. 55 pp.

GREECE. *Développement de l'éducation: Rapport national de la Grèce*. Athens, Institut Pédagogique du Ministère de l'Éducation Nationale et des Cultes, 1994. 62 pp.

GUINEA. *Développement de l'éducation, 1992–1994: Rapport national de la République de Guinée*. Conakry, Ministère de l'Enseignement Préuniversitaire et de la Formation Professionnelle, 1994. 19 pp.

HUNGARY. *The Development of Education, 1992–1994*. Budapest, Ministry of Education and Culture, 1994. 33 pp.

INDIA. *Development of Education in India, 1993–1994*. New Delhi, Department of Education, Ministry of Human Resource Development, 1994. 87 pp.

INDONESIA. *The Development of Education System in Indonesia: A Country Report*. Jakarta, Ministry of Education and Culture, 1994. 109 pp.

IRAN (Islamic Republic of). *The Development of Education: National Report from the Islamic Republic of Iran*. Tehran, Ministry of Education, Ministry of Culture and Higher Education, 1994. 90 pp.

ISRAEL. *Facts and Figures about Education and Culture in Israel*. Jerusalem, Ministry of Education, Culture and Sport, 1994. 100 pp.

ITALY. *Paper prepared for the 44th International Conference on Education*. Rome, Ministry of Education, 1994. 8 pp.

JAMAICA. *National Report on the Development of Education – Jamaica*. Kingston, Ministry of Education and Culture, 1994. 14 pp.

JAPAN. *Development of Education in Japan 1992–1994*. Tokyo, Ministry of Education, Science and Culture, 1994. 91 pp.

JORDAN. *The Development of Education in the Hashemite Kingdom of Jordan, 1993–1994*. Amman, The General Directorate of Planning, Research and Development, Ministry of Education, 1994. 66 pp., appendices.

KENYA. *Development of Education, 1993 to 1994: National Report from Kenya*. Nairobi, Ministry of Education, 1994. 70 pp., appendices.

KUWAIT. *The Development of Education: National Report from the State of Kuwait, 1993–1994*. Kuwait, Ministry of Education, 1994. 124 pp. (Ar)

LESOTHO. *Lesotho's Country Paper on Development of Education, 1992–1994*. Maseru, Ministry of Education, 1994. 25 pp.

LIBERIA. *The Development of Education: National Report from Liberia*. Monrovia, Ministry of Education, 1994. 125 pp.

LIBYAN ARAB JAMAHIRIYA. *National Report on the Development of Education in the Great Socialist People's Libyan Arab Jamahiriya during the period 1992–1993–1994*. Tripoli, Secretariat of Education and Scientific Research, National Commission for Education, Culture and Science, 1994. Bilingual: English (60 pp.)/Arabic (72 pp.).

LUXEMBOURG. *Rapport national sur le développement de l'éducation*. Luxembourg, Ministère de l'Éducation Nationale, 1994. 72 pp.

MADAGASCAR. *Développement de l'éducation: Rapport national de Madagascar*. Antananarivo, Ministère de l'Éducation Nationale, 1994. 24 pp., annexes.

MALAWI. *Educational Development in Malawi, 1993–1994*. Lilongwe, Malawi National Commission for UNESCO, 1994. 50 pp., appendices.

MALAYSIA. *The Development of Education: National Report from Malaysia*. Kuala Lumpur, Ministry of Education, 1994. 45 pp.

MALDIVES. *Developments in Education: 1992–1994*. Male', Ministry of Education, 1994. 32 pp.

MALI. *Développement de l'éducation au Mali, 1992–1994*. Bamako, Ministère de l'Éducation de Base, Ministère des Enseignements Secondaire, Supérieur et de la Recherche Scientifique, Commission Nationale Malienne pour l'UNESCO, 1994. 39 pp.

MALTA. *The Development of Education, 1992–94: National Report for Malta*. Floriana, Educational Planning and Post-secondary Sections, Education Division, 1994. 46 pp.

MEXICO. *The Development of Education: National Report from Mexico, 1990–1994*. Mexico City, Secretariat of Public Education, 1994. 34 pp. (S)

NAMIBIA. *The Development of Education: National Report from Namibia*. Windhoek, Ministry of Education and Culture, 1994. 10 pp.

NEPAL. *Country Report on Education for International Understanding, Co-operation and Peace and Education Relating to Human Rights and Fundamental Freedoms*. Kathmandu, Ministry of Education, Culture and Social Welfare, 1994. 4 pp.

NETHERLANDS. *Education Policy in the Netherlands: 1992–1994. The Development of Education: A National Report from the Netherlands*. Zoetermeer, Ministry of Education, Culture and Science, 1994. 35 pp.

NEW ZEALAND. *Three Years On: The New Zealand Education Reforms 1989 to 1992*. Wellington, Ministry of Education, 1993. 63 pp.

NICARAGUA. *Informe nacional sobre el desarrollo de la educación en Nicaragua*. Managua, Ministerio de Educación, 1994. 48 pp., annexes.

NIGERIA. *The Development of Education, 1992–1994: National Report from Nigeria*. Lagos, Nigerian National Commission for UNESCO, Federal Ministry of Education and Youth Development, 1994. 49 pp.

NORWAY. *The Development of Education, 1992–94: National Report*. Oslo, Royal Ministry of Education, Research and Church Affairs, 1994. 47 pp.

OMAN. *The Educational Innovation in the Sultanate of Oman during the School Years 1992/93–1993/94*. Muscat, Ministry of Education, Omani National Commission for Education, Culture and Science, 1994. 68 pp. (Ar)

PAKISTAN. *The Development of Education in Pakistan*. Islamabad, Ministry of Education, 1994. 33 pp.

PANAMA. *Balance y perspectivas de la educación para la comprensión internacional*. Panama, Ministerio de Educación, 1994. 155 pp., annexes.

PARAGUAY. *Desarrollo de la educación: Informe nacional.* Asunción, Ministerio de Educación y Culto, 1994. 31 pp. + 23 pp. annexes.

PHILIPPINES. *National Report on the Development of Education.* Manila, Department of Education, Culture and Sports, 1993. 60 pp.

POLAND. *Development of Education in Poland in 1992–1993.* Warsaw, Ministry of National Education, 1994. 33 pp., appendices.

PORTUGAL. *Rapport national du Portugal.* Lisbon, Ministère de l'Éducation, Direction des Services des Relations Internationales, 1994. 128 pp., annexes.

QATAR. *Education for International Understanding in the State of Qatar.* Doha, Ministry of Education, Qatar National Commission for Education, 1994. Bilingual: English (37 pp.)/Arabic (46 pp.).

REPUBLIC OF KOREA. *Educational Development in the Republic of Korea: 1993–1994.* Seoul, Ministry of Education, 1994. 96 pp.

ROMANIA. *The System of Education.* Bucharest, Ministry of Education, 1994. 28 pp. (F)

RUSSIAN FEDERATION. *The Development of Education: National Report of the Russian Federation.* Moscow, Ministry of Education, 1994. 52 pp. + 22 pp. appendices. (R)

SAN MARINO. *Rapport national de la République de Saint-Marin.* San Marino, Ministère de l'Éducation Nationale, Commission Nationale de Saint-Marin pour l'UNESCO, 1994. 7 pp.

SAUDI ARABIA. *Development of Education in the Kingdom of Saudi Arabia, 1992–1994.* Riyadh, Ministry of Education, 1994. Bilingual: English (88 pp.)/Arabic (90 pp.).

SENEGAL. *Rapport national sur le développement de l'éducation au Sénégal.* Dakar, Ministère de l'Éducation Nationale, 1994. 15 pp.

SIERRA LEONE. *The Development of Education: National Report from Sierra Leone.* Freetown, Department of Education, 1994. 7 pp.

SLOVAKIA. *Development of Education, 1992–1994.* Bratislava, Institute of Information and Prognoses of Education, Youth and Sports, 1994. 113 pp.

SLOVENIA. *National Report: Development of Education, 1992/1994.* Ljubljana, Ministry of Education and Sport, 1994. 93 pp.

SPAIN. *Informe nacional de educación. Desarrollo de la educación/Education: National Report. Development of Education.* Madrid, Ministerio de Educación y Ciencia/Ministry of Education and Science, 1994. Bilingual: Spanish (142 pp.)/English (134 pp).

SUDAN. *Sudan's Report to the International Conference on Education.* Khartoum, Ministry of Education and Scientific Research, 1994. 58 pp. (Ar)

SWAZILAND. *National Report: Kingdom of Swaziland.* Mbabane, Ministry of Education, 1994. 9 pp.

SWEDEN. *The Development of Education: National Report from Sweden.* Stockholm, Ministry of Education and Science, 1994. 32 pp., appendix.

SWITZERLAND. *Développement de l'éducation: Rapport national de la Suisse.* Bern, Secrétariat Général de la Conférence Suisse des Directeurs Cantonaux de l'Instruction Publique, 1994. 56 pp., annexes.

SYRIAN ARAB REPUBLIC. *National Report on Education Development in the Syrian Arab Republic.* Damascus, Ministry of Education, 1994. 43 pp. (Ar)

THAILAND. *Development of Education.* Bangkok, Ministry of Education, 1994. 52 pp.

TOGO. *Développement de l'éducation: Rapport national du Togo.* Lomé, Ministère de l'Éducation Nationale et de la Recherche Scientifique, 1994. 11 pp.

TUNISIA. *Développement de l'éducation en Tunisie, 1992–1994.* Tunis, Ministère de l'Éducation et des Sciences, Commission Nationale Tunisienne pour l'Éducation, la Science et la Culture, 1994. 100 pp. (Ar)

TURKEY. *Developments in National Education: Turkey.* Ankara, Ministry of National Education, 1994. 87 pp.

UKRAINE. *The Development of Education in Ukraine, 1992–1993.* Kiev, Ministry of Education, 1994. Bilingual: Ukrainian (66 pp.)/English (51 pp.).

UNITED ARAB EMIRATES. *The Development of Education from 1991/1992–1993/1994.* Abu Dhabi, Ministry of Education, 1994. Bilingual: English (41 pp.)/Arabic (51 pp.).

UNITED REPUBLIC OF TANZANIA. *The Development of Education: 1993–1994. National Report of the United Republic of Tanzania.* Dar es Salaam, Ministry of Education and Culture, 1994. 67 pp., annexes.

UNITED STATES OF AMERICA. *Progress of Education in the United States of America: 1990 through 1994.* Washington, D.C., United States Department of Education, 1994. iv + 133 pp., appendices.

VIET NAM. *The Development of Education in S. R. Viet-nam.* Hanoi, Ministry of Education and Training, 1994. 24 pp.

ZAMBIA. *Education for International Understanding: A National Report from Zambia.* Lusaka, Ministry of Education, National Commission for UNESCO, 1994. 7 pp.

ZIMBABWE. *The Development of Education, 1992–1994: National Report from Zimbabwe.* Harare, Ministry of Education and Culture, Ministry of Higher Education, 1994. 43 pp., appendices.

Reports of UNESCO meetings

Across the Divide: Quality Education for Girls and Women. A Workshop Report. Innovations in Quality Education for Girls and Women. Bangladesh, 28 May–2 June 1994. Paris, UNESCO, 1994. 44 pp.

Advisory Committee of the Regional Programme for the Universalization and Renewal of Primary Education and the Eradication of Adult Illiteracy in the Arab States (ARABUPEAL), Second Session. Cairo, Egypt, 5–8 June 1994. Final Report. Cairo, UNESCO/UNEDBAS, 1994. 18 pp. (Ar)

Advisory Committee on Regional Co-operation in Education in Asia and the Pacific, Seventh Session. Kuala Lumpur, Malaysia, 14–17 June 1993. Final Report. Bangkok, UNESCO/PROAP, 1993. 71 pp. (PROAP Document, BKR/93/M/229–400.)

Audience Africa. Social Development: Africa's Priorities. UNESCO, Paris, 6–10 February 1995. Final Report. Paris, UNESCO, 1995. 20 pp. (BRX-95/CONF.006/7.) (F)

Book Sector Studies – A Comprehensive Approach to a Complex Reality. By P. Askerud. Paris, UNESCO, 1994. 4 pp.

(Paper prepared for the Technical Consultation on Basic Learning Materials for Developing Countries held at UNESCO, Paris, 29 November–1 December 1993.)

Compte rendu de l'atelier régional sur l'analyse de politiques éducatives, en vue de la formulation d'une politique et d'un programme d'investissement pour le secteur de l'éducation. Cotonou (Bénin), 3–6 Mars 1993. Paris, UNESCO/UNDP/Ministère

de l'Éducation Nationale du Bénin, 1994. 260 pp.

Consultative Committee on Steps to Promote the Full and Comprehensive Implementation of the Recommendation Concerning Education for International Understanding, Co-operation and Peace and Education Relating to Human Rights and Fundamental Freedoms, Fourth Session. Paris, 14–17 December 1992. Final Report. Paris, UNESCO, 1993. 24 pp., annexes. (ED-92/CONF. 502.) (F)

La educación de adultos en América Latina ante el próximo siglo. Seminario consulta: educación de adultos. Prioridades de acción estratégicas para la última década del siglo. Bogotá, Colombia, 22–27 mayo 1992. Santiago (Chile), UNESCO/UNICEF, 1994. 270 pp.

Educating Girls and Women in Africa. Pan-African Conference on the Education of Girls, in Co-operation with the Government of Burkina Faso. Ouagadougou, Burkina Faso, 28 March–1 April 1993. Paris, UNESCO/UNICEF, 1995. 56 pp. (ED.95/WS.30.) (F)

Education For All. Summit of Nine High-Population Countries. New Delhi, 12–16 December 1993. Final Report. Paris, UNESCO, 1994. 88 pp.

The Education of Girls and Women. Towards a Global Framework for Action. Paris, UNESCO, 1995. 59 pp., annexes. (ED-95/WS.34.) (Ch, F, S)

80th Session of the Standing Committee of UIE. UNESCO, Paris, 2–3 November 1993. Progress Report. Hamburg, UNESCO-UIE, 1994. (Various pagination.) (80 SC/93.)

Eleventh Meeting of Experts on Regional Co-operation in UNESCO Cultural Activities in Asia and the Pacific. 16–20 February 1993, Tokyo. Report. Tokyo, UNESCO/ACCU, 1993. 118 pp.

Enhancing Humanistic, Ethical, Cultural and International Dimensions of Education in Asia and the Pacific: Final Report of a Workshop. Tokyo, UNESCO/National Institute for Educational Research (NIER), 1994. 92 pp.

(Report of a UNESCO regional workshop held at the NIER, Tokyo, 19 January–2 February 1994.)

Fifth Conference of Ministers of Education and those Responsible for Economic Planning in the Arab States (MINEDARAB V). Cairo, 11–14 June 1994. Final Report. Paris, UNESCO/ALECSO/ISESCO, 1994. 86 pp., annexes. (ED/MD/98.) (Ar, F)

Fifth Meeting of the Intergovernmental Regional Committee for the Major Project in the Field of Education in Latin America and the Caribbean. Santiago, Chile, 8–11 June 1993. Final Report. Paris, UNESCO, 1993. 118 pp., annexes. (ED/MD/96.) (S)

First Consultative Meeting of the Culture of Peace Programme. UNESCO, Paris, 27–29 September 1994. Final Report. Paris, UNESCO, 1994. 22 pp., annexes. (CPP-94/CONF.601/3.) (F)

First International Congress on Population Education and Development. Istanbul, Turkey, 14–17 April 1993. Final Report. Paris, UNESCO/UNFPA, 1993. 76 pp. (ED-93/CONF.401.) (F)

46th Session of the Governing Board of UIE. Hamburg, 11–13 April 1994. Hamburg, UNESCO-UIE, 1994. (Various pagination.) (46/GB/94.)

Fourth Consultation with UN Agencies and Relevant Intergovernmental and Non-governmental Organizations Concerned with Environmental Education and Information. Paris, 13–14 September 1993. Final Report. Paris, UNESCO/UNEP, 1993. 15 pp. + 25 pp. annexes.

The Impact of HIV/AIDS on Education. Report of an IIEP Seminar. Paris, 8–10 December 1993. Paris, UNESCO-IIEP/SIDA/IDRC, 1994. 81 pp.

International Commission on Education for the Twenty-first Century:

First Session. UNESCO Headquarters, 2–4 March 1993. Report. Paris, UNESCO, 1993. 26 pp., annexes. (EDC.93/CONF.001.) (F)

Second Session. Dakar (Senegal), 18–21 September 1993. Report. Paris, UNESCO, 1993. 14 pp. (EDC.93/CONF.002.) (F)

Third Session. UNESCO Headquarters, 12–15 January 1994. Report. Paris, UNESCO, 1994. 9 pp. (EDC.94/CONF.002.) (F)

Fourth Session. Vancouver (Canada), 13–15 April 1994. Report. Paris, UNESCO, 1994. 15 pp., annexes. (EDC/6.) (F)

Fifth Session. Santiago (Chile), 26–28 September 1994. Report. Paris, UNESCO, 1994. 16 pp., annexes. (EDC-94/CONF.005.) (F)

International Conference on Education, 44th Session. Geneva, 3–8 October 1994. Final Report. Paris, UNESCO-IBE, 1995. 118 pp., annexes. (F, S)

International Forum on Scientific and Technological

Literacy for All. Paris, 5–10 July 1993. Final Report. Paris, UNESCO, 1993. 127 pp. (ED-93/CONF.016.) (F)

International High-level Consultation on Policy Issues of Quality Assessment and Institutional Accreditation in Higher Education. 5–7 May 1993, Oradea. Final Report. Bucharest, UNESCO/CEPES, 1993. 10 pp. (ED-93/CEPES/CONF.8.2/13.) (F)

International Project on Technical and Vocational Education (UNEVOC). International Advisory Committee, First Session. Berlin, 20–22 September 1993. Final Report. Paris, UNESCO/UNEVOC, 1993. 20 pp. (ED/93/504.10.) (F)

International Project on Technical and Vocational Education (UNEVOC). International Advisory Committee, Second Session. Paris, 12–14 December 1994. Final Report. Paris, UNESCO/UNEVOC, 1994. 29 pp. (F)

International Project on Technical and Vocational Education (UNEVOC). International Consultation Meeting on the Role of Technical and Vocational Education in Educational Systems. Turin, Italy, 14–18 June 1993. Final Report. Paris, UNESCO/UNEVOC, 1993. 19 pp. (ED/93/ C.19.) (F)

International Project on Technical and Vocational Education (UNEVOC). International Workshop on Curriculum Development in Technical and Vocational Education. Turin, 30 August–3 September 1993. Final Report. Paris, UNESCO/UNEVOC, 1993. 24 pp. (ED/93.C/20.) (F)

Interregional Seminar on Establishing Sustained Literacy Mechanisms. UNESCO, Paris, 24–27 October 1994. Final Report. Paris, UNESCO/UNDP, 1994. 31 pp.

Jomtien, trois ans après. L'éducation pour tous dans les pays du Sahel. Rapport du Séminaire sur les politiques de développement de l'éducation pour tous dans les pays du Sahel, organisé à Ouagadougou, Burkina Faso, 6–8 avril 1993. By I. Deblé and G. Carron. Paris, UNESCO-IIEP, 1993. 175 pp.

Mobilizing Project Workshop. Report of the Subregional Workshop on Universalization of Basic Education, Held by UNESCO at the Indian Institute of Education, Pune (India), 15–20 March 1993. Pune, UNESCO/Indian Institute of Education, 1993. 50 pp.

1993 Planning Meeting on Asian/Pacific Joint Pro-

duction Programme of Materials for Neo-literates in Rural Areas. Tokyo, 7–9 June 1993. Report. Tokyo, UNESCO/ACCU, 1994. 105 pp.

9th Regional Consultation Meeting. Lagos, Nigeria, 29–31 March 1993. Final Report. Dakar, UNESCO/BREDA/NEIDA, 1993. 38 pp. (F)

Policy and Planning for Vocational Education and Training. Report of an IIEP Sub-regional Training Workshop. Barbados, 20 September–1 October 1993. By D. Atchoarena. Paris, UNESCO-IIEP, 1994. 226 pp.

Quality Education for All. Second Meeting of the International Consultative Forum on Education for All. New Delhi, 8–10 September 1993. Final Report. Paris, UNESCO, 1994. 48 pp. (F)

Quality Improvement in Initial Teacher Training and Co-operation in Distance Education in Asia. Report of a Regional Roundtable. Bangkok, UNESCO/PROAP, 1993. 54 pp. (PROAP Document, BKA/93/M/203-500.)

Regional Expert Forum on Education for All: Present and Future Challenges. Jomtien, Thailand, 12–16 December 1994. Draft Final Report. Bangkok, UNESCO/PROAP, 1995. 124 pp.

Regional Training Workshop for the Preparation of Post-literacy Materials for Rural Women in the Arab Countries. Tunis, 9–21 June 1993. Paris, UNESCO, 1993. 345 pp. (Only published in Arabic.)

Research Design for Functional Literacy. Report of a Sub-regional Workshop. Seoul, Republic of Korea, 26 April–1 May 1993. Bangkok, UNESCO/PROAP, 1994. 79 pp. (PROAP Document, BKL/94/M/82-200.)

The Seventh Regional Consultation Meeting of the Educational Innovation Programme for Development in the Arab States. Amman, 17–19 May 1993. Final Report. Amman, UNESCO/UNEDBAS/EIPDAS, 1993. 34 pp. (Ar)

Sixth Regional Conference of Ministers of Education and those Responsible for Economic Planning in Asia and the Pacific. Kuala Lumpur, 21–24 June 1993. Final Report. Paris, UNESCO/ESCAP, 1993. 32 pp. + 60 pp. annexes. (ED/MD/97.)

Syrian Arab Republic's Workshop for Rural Education Personnel. 20–27 September 1994, Homs, Syria. Final Report. Amman, UNESCO/UNEDBAS, 1994. 69 pp. (Only published in Arabic.)

Taller sobre la recolección de información sobre educación y desarrollo humano en la región de la América Latina y el Caribe. Santiago de Chile, 7–9 de junio de 1994. Informe final. Santiago, UNESCO/OREALC, 1994. 35 pp.

Towards Appropriate and Effective Pedagogies. Is there a Pedagogy for Girls? Report of UNESCO/ULIE Colloquium. By Professor Caroline Gipps. London, University of London Institute of Education, 1995. 30 pp.

Towards Meeting the Challenges of the Present and the Future. Report and Recommendations of a Consultative Group. Jomtiem, Pattaya City, Thailand, 29 November–3 December 1993. Bangkok, UNESCO/PROAP, 1994. 35 pp. (PROAP Document, BKA/94/M/102-1000.)

UNESCO's Involvement in Efforts to Strengthen the Provision of Basic Learning Materials to Schools and Non-formal Education Programmes. By P. Akserud. Paris, UNESCO, 1993. 10 pp.
(Papers prepared for the Technical Consultation on Basic Learning Materials for Developing Countries held at UNESCO, Paris, 29 November–1 December 1993.)

UNESCO Meeting of Experts from the Asia and Pacific Region to Prepare for the 44th Session of the International Conference on Education. Tagaytay City, Philippines, 1–4 March 1994. Final Report. Bangkok, UNESCO/PROAP, 1994. 156 pp.

Women's Education and Empowerment. Report of the International Seminar Held at UIE, Hamburg, 27 January–2 February 1993. Hamburg, UNESCO-UIE, 1993. 129 pp.

World Conference on Special Needs Education: Access and Quality. Salamanca, Spain, 7–10 June 1994. Final Report. Paris, UNESCO/Ministry of Education and Science of Spain, 1995. 121 pp. (F, S)

Publications

Academic Freedom and University Autonomy. Bucharest, UNESCO/CEPES, 1993. 309 pp. (Papers on Higher Education.) (Bilingual: English/French.) ISBN 92-9069-126-3.

Acreditación universitaria en América Latina: antece-

dentes y experiencias. Caracas, UNESCO/CRESALC/CINDA, 1994. 267 pp.
ISBN 980-6226-86-0 (UNESCO/CRESALC);
ISBN 956-7106-15-0 (CINDA).

Blossoms in the Dust. Street Children in Africa. By J.-P. Vélis. Paris, UNESCO, 1995. 169 pp. (Youth *Plus*.) (F)
ISBN 92-3-102924-X.

Coping with Crisis. Austerity, Adjustment and Human Resources. Edited by J. Samoff. Paris/London, UNESCO/ILO/Cassell, 1994. 284 pp. (Education on the Move.)
ISBN 92-3-102973-8 (UNESCO);
ISBN 0-304-33094-9 (Cassell).

Cost Analysis of Educational Inclusion of Marginalized Populations. By M. C. Tsang. Paris, UNESCO-IIEP, 1994. 106 pp. (Fundamentals of Educational Planning, 48.) (F)
ISBN 92-803-1152-2.

Culture of Democracy: A Challenge for Schools. By P. Meyer-Bisch (ed.). Paris, UNESCO, 1995. 143 pp. (F, S; Ar, Ch, R to appear)
ISBN 92-3-103093-0.

Development, Culture and Education. By L. F. B. Dubbledamm et al. Paris, UNESCO-IBE, 1994. 236 pp. (International Yearbook of Education, Vol. XLIV.)
ISBN 92-3-103038-8.

Early Intervention and Culture. Preparation for Literacy: The Interface between Theory and Practice. Edited by L. Eldering and P. Leseman. Paris, UNESCO/Netherlands National Commission for UNESCO, 1993. 352 pp. (Focus on Literacy.)
ISBN 92-3-102937-1.

Education for Human Rights: An International Perspective. By D. Ray. Paris, UNESCO-IBE, 1994. 304 pp.
ISBN 92-3-103039-6.

Educational Research for Development in Africa. Dakar, UNESCO/BREDA/ASEP, 1993. 144 pp.
ISBN 92-9091-022-4.

An Efficiency-based Management Information System. By W. W. McMahon. Paris, UNESCO-IIEP, 1994. 84 pp. (Fundamentals of Educational Planning, 49.) (F)
ISBN 92-803-1153-0.

L'enseignement intégré des sciences au Nigéria et au Ghana. Dakar, UNESCO/BREDA, 1993. 208 pp.
ISBN 92-9091-021-5.

Les entretiens du Courrier de l'UNESCO. Vol. 1. Paris, UNESCO, 1994. 285 pp.
ISBN 92-3-203054-3.

Families: Celebration and Hope in a World of Change. By J. Boyden. Paris/London, UNESCO/Gaia Books, 1993. 175 pp. (Family *Plus*.)
ISBN 92-3-102873-1 (UNESCO);
ISBN 1-85675-041-8 (Gaia Books).

Formation d'éducateurs et production de matériels didactiques en Afrique. By A. Fofana. Dakar, UNESCO/BREDA, 1993. 96 pp.
ISBN 92-9091-024-0.

Higher Education in Perspective: Toward the 21st Century. By Z. Morsy and P. Altbach. Paris/New York, UNESCO/Advent Books, 1993. 218 pp.
ISBN 92-3-102827-8 (UNESCO);
ISBN 0-89891-066-8 (Advent Books).

Higher Education Reform in Romania. A Study. Edited by L. C. Barrows. Bucharest, UNESCO/CEPES, 1994. 143 pp.
ISBN 92-9069-128-X.

Innovations in Science and Technology Education. Vol. V. Edited by D. Layton. Paris, UNESCO, 1994. 258 pp.
ISBN 92-3-102975-4.

Interdisciplinary Round Table on Education and Learning for the 21st Century in Africa. Dakar, UNESCO/BREDA, 1993. 80 pp. (F)
ISBN 92-9091-023-3.

International Education and the University. Edited by J. Calleja. Paris/London, UNESCO/Jessica Kingsley Publishers, 1995. 262 pp. (Education on the Move.)
ISBN 92-3-102950-9 (UNESCO);
ISBN 1-85302-274-8 (J. K. P.).

Interpreting International Comparisons of Student Achievement. By H. Goldstein. Paris, UNESCO, 1994. 38 pp. (Educational Studies and Documents, 63.) (F)
ISBN 92-3-103082-5.

Junior Secondary Education: the West African Experience. Dakar, UNESCO/BREDA, 1994. 94 pp.
ISBN 92-9091-031-3.

Literacy, Socialisation and Employment. By C. Stercq Hamburg/London, UNESCO-UIE/Jessica Kingsley Publishers, 1993. 103 pp. (F, S)
ISBN 1-85302-209-8 (J. K. P.).

Memory of the Future. By F. Mayor. Paris, UNESCO, 1995. 208 pp. (Challenges.) (F, S)
ISBN 92-3-103030-2.

National Examinations: Design, Procedures and Reporting. By J. Keeves. Paris, UNESCO-IIEP, 1994. 107 pp. (Fundamentals of Educational Planning, 50.) (F)
ISBN 92-803-1154-9.

A New Partnership: Indigenous Peoples and the United Nations System. By J. P. Zinsser. Paris, UNESCO, 1994. 120 pp. (Educational Studies and Documents, 62.) (F, S)
ISBN 92-3-103046-9.

Les nouvelles technologies, outils d'enseignement. By H. Dieuzeide. Paris, UNESCO/Éditions Nathan, 1994. 248 pp.
ISBN 92-3-203056-X (UNESCO);
ISBN 2-09-120473-0 (Éditions Nathan).

Una nueva manera de comunicar el conocimiento. Caracas, UNESCO/CRESALC, 1993. 345 pp.
ISBN 980-6226-82-8.

Recent Trends and Developments in Educational Psychology: Chinese and American Perspectives. Paris, UNESCO, 1994. 52 pp. (Educational Studies and Documents, 61.)
ISBN 92-3-102980-0.

Réussir l'école, réussir à l'école. Stratégies de réussite à l'école fondamentale. By E. Brunswic. Paris, UNESCO, 1994. 143 pp. (La bibliothèque de l'enseignant.)
ISBN 92-3-203048-9.

The Role of African Student Movements in the Political and Social Evolution of Africa from 1900 to 1975. Paris, UNESCO, 1994. 210 pp. (The General History of Africa: Studies and Documents, 12.) (F)
ISBN 92-3-102804-9.

The Scientific Education of Girls. Education beyond Reproach? Work carried out by the French Commission for UNESCO under the supervision of Renée Clair. Paris/London, UNESCO/Jessica Kingsley Publishers, 1995. 214 pp.
ISBN 92-3-103168-6 (UNESCO);
ISBN 1-85302-346-9 (J. K. P.).

A Sourcebook for Literacy Workers: Perspective from the Grassroots. Paris/London, UNESCO/Jessica Kingsley Publishers, 1994. 200 pp. (Focus on Literacy.)
ISBN 92-3-102947-9 (UNESCO);
ISBN 1-85302-263-2 (J. K. P.).

Special Needs in the Classroom. A Teacher Education Guide. Paris/London, UNESCO/Jessica Kingsley Publishers, 1994. 225 pp. (The Teacher's Library.)
ISBN 92-3-102934-7 (UNESCO);
ISBN 1-85302-248-9 (J. K. P.).

Study Abroad/Études à l'étranger/Estudios en el extranjero. Vol. XXIX. Paris, UNESCO, 1995. 1,376 pp. (Trilingual: E/F/S)
ISBN 92-3-003148-8.

UNESCO's Commitment to the Success of Higher Education in Africa. By H. Aguessy. Dakar, UNESCO/BREDA, 1994. 105 pp. (F)
ISBN 92-9091-031-3.

UNESCO Statistical Yearbook/Annuaire statistique de l'UNESCO/Anuario estadístico de la UNESCO: 1994. Paris, UNESCO, 1994. 900 pp. (Trilingual: E/F/S)
ISBN 92-3-003032-5.

UNESCO-UIE Literacy Exchange Network on Industrialized Countries. Directory of Members/Répertoire des membres/Directorio de los miembros/Mitgliederverzeichnis. Edited by U. Giere. Paris, UNESCO-UIE, 1994. 352 pp. (Multilingual: E/F/S/G)
ISBN 92-820-0068-X.
(Directory of individuals/institutions throughout the world working on literacy in industrialized countries.)

Universidad, modernidad y desarrollo humano. By O. Silva and L. Enrique. Caracas, UNESCO/CRESALC, 1994. 125 pp.
ISBN 92-9143-001-3.

Universidad y mundo productivo. Caracas, UNESCO/CRESALC, 1994. 197 pp.
ISBN 92-9143-002-1 (CRESALC);
ISBN 980-6226-88-7 (UNESCO/CARACAS).

The University as an Institution Today. Topics for reflection. By A. Borrero Cabal. Paris/Ottawa, UNESCO/International Development Research Centre (IDRC), 1994. xxiv + 238 pp. (F)
ISBN 92-3-102939-8 (UNESCO);
ISBN 0-88936-685-3 (IDRC).

Vers une culture multilingue de l'éducation. Edited by Adama Ouane. Hamburg, UNESCO-UIE, 1995. xv + 472 pp., annexes. (UIE Studies, 3.)
ISBN 92-820-2066-5.

Visión iberoamericana 2000. I: Cumbre del pensamiento. Paris, UNESCO, 1994. 101 pp. (Dimensión Americana.)
ISBN 92-3-302963-8.

Women, Education and Empowerment: Pathways towards Autonomy. Report of an International Seminar Held at UIE, Hamburg, 27 January– 2 February 1993. Edited by Carolyn Medel-Añonuevo. Hamburg, UNESCO-UIE, 1995. 69 pp. (UIE Studies, 5.)
ISBN 92-820-1013-9.

Working with Street Children. Paris, UNESCO/International Catholic Child Bureau, 1995. 303 pp. (Youth *Plus.*) (F, S)
ISBN 92-3-103096-5.

World Directory of Teacher-Training Institutions/ Répertoire mondial des institutions de formation d'enseignants/Repertorio mundial de instituciones de formación de docentes. Paris, UNESCO/ICET, 1993. 515 pp. (Trilingual: E/F/S)
ISBN 93-3-002800-2.

World Education Report 1993. Paris, UNESCO, 1993. 172 pp., figs., tables. (Ar, Ch, F, R, S)
ISBN 92-3-102935-5.

World Guide to Higher Education. A Comparative Survey of Systems, Degrees and Qualifications (3rd ed.). Paris, UNESCO, 1995. (In press.)
ISBN 92-3-102766-2.

Periodicals

Bulletin of the Major Project of Education in Latin America and the Caribbean (Santiago (Chile), UNESCO/OREALC). Bulletin published three times a year. (S):
1993. Nos. 30 to 32.
1994. Nos. 33 to 35.
1995. No. 36.

L'éducation nouvelle (Amman, UNESCO/UNEDBAS). Three issues a year. (Published in Arabic only, résumés in French.)

Higher Education in Europe (Bucharest, UNESCO/ CEPES). Quarterly review. (F, R):
1993. Vol. XVIII, No. 1: Conflict of Interest in Higher Education.
Vol. XVIII, No. 2: Higher Education and the Labour Market.
Vol. XVIII, No. 3: Policy Issues of Quality Assessment and Institutional Accreditation.
Vol. XVIII, No. 4: Careers for Women at European Universities: Obstacles and Opportunities.
1994. Vol. XIX, No. 1: Trends, Issues and New Laws in Higher Education.

International Review of Education/Internationale Zeitschrift für Erziehungswissenschaft/Revue internationale de l'éducation (Hamburg, UNESCO-UIE/ Kluwer Academic Publishers). Six issues a year. (Trilingual: E/G/F):
1994. Vol. 40, Nos.1 and 2; No. 3/5: Special issue: Life-long Education; No. 6.
1995. Vol. 41, No. 1/2: Special Issue: Moral Education.

Prospects: Quarterly Review of Education. Review published in Paris by UNESCO until No. 85/86 (Vol. XXIII, No. 1/2), 1993. From No. 87/88 (Vol. XXIII, No. 3/4), 1993, published in Geneva by UNESCO and IBE. (Ar, Ch, F, R, S):
1993. No. 85/86 (Vol. XXIII, No. 1/2): Thinkers on Education, 1.
No. 87/88 (Vol. XXIII, No. 3/4): Thinkers on Education, 2.
1994. No. 89/90 (Vol. XXIV, No. 1/2): Thinkers on Education, 3.
No. 91/92 (Vol. XXIV, No. 3/4): Thinkers on Education, 4.

UNESCO-AFRICA (Dakar, UNESCO/BREDA). Two issues a year. (F):
1993. Nos. 6 and 7.
1994. Nos. 8 and 9.